*Early German and
Austrian Detective Fiction:
An Anthology*

Early German and Austrian Detective Fiction

An Anthology

Translated and edited by
Mary W. Tannert
and Henry Kratz

McFarland & Company, Inc., Publishers
Jefferson, North Carolina, and London

British Library Cataloguing-in-Publication data are available

Library of Congress Cataloguing-in-Publication Data

Early German and Austrian detective fiction : an anthology /
    translated and edited by Mary W. Tannert and Henry Kratz.
        p.   cm.
    Includes bibliographical references.
    Contents: The caliber / Adolph Müllner — The dead man
of St. Anne's Chapel / Otto Ludwig — The star tavern /
Adolf Streckfuss — The golden bullet / Auguste Groner —
The detective / Maximilian Böttcher — The vault break-in /
Balduin Groller.
    ISBN 0-7864-0659-3 (library binding : 50# alkaline paper) ∞
    1. Detective and mystery stories, German—Translations into
English.   2. German fiction—19th century—Translations into
English.   3. German fiction—20th century—Translations into
English.   4. Detective and mystery stories, Austrian—
Translations into English.   5. Austrian fiction—19th century—
Translations into English.   6. Austrian fiction—20th century—
Translations into English.   I. Tannert, Mary W., 1957–   .
II. Kratz, Henry.
PT1327.E27   1999
833'.087208—dc21   98-54255
                                                                CIP

Manufactured in the United States of America

McFarland & Company, Inc., Publishers
    Box 611, Jefferson, North Carolina 28640

Acknowledgments

We had many who encouraged us during the years we worked on this project. We would like first to thank a fellow scholar whom we have never met, but to whom we owe, indirectly, the existence of this book: Hans-Otto Hügel, whose ground-breaking analysis of the history of the German-language detective story—*Untersuchungsrichter, Diebsfänger, Detektive: Theorie und Geschichte der deutschen Detektiverzählung im 19. Jahrhundert.* Stuttgart: J.B. Metzler, 1978—was the beginning of our fascination with this forgotten body of work and our determination to retrieve it and make its best examples available to readers of English. Jeffrey L. Sammons, general editor of the series *North American Studies in Nineteenth-Century German Literature*, read the manuscript in an early form and gave us several thoughtful and invaluable suggestions. Thanks also to all the other scholars of detective fiction in the United States who shared our enthusiasm at academic conferences and in detective-fiction newsletters.

We are most grateful to Gerhard Lindenstruth of Giessen, Germany, whose bibliographic expertise helped us locate biographical and bibliographic information we needed, and also some of the detective stories we considered for this anthology. It is to Gerhard that we owe the discovery of Böttcher's *The Detective*.

Finally, thanks to Joel Haden (especially for his computer expertise) and Peggy Hogg, our spouses, for enduring our "shop talk" so patiently and lending us their moral support.

Table of Contents

Notes on Sources

The works in this anthology present bibliographic challenges. Some were first printed in serial form; literary newspapers and journals were a common way of introducing popular fiction during the nineteenth century. A whodunit had a particular advantage when published in installments: each cliffhanger insured that the reader bought the next edition of the paper to find out what happened.

A successful serial publication generally led to a reprint in book form, either alone or together with other short works in one volume. If the serial version was an edited one, the work might be published in its entirety for the first time when it appeared in book form. The book publisher was often not the publisher responsible for the serial version. If the work was popular and durable, several publishers might undertake reprints over the years, and each publisher had a different approach. Thus, occasionally, titles, subtitles or author names were altered between serial and book versions, or between early and later book versions. Introductions or forewords might appear in one edition but not in others. Some books were published without dates, leaving the chronology of various editions unclear. And many publishing houses do not exist anymore. The past hundred and fifty years have seen much war and social upheaval on the European continent.

Through all this, the translator has two tasks: to determine the earliest date of publication of a particular work, in order to understand its place both in the author's career and in the history of detective fiction; and to discover, if possible, which version of a work is the most authentic. We've used the earliest most complete edition we could locate as the basis for our translations. In each case, the edition we used is cited below.

Adolph Müllner. *The Caliber.* Originally published in German under the title *Der Kaliber. Aus den Papieren eines Criminal-Beamten.* Novelle von Adolph Müllner. In *Mitternachtblatt.* Nos. 1-20, 1828. Ed. Adolph Müllner. The edition used for the present translation is *Der Kaliber. Aus den Papieren eines Kriminalbeamten.* Leipzig: Philipp Reclam, n.d.

Otto Ludwig. *The Dead Man of St. Anne's Chapel.* Originally published in German under the title *Der Tote von St.-Annas Kapelle. Ein Criminalfall. Nach Akten und brieflichen Mitteilungen erzählt.* Reprinted from *Urania. Taschenbuch auf das Jahr 1840* (Leipzig: Brockhaus Verlag, 1840 [1839]) pp. 289–422.

Adolf Streckfuss. *The Star Tavern.* Originally published in German under the title *Der Sternkrug. Criminal-Novelle.* Berlin: B. Brigl, 1870.

Auguste Groner. *The Golden Bullet.* Originally published in German under the title *Zwei Kriminalnovellen: Der Neunundsiebzigste. Die goldene Kugel.* Leipzig: Philipp Reclam, 1893.

Maximilian Böttcher. *The Detective.* Originally published in German under the title *Der Detektiv. Kriminalnovelle.* In *Willkommen!* Vol. 10. (1899), pp. 180–195.

Balduin Groller. *The Vault Break-In.* Originally published in German under the title *Der Kasseneinbruch.* In *Detektiv Dagoberts Taten und Abenteuer. Ein Novellen-Zyklus* (Vol. 3. Universal-Bibliothek 5216) Leipzig: Philipp Reclam, 1909.

Introduction

The romance of police activity keeps in some sense before the mind the fact that civilization itself is the most sensational of departures and the most romantic of rebellions..... The romance of the police force is thus the whole romance of man. It is based on the fact that morality is the most dark and daring of conspiracies.

G. K. Chesterton
"A Defence of Detective Stories"

I The translators of this anthology offer mystery readers a glimpse into the history of German-language detective fiction, a tradition unknown to most devotees of the genre. Indeed, to judge from the essays of the detective story's seminal scholars, the genre has always been a nearly exclusively Anglo-American and French affair, proceeding from Poe to Conan Doyle and beyond with brief pauses for Collins, Dickens, Green, and Gaboriau, to name a few examples. But in the lands of Johann Wolfgang von Goethe and Thomas Mann, of Rainer Maria Rilke and Friedrich Dürrenmatt, there has always been a love of literature and a large community of readers. And indeed, the German-speaking countries of Europe developed a taste for crime fiction on much the same terms and timetable as the other industrialized societies of Europe. The stories are there. We have merely overlooked their existence.

As in the rest of Europe, the development of detective fiction in the German-speaking world closely followed certain key advancements in nineteenth-century judicial procedure, particularly the abolition of torture and the subsequent development of a trial system in which physical evidence of guilt was definitive for judge and jury. Torture was formally eradicated from the last of the German states in 1831, after having been gradually reduced in practice (often by law) during the late eighteenth century to the most egregious cases, generally capital crimes, and retaining its greatest applicability when there was a prime suspect; in such a case, the point of the physical evidence of guilt was merely to assist torture

1

in provoking a confession from that suspect.[1] The procedures that replaced this system of inquisition included both jury trials and the practice of "ruling on the record," that is, of a written decision by one or more judges handed down upon the basis of a written defense presented by a defense lawyer. With these new methods, the importance of physical evidence was enhanced: once a suspect could no longer be forced to incriminate himself, falsely or otherwise, other evidence of guilt had to be found, and it had to be someone's task to find and evaluate that evidence.

The latter task usually fell to a professional (though the reader of this volume will also meet a few amateur detectives). Detective fiction from the first part of the nineteenth century usually features an investigating magistrate, who combined the functions of detective and district attorney in one (as in *The Caliber*). As the century wore on, in most novels a police officer, usually with the rank of "inspector" or even "superintendent," supervised or carried out the detection of a crime for the state. Sometimes this detective was sent out undercover, as in *The Star Tavern*; in urban areas he was more likely to be assisted by a phalanx of police officers of lesser rank, as in *The Vault Break-In*. To those interested in a more complete history of the development of—actual, not fictional—police forces in German-speaking Europe, we recommend the research of Hsi-Huey Liang and Elaine Glovka Spencer.

The reader will see mirrored in this anthology all the developments of the nineteenth century in judicial and criminological sophistication, in physical and social responses to crime. We begin with the oldest known German detective story—the journalist and dramatist Adolph Müllner's 1828 novella *The Caliber*, which offers the first fictional instance of the use of bullet caliber to determine a suspect's guilt or innocence.[2] We have also included the 1840 novella *The Dead Man of St. Anne's Chapel*, by Otto Ludwig Emil von Puttkammer. An early courtroom drama, it features a fascinating debate on the merits and meaning of the evidence in a murder case, showing how adept the judicial manipulation of evidence had become in the short time since it was deemed authoritative.

As occupational and scientific concepts of detecting evolved, crime fiction changed, too: with the means to claim the foreground in the plot, the activity of detection gradually consumed the entire novel, avoiding both subplot status and being padded with subplots, as often was its fate in novels of the early and mid-nineteenth century (Charles Dickens' *Bleak House* being perhaps the most well-known English example of this

---

[1]For more information on the abolition of torture in Germany, see Hügel pp. 92–97, 261.

[2]In 1823, the Danish-born journalist Laurids Kruse published *Der krystallene Dolch* (*The Crystal Dagger*) in Germany, a romantic tale with strong elements of detection. However, because it is less detective fiction than Gothic novel, we believe Müllner's *Der Kaliber* (*The Caliber*) is more deserving of the title of the first German-language detective story.

phenomenon). This growth is illustrated by Adolf Streckfuss's 1870 rural novel *The Star Tavern*. By this time, in the hands of Streckfuss and others (Ludwig Habicht, Ewald August König, and J.D.H. Temme, for example), German-language detective fiction had reached an early maturity that was not to be England's or America's for another fifteen to twenty years. As Hans Otto Hügel, German detective fiction's foremost historian, has written, "as important as the developments were that the detective story made in Germany after 1890, ... between 1860 and 1880 it had already won its independence and [completed] its formal development. The breakthrough success that was Conan Doyle's after 1890 encountered in Germany a genre already existent in a variety of forms" (174; editors' translation). Real criminological practice undoubtedly provided some impetus: by the 1890s, Austrian professor of criminal law Dr. Hans Gross had developed a criminology handbook that came to be used all over the world in criminology and law enforcement studies (and was particularly beloved of H.R.F. Keating's fictional detective, Inspector Ghote of the Bombay Police).

Although early and mid-nineteenth-century detective fiction appears to have been the province of men, by the end of the century a number of women had been attracted to the genre. Their work suggests that they saw in the detective figure vicarious possibilities for the freedom and adventure that bourgeois life then denied respectable women in Europe. In their hands the detective story gained new settings and dimensions, and though their detective figures were still mostly male, prototypes for women detectives began to emerge. Among the many women who could represent this trend (including Luise Westkirch and Eufemia von Adlersfeld-Ballestrem), we have chosen Auguste Groner, who wrote more than three dozen detective novels and novellas between the late 1880s and 1927, and developed the first known German-language series police detective, Joseph Müller; he makes an early appearance here in her 1893 novella *The Golden Bullet*.

With the fin de siècle, the stability of the genre made possible the appearance of parodies and pastiches and the poking of gentle fun at the professions of law enforcement and detection. Thus we could not resist including a clever parody of Sherlock Holmes, namely Maximilian Böttcher's short story *The Detective*. And to demonstrate the adaptability of the Sherlock Holmes model to other cultures, we offer one of Balduin Groller's 1909 *Detective Dagobert* capers to give the reader a glimpse of high-society Viennese crime and the justice of the wealthy and noble.

Space limitations preclude our featuring any detective stories from the growing numbers of post–World War II crime fiction writers in Germany, Austria, and Switzerland. Yet the genre flourishes at the end of the twentieth century as never before in many cultures and languages. Just as scholars of canonical literature acknowledge the contributions of other languages to the world's *belles lettres*, we recommend that serious readers of detective fiction reach beyond British and American borders to the detective fiction of other cultures, whether in translation or in the original language.

II When one considers the variety and numbers of detective stories the German-language popular presses produced from the early nineteenth century to the rise of National Socialism, it is astonishing that so little is known about them. It may therefore be useful to offer a brief explanation of why the scholars of detective fiction have been so quick to accept the conclusion that there was no German detective story tradition to compare with those of Great Britain, the United States, and France.

There are three principal reasons. Foremost among them is German academia's traditional disapproval of popular literature. When the detective story loomed large enough to demand the attention even of those in belles lettres, German academia simply went through the Germanistics canon, identifying in it those prose works that featured crimes and offering them to detective fiction posterity as Austria's and Germany's contributions (see, for example, Schönhaar, Freund, and Reinert). Works frequently found in this grouping usually include:

—Friedrich Schiller, *Verbrecher aus verlorener Ehre* (Criminal from Lost Honor), 1786
—Heinrich von Kleist, *Der Zweikampf* (The Duel), 1810
—E.T.A. Hoffmann, *Das Fräulein von Scuderi* (Miss von Scuderi), 1819
—Annette von Droste Hülshoff, *Die Judenbuche* (The Jew Beech), 1842
—Theodor Fontane, *Unterm Birnbaum* (Under the Pear Tree), 1885
—Wilhelm Raabe, *Stopfkuchen* (Stopfkuchen), 1891

Although all feature a crime, none is a genuine detective story, which for our purposes we define as a story in which the goal and focus of the narration is the use of human ratiocination to solve a puzzle on the basis of physical evidence. The first three titles are Romantic tales of a suspenseful or metaphysical nature, constructed around an initially mysterious crime. The last three, from the traditions of Realism, are studies of human failing with elements of the psycho-thriller. For German academia's purpose, they were simply relabeled "crime fiction" (*Kriminalgeschichte* or *Kriminalerzählung*), a half-measure that permitted the scholar to remain with familiar texts even when a close reading revealed that they were not genuine examples of detective fiction.

Such false representation has many ramifications. First, serious readers, who look to scholarship for objectivity and guidance, do not discover the huge body of genuine detective fiction from Germany and Austria's popular presses. Second, such novels and novellas as those cited above were never intended as detective stories, and unsuccessful attempts to press them into that mold do nothing for the reader's appreciation of the work, and fuel the flames of those who find no reason to take German-language detective fiction seriously.

Germans who write about genuine detective fiction tend also to regard it as an Anglo-American affair with French contributions (see, for example, Boileau-Narcejac, Gerteis, Skreb, Vogt, and Zmegac), although, ironically, they do not feel the need to limit themselves to canonical figures like Edgar Allan Poe or Charles Dickens.

A second reason for German-language detective fiction's obscurity is its treatment by Anglo-American scholars of the genre, especially by influential "Golden Age" writers (those of the 1920s–1940s). They generally ignored German-language contributions (along with those of many other cultures) or dismissed them for specious and often contradictory reasons. For example, in his 1927 introduction to the anthology *The Great Detective Stories*, Willard Huntington Wright wrote:

> Germany's efforts at the exacting art of detective-story writing are, in the main, abortive and ponderous.... The hero is generally a hide-bound, system-worshiping officer of the *Polizei*.... Even the best of the Germanic attempts at this literary *genre* read somewhat like painstaking official reports, lacking imagination and dramatic suspense.... The Austrian authors who have devoted their energies to crime-problem fiction follow closely along German lines ... [30–31].

To give Wright his due, he cites a number of novels in support of his conclusions. But his citations suggest that he drew only from the most readily available contemporary examples, irrespective of quality. In contrast, his discussions of English, American, and French detective stories in the same essay suggest careful attention to historical continuity and qualitative differences among individual works.

Two years later, Dorothy Leigh Sayers offered a contradictory reason for the same outcome, relying on the comments of a visiting German novelist and playwright. In her 1929 introduction to *The Omnibus of Crime*, she says:

> Some further light is thrown on the question by a remark made by Herr Lion Feuchtwanger when broadcasting during his visit to London in 1927. Contrasting the tastes of the English, French, and German publics, he noted the great attention paid by the Englishman to the external details of men and things. The Englishman likes material exactness in the books he reads; the German and the Frenchman, in different degrees, care little for it in comparison with psychological truth. It is hardly surprising, then, that the detective-story ... should appeal far more strongly to Anglo-Saxon taste than to that of France or Germany [11].

Sayers' mode of presenting Feuchtwanger's views (note the seamless transition from his thoughts to hers) suggests that she simply extended Feuchtwanger's analysis from its original, undescribed context to her own, without worrying about its accuracy (was he referring to fiction or journalism? *Which* Germans and Frenchmen? And does he speak for Austria and Switzerland, too?). And Sayers cites no titles; evidently she did not see the need to support her position with concrete examples.

Howard Haycraft's well-known 1940 treatise, *Murder for Pleasure*, contains a chapter called "The Continental Detective Story." In it he dismisses all but French detective fiction in a sweeping claim that Europe outside of France "simply lacked the essential political and legalistic backgrounds of the established democracies, and was consequently able to produce at best feeble imitations of the real thing" (103).

Like Sayers, Haycraft does not cite any detective stories or historical sources to support his assertions. His analysis largely addresses French detective novels and closes with a final dismissal:

> Continental contributions to the detective story, aside from the French, have been so few, so indirect, and so unimportant that there would be no sensible object in discussing them here: the result would be only a list of authors obscure at best and for the great part untranslated and unavailable in England or America ... and the explosion of the totalitarian cataclysm over Europe would seem to have halted effectively further development in any part of the Continent for at least a number of years [110–111].

Haycraft's allusion to "totalitarian cataclysm" points to the third—if minor—reason for current unfamiliarity with early German-language detective fiction. National Socialist cultural policies, developed after Hitler's election as Chancellor in 1933, functioned largely to suppress and destroy art and literature produced by so-called "enemies of the state." Detective fiction was among the genres targeted for destruction. What was not deliberately destroyed in the book burnings of the 1930s was often lost to the physical upheaval of the war years, and of course during the war new publications were infrequent. Even so, surviving bibliographic records provide scholars with ample evidence of a vigorous tradition prior to the war years.

In summary, Wright's and Sayers' opinions are typical of judgments of German-language detective fiction during the first part of the Golden Age. They are characterized primarily by ignorance and underscored by crime-fiction chauvinism. They reveal an insufficient knowledge base and no effort to judge German-language detective fiction by its best rather than its worst examples, as mystery scholars constantly exhort the genre's critics to do.

Haycraft's reaction to contemporary events (see, for example, Chapter XV, "Dictators, Democrats, and Detectives") reveals a different but equally serious kind of bias. Haycraft probably did not allow the advent of Nazism to ruin Goethe or Mozart for him, yet it clearly affected his judgment of German-language detective fiction, which he seems to be dismissing primarily because it was unavailable in English and because Hitler was totalitarian. Unfortunately, one cannot help wondering how many of

Haycraft's detective fiction contemporaries also confused the value of a literary tradition with current events in the land of its origin.

Between them, these influential scholars managed to damn German-language detective fiction on literary, linguistic, and political-social grounds without very much actual knowledge or experience of it. Even if we excuse their carelessness because they were writing essayistically about a popular fiction genre, we must acknowledge that their critiques had a deleterious effect on the exploration of German-language detective fiction, an exploration that would ideally have accompanied the Golden Age's renewed interest in the history of the genre in England, America, and France.

III Like its English and American counterparts, German-language detective fiction was shaped by social experience, diversity of narrative approach and scientific progress. However, pre–World War I detective stories from the German and Austro-Hungarian empires are also characterized by a unique and complex set of questions about the nature of justice in a classed society, and its effects on the lives of detectives working within it. For German and Austrian writers of the nineteenth and early twentieth centuries, the socially detached approach of a Dupin, an Inspector Bucket or a Sherlock Holmes was dangerous: the detective's very survival in a rigidly classed society depended on his awareness of the way others viewed his work, and he could not afford to behave as if he did not care whom he alienated or exposed.

Golden Age notions of what was proper in a detective story tended to ignore socio-historic differences that influence literature in other cultures, and to impose upon the detective story a standard rooted largely in Anglo-American middle-class values and reflective of a society in which justice has a structure and an accessibility that render certain discussions unnecessary—in effect, measuring detective fiction of every century and place with what is essentially a twentieth-century, culturally limited set of tools. We note this with the goal of enhancing reader awareness: the act of solving serious crimes, especially murder (and there is nearly always a murder in a detective story), involves not merely ratiocination applied to the physical evidence, but—even if unconsciously—also *the whole of a society's values with regard to justice and punishment.* For us, a major source of fascination in working with these texts has been the discovery of the differences between Anglo-American values and those of the principalities that made up the German Empire during most of the nineteenth century, of the Germany unified under Bismarck and during the Weimar Republic, and of the Austro-Hungarian Empire and the Austria that emerged from World War I. This study alone has much to teach us about societies that, thanks to two world wars, are gone forever.

The works we have included in this anthology represent only the tip of a large iceberg of German-language detective fiction. With our selections, ranging in date from 1828 to the eve of World War I, we have attempted to make the history of the German-language detective story transparent, to give some indication of the nature of the iceberg. In order to keep the size of this volume manageable, it was necessary to abridge the first four works. In each case, our foremost aim was to preserve the detective plot as completely as possible, and in no case has any text been condensed by more than 13 percent. While we would not claim that they make exactly the same literary impression as the unabridged originals, we are confident that these four stories still make good detective story reading, and that all the works in this volume can be judged on their own merits and in the context of their historical place in one of the most fruitful genres in popular fiction.

Adolph Müllner
(1774–1829)

Amandus Gottfried Adolph Müllner was born in Langendorf, a town in Saxony. He studied law in Leipzig from 1793 to 1797, and later received his doctorate from the University of Wittenberg. He practiced law in Delitzsch, and later in Weissenfels, where he lived most of his life. In 1802 he married Amalie von Logau, whom he had long loved but who had first been engaged to Müllner's stepbrother; the latter died before the marriage could take place.

Müllner was a prolific writer, and his interests extended beyond the law to the theater and journalism. Within the legal field, he wrote numerous reviews of juridical works and a number of articles and books on various aspects of jurisprudence. He also founded a private theater and edited various literary magazines. His first belletristic work was a lurid novel called *Incest*, published in 1799. He was best known for his dramas, which attracted the attention of Goethe, who produced several of them in Weimar. In particular, Müllner was regarded as one of the foremost representatives of the so-called *Schicksalstragödie* ("fate-tragedy"), including *Der neunundzwanzigste Februar* (*The Twenty-Ninth of February*), 1812, and *Die Schuld* (*Guilt*), 1816. The latter is quoted in *The Caliber*, as are two other Müllner dramas, *König Yngurd* (*King Yngurd*) 1817, and *Die Albaneserin* (*The Albanian Woman*) 1820.

Müllner's sole contribution to detective fiction is his 1828 novella *Der Kaliber* (*The Caliber*). It is regarded as the first genuine detective story in the German language (some thirteen years, let it be noted, before Poe's first Dupin story). The plot of *The Caliber* deals with fratricide, a topic of interest to Müllner from his days as a law student (doubtless because fraternal rivalry played a part in Müllner's own life), and one that also features largely in the fate-tragedy *Guilt*. In the novella, a young man believes he has murdered his brother, with whose fiancée he has fallen in love, and is proved innocent when the bullet removed from his brother's body is of a caliber different from the ones in his own pistol.

Of the works included in this anthology, this is the most closely allied with the canon literature of Germanistics. The story has many hallmarks of Romanticism, and echoes self-consciously some of the great robber-hero themes of the turn of the century. The prime suspect, Ferdinand Albus, is a romantic figure in his passion for the beautiful Mariane and the depths of his torment when he believes himself to be his brother's murderer. The narrator, the investigating magistrate whose duty it is to administer the case, and the lawyer for the defense, Dr. Rebhahn, offer the reader the cool influences of science and reason that mark the detection in the novella. The resolution of the conflict between passion and reason is brought about by Ferdinand's beloved Mariane, a strong and beautiful woman much like the "beautiful Amazon" of Goethe's *Wilhelm Meisters Lehrjahre*.

Because of Müllner's training, the details of juridical procedure in the novella are quite realistic. Of note is the fact that the courts of Müllner's day still relied largely on the confession of the prime suspect for the outcome of a case like this one. Although by 1828 torture had largely been outlawed in Germany as a means for extracting a confession, physical evidence was still regarded primarily as a vehicle for convincing the prime suspect to confess rather than as an independent means of demonstrating guilt or innocence. Here, ironically, the physical evidence *disproves* the prime suspect's guilt, even though he himself is initially reluctant to believe this.

Müllner himself provides additional irony in his dismissive references to the state of German drama. At the beginning of chapter VII, "Quiet Intimacies," he notes the "sensationalistic nonsense of every sort" that had begun to appear on the German stage at that time, ca. 1816. That is the year, as mentioned above, in which Müllner's own fate-tragedy *Guilt* first appeared, and in the novella a production of the play precipitates the prime suspect's confession of fratricide and episode of mania. History has consigned Müllner's dramas to literary obscurity; Müllner's self-irony suggests that he might have anticipated this. Unfortunately his death in 1829 cut short any possibility of his earning a more enduring reputation, but if *The Caliber* is anything to judge by, he might have done worse than to try more detective fiction.

The Caliber
by Adolph Müllner

CHAPTER I. *The Forest*

"Hell freely offers opportunities for misfortune."
King Yngurd, IV, 7

A file, which the pursuit of an apparently still widely dispersed band of thieves had swelled in recent weeks to uncomfortable proportions for its reader, kept me at my desk until twilight, which, because of the unfriendly autumn storm, fell earlier than the hour when my servant at this time of year was accustomed to bring me a light. The need of a small rest for both the mind and the eyes convinced me to wait for that moment in my armchair. Through the near window and the sparsely falling flakes of the first snow my idle gaze swept the rooftops of the village up to the edge of the boundary woods, which, a few miles away, separated my small fatherland from the neighboring larger state but largely belonged to the former. This expansive dark forest, full of ravines and encompassing several mountain ridges, during recent months had been a silent witness to many attacks upon travelers that indicated the work of an armed band, although no murder had as yet been committed. It was my profound wish to discover such a thing, to produce from the woods a corpse covered with wounds, and — as paradoxical as it may sound — I may call this wish benevolent. Without strong measures, public safety was difficult to restore, and the closest public safety officer[1] of the neighboring land had refused my request to commandeer its numerous idle border guards to purge the forest of the dangerous den of bandits with the excuse that, given the present system of a "permanent drill-period," he did not dare apply to his government for such use of the border troops before it had been proved that the supposed bandits had sullied the forest with human blood.

Thence comes my longing for the *corpus delicti* of a murder, the more daring, cruel, and outrageous, the better. For this reason I had read, page for page, through the thick research files and the reports of other courts and police stations contained therein, and now as I rested from many hours' exertion of my deductive powers, my mind strayed involuntarily from the province of wishful thinking into the realm of imagination. In the dark forest, which in the thickening twilight gradually receded from my view, I saw murderous thieves with hunting rifles under their arms stealthily slipping out of their ravines; I saw them shooting down wealthy travelers from their ambushes, uniting at the signal of a bandit's whistle, stopping heavy-laden traveling coaches, tearing the postillions from the horses, the footmen from the coach-boxes, the passengers from the coaches, gagging the women who screamed for help, tying them to trees and stabbing them to death with dagger thrusts: in a word, I saw Schiller's Spiegelberg band of thieves,[2] carrying out all the horror of their handiwork in an increasing progression of insolence and cruelty, without myself feeling anything other than what a writer may feel who is working on the bloodiest scene of a tale of robbery, a new *Rinaldo Rinaldini*,[3] the story of a great bandit.

My servant woke me from these delectable dreams by setting the chimney

---

[1]"Kriminal-beamte."

[2]Spiegelberg was a villain in Schiller's 1781 drama *Die Räuber (The Bandits)*.

[3]This is a reference to the 1799 prose tale *Rinaldo Rinaldini, der Räuberhauptmann*, the story of the great robber-baron of the title. This three-part romance, written by Goethe's brother-in-law, Christian August Vulpius, was part of the wave of robber-hero tales which followed the appearance in 1781 of Schiller's play *Die Räuber*.

lamp in front of me while announcing a stranger who wished to speak to me about an urgent official matter. He had introduced himself as Ferdinand Albus, a businessman from B..., and his request to speak to me in my capacity as investigating magistrate had been presented with such respectable manners that my servant had deemed it proper to take his hat and snow-dusted coat and to show him into the parlor, although it was neither heated nor lighted. I ordered him to repair this impropriety by showing the stranger into my study and bringing stronger light. The stranger came in. With a polite bow I moved several steps toward him, and I found it strange that he, whom my servant had announced as a "fine and respectable gentleman," did not return my bow, but rather remained upright like a distracted man who does not know where he is or has forgotten what he wanted.

"To what business, sir, do I owe the honor?" I addressed him.

"To the most horrible, sir!" he answered with a hoarse voice which he only rendered comprehensible with great effort, "My brother — my own brother, the merchant Heinrich Albus, has just this moment — before my eyes, at my side — been shot dead by a bandit."

"Where?" I asked quickly, and surely with a tone which must have taken him aback, for probably it better fit my aforementioned longing for the discovery of a corpse than it did his horror.

He hesitated some seconds with his answer and then said, "In the boundary woods, sir."

I had expected this answer because I wished for it; but now I became aware of the contradiction which appeared to exist in the words of the report. "Just this moment, you said? It is a fair distance —"

"Oh, my God!" he cried out, his voice shaking, "what are moments, what is time, what is eternity, in my condition?"

Breath seemed to fail him. The servant brought the lights. "Compose yourself, sir," I said as I took him by the hand and led him from the door to the sofa.

"You must excuse me," he said again, after having recovered somewhat, "if I do not report with clarity and order, as I should to an official."

"Permit me to spare you by questioning you about the course of events, as we investigators are accustomed to do. Your brother was struck by a bullet?"

"Yes."

"At your side?"

"He died in my arms."

"You were both traveling alone? On foot?"

"Yes. My brother had a payment to make in M.... He hoped to transact the business more easily if he did it in person. It is only four hours from B... upon the footpath through the woods. I accompanied him."

"And here you were attacked? By one or more persons?"

"By one, as far as I know."

"As far as you know? But it was still daylight?"

"Yes. I only saw the bandit when he fled. We were about one hundred paces apart; a call of nature had occupied me. I hear an exchange of words, a cry for help. I hurry, I catch sight of him again. He is struggling with a wild man. A shot is fired — oh Jesus! Jesus! my Savior!"

"Your brother was unarmed?" I asked, after a moment during which I believed he would be able to collect himself.

"A flimsy sword cane, nothing else."

"And you —"

"A double-barreled pocket-pistol, a tercerole. Oh, God, God! that was his death!"

"What? Your weapon?"

"I am afraid so. I tore it from my belt as I hurried to help him. As the robber saw me, he fired and plunged into the undergrowth. Heinrich collapsed. I sprang into the bushes, sent a bullet flying toward the fleeing man, and hurried back — useless hope! He was mortally wounded, in the chest. But yet he lived, in my arms, 'save yourself—*yourself*, Ferdinand' — Oh, Lord! Oh, God!"

He threw his arms around me, and hot tears flowed from his eyes. Comforting words would not have been appropriate. I lifted him gently from my shoulder, gave him my handkerchief to dry his wet cheeks, and waited a few moments before continuing with my painful inquiry.

"At that moment, the warning of the dying man about your own danger was as noble-hearted as it was sensible; the flight of the thief and the shot you sent after him did not secure your safety from a bullet fired from the bushes. Did you leave that dangerous spot immediately?"

He nodded silently.

"Did you remain in possession of your weapon?"

He appeared to reflect and opened his cloak. Underneath it he wore a wide leather belt which was fitted with pistol holsters. But both were empty.

"The pistol —" he said. "By God, I do not exactly know —"

"It is not important. Perhaps you left it behind in the confusion. But — you are not wounded yourself?"

"No."

"The unfortunate man died in your arms ... and the blood flecks upon your chest? —"

He stared down at them. "My blood," he said slowly and dully, "my father's blood! Oh horrible color!"

"My chest," he continued sorrowfully, "pressed against his death-wound, as did my mouth against his fading lips. I do not know how long it was before I thought about what I should do. I took his purse, his pocket-book, and his watch. Here they are. I wanted to reach the nearest authorities before nightfall. But in the village in front of the woods it occurred to me that I could also notify the constable of what happened. I described to him the path and the place, and learned from him your name and place of residence. He assembled farmers armed with pitchforks, and assured me that the body, if it could still be found, would be guarded where it lay until you gave further orders."

Thus I had, then, the desired case that the neighboring administration wished to await before it consented to release the border troops from drills. I ordered that my carriage be readied, that official forces be summoned, that the people be equipped with torches, and that both medical officers of the district be invited so that they could either accompany me forthwith or follow me as soon as possible to Waldrainsdorf to perform their duty upon the murdered man. Meanwhile Albus's statement was duly recorded. His memory failed to serve him only as regards an exact description of the person and clothing of the bandit, which lapse he excused with the words, "Actually, I saw nothing but Heinrich; his collapse left me no thought, no eye, no consciousness to acquire an impression of the fleeing bandit's form or the color of his clothing. The dreadful thought that he could be mortally wounded numbed me to any other idea."

"Perhaps," I said, "other features will be reawakened in your memory when you return to the place."

"Must I?" he asked, with an expression of reluctance in the face of this new emotional shock.

"It is necessary. Your identification of your brother cannot be avoided."

To this he offered no objection. In the carriage he was silent, and appeared now and then to be beset by feverish shudders. As we drove slowly over the high arched bridge of the stream, he became attentive, looked out of the carriage and said, more to himself than to me, "Here, it was here."

"You had to walk over this bridge," I replied. "Did something happen to you here?"

He leaned back in the carriage, pressed a handkerchief to his eyes, and answered heavily, "The thought of suicide!— Yes," he continued, again looking timidly out of the carriage, "the view of this weak railing reminds me of it! The torchlight illuminates the chasm, the eternal abyss to which despair had driven me."

I was struck by his confession of such a thought. This degree of despair seemed disproportionate to the case. "Is the unfortunate man the first close relative you have lost?" I asked.

"But under such circumstances, sir?" he replied, in a tone of such pain that sympathy bade me keep silent.

Chapter II. *The Corpse*

I beg, ye cranes who fly on high,
If no one else will raise his voice,
That you will tell by whom I die.
Schiller, "The Cranes of Ibycus"

On the other side of the bridge, a mounted messenger came toward me with the news that the body had been found. This made no impression upon my

companion. We drove to the edge of the woods without stopping in Waldrainsdorf. Here we got out and went on foot among the trees. Albus followed, wrapped
deeply in his cloak, silent, apparently lost in his thoughts; but with firm steps
which he quickened the closer we came to the lanterns of the farmers who were
guarding the body. Timidity in the face of death, the fear of ghosts, had made
them keep considerable distance between themselves and the corpse. "Not yet,"
said Albus as we reached the farmers, and hurried onward. The torchbearers and
I found it hard to keep up with him. Suddenly he stood still as if rooted to the
ground. Three steps away, close to the edge of the path, lay the lifeless man. Albus
threw back his cloak; holding his hands folded above his head, he stared down
at him for some seconds. "Oh, horror, horror, horror!" he cried out — it was
enough to curdle our blood. Then he threw himself upon the dead man and hid
his face upon the latter's bloody breast. His voice woke the ravens from their slum-
ber in the tops of the tall trees. Screeching, they took flight. Albus straightened
up, stretched one hand to the heavens, and called out, "Hah, cranes — cranes of
Ibycus! Pursue the murderer! Caw overhead in the theater — in the church — at
the altar!" In this pose he appeared to have become a statue. Yet now he made a
fist of his outstretched hand, pressed it against his forehead like a desperate man,
and cried out in tones of the most violent anguish: "No, no, no! It's impossible!
Mariane — Mariane! You cannot bear it — I cannot bear it! Both — both lost!" The
pallor of death spread over his cheeks. A sigh like a death rattle escaped his breast
and before my signal for help from those standing closest could be attended, he
sank down unconscious against me.

As I was provided with none of the remedies with which one ordinarily
brings the unconscious back to consciousness, there was nothing else for it but
to carry him to my carriage upon the stretcher which had been destined for the
murdered man. I ordered that he be swiftly conveyed to Waldrainsdorf, where
the doctor could have arrived meanwhile.

Many thoughts ran through my mind. Even the unworthy suspicion that
the witness to the murder could himself be the murderer arose from the confusion of my thoughts and tried to intrude itself upon my judgment even as my
agitated feelings rejected it with indignation. One may pardon an investigating
magistrate for such a thought. This occupation accustoms even the best-natured
man to believe others capable of the greatest malevolence.

In Waldrainsdorf I found the doctor and the surgeon occupied with Ferdinand in the constable's house. He had regained consciousness, but did not appear
to have completely recovered his senses. He did not speak, and only doubtful
signs indicated that he understood us. According to the doctor Ferdinand was
falling ill. He thought it unwise to await the outbreak of the illness in the constable's house. I gladly offered to take the sufferer into my house, and my servant received the order to accompany Ferdinand thither and, until our return,
to care for him in such a fashion as the doctor should ordain.

We proceeded with the autopsy, which in criminal cases should not be delayed except for urgent reasons. There was no doubt about the cause of the violent death of the young and perfectly healthy man. The bullet had entered the breast on the left side, had damaged heart and lung, and had come to rest, scarcely visibly out of shape, at the right shoulder blade, which it had no longer had the force to shatter. The sword cane of the murdered man had been found at the site of the murder. It appeared that he had tried to unsheathe it, since it was pulled out of its sheath a hand's breadth. Ferdinand's pocket pistol, which I had suspected would be there, was missing. The farmers, who had arrived at the body by the light of day, claimed not to have noticed a pistol, and our torch-lit search for it in the brush nearby had been to no avail.

CHAPTER III. *The Sick Man*

"Good Lord!
His brother's bride! And love?"
Basil in *The Albanian Woman*, III, 4

I returned about midnight. My mother and sister had attended to the sick man with care; he lay in bed. The doctor found him feverish but fully conscious. I therefore asked Ferdinand without delay for the necessary information about the domestic situation of the unfortunate dead man. The latter had no other living blood relatives besides Ferdinand and a maternal uncle in Philadelphia. A clerk, an apprentice, and a handyman completed his household. Ferdinand himself was second assistant to Councillor Brand, the banker, and lived in the home of his employer. It was thus necessary to send a report of the accident to the probate court in B... in order that Heinrich Albus's personal property might be sealed off, his business inventoried, and an administrator appointed for said business. "Perhaps," I remarked, "these complications might be avoided or reduced if you yourself could return tomorrow, since you are the heir."

"Who? I?" he answered with astonishment.

"Without doubt, if there is no will."

This appeared to discomfort him. He asked me anxiously whether he would be obliged to assume the inheritance. When I replied that he could refuse it if he did not find the assets sufficient to meet the debts, he revealed the sensitivity of an ambitious merchant and explained his concern about the acceptance of the inheritance by saying that he had never thought to inherit from a brother who was only a few years older than he himself and who would doubtless have married. When he understood that I would send the official notice to B... at daybreak, he asked for materials to write a few lines to his employer. The attempt to write with pen and ink was beyond his strength. But with a pencil he was able to put the words to paper: "Heinrich has been murdered, I lie ill, but only with exhaustion. Inform your daughter with care before she hears it as a rumor. Please send fresh clothing." I sealed the note, addressed it to Councillor Brand "to be opened only by addressee," spoke these words aloud, and deliberately remarked that they appeared to me to be necessary so that the letter would in no case be opened by Mariane. It did not occur to him that I was aware of the name.

"She will not," he said, "and in the end —" He turned away, sighed anxiously, and buried his face in the pillow.

CHAPTER IV. *Mariane*

Fernando —
She cannot hate, because she burns for him.
The Albanian Woman, II, 5

On the following midday, before my messenger could return, a coach arrived and Councillor Brand was announced. I received him in my mother's sitting room, which was heated but unoccupied at the moment. He walked in, a young woman upon his arm. It was his daughter Mariane. She was not of a classic or artist's type of beauty, but I have never seen a woman's form and face which at first glance could have captivated with equal power the sensual nature of the stronger sex. Something above middle height, a majestic physique, too strong and voluptuous to be considered slim alongside the artificial wasp-waists of our ballrooms, but adorned with all the charms of symmetry: dark-brown hair, fiery and soulful eyes, the bloom of youth and health upon her cheeks and lips; a beautifully curved neck, a throat the color of the lily when the shimmer of twilight plays upon its leaves; a gently curving figure, a bosom whose covering only contained it by sacrificing its folds; full, softly rounded arms and hips; in a word, everything that, communicated by the eyes, sets the sensual desires in motion without offending one's sense of beauty, of taste.

After the father, a lean man of friendly but not captivating expression and rather Jewish features, had brought forth the usual request for forgiving the disturbance, and I had replied in the usual fashion, I led the charming girl to the ottoman and requested with a gesture that she be seated there. "Thank you, sir," she said with a pleasant, bell-like voice, whose vibrations betrayed agitation. However, it was not pain but anxiety which struck me about those tones; I felt a light trembling in her hand and she sank down in a fashion which revealed that her calmness was not at one with her state of mind. Quickly I turned again to the old man.

"Doubtless you come, councillor, to discover how long you must do without your assistant. Sleep has strengthened him, the doctor's concerns have greatly vanished, but he should not yet leave his room, and my mother has settled in there, so to speak, so that loneliness cannot increase his melancholy."

"Merely melancholy?" said Mariane animatedly as she rose, approached me and laid a trembling hand upon my arm. "Oh, I ask you, sir, tell me everything! Is it only melancholy, not despair, not rage against himself? If he is responsible for anything, if he believes himself to have been responsible for anything, if he imagines that he could have saved his brother; then his melancholy is horrible, then he is capable of the most extreme deed."

All this was spoken so quickly that I could not have answered the individual questions even if my surprise had allowed me to realize that the affairs of the heart in this matter were completely other than I had suspected. This was clearly not the murdered man's sweetheart, but Ferdinand's; or it was at least not the former, but the latter, whom she loved. Did Ferdinand not know this himself, when, beside the body of his brother, he cried out, "Mariane, you cannot bear it!" Criminalistically, this improbability struck me at once.

"Indeed, miss," I replied, "Mr. Albus has shown signs of a despair which could have endangered his own life. He even confessed to me that after the accident he was overcome with the thought of suicide while upon the bridge at Eichdorf—"

"Oh, you see, you see there, father!" interrupted Mariane.

"And yet," I continued, "he admitted the thought with the abhorrence of a Christian; this danger is past."

"You do not know him, sir! You have no conception of this dreadful sensitivity, this awful vehemence in the face of misfortune. Not the misfortune which he experiences, but that which he causes. Oh, no one knows this as I do, who for months trembled in fear of hearing the shot fired which would shatter his brain!"

"That was a very different case, daughter," said Mr. Brand pacifyingly.

"Who knows? Who guarantees that the cases are not as similar as one egg is to another, at least in his mind? Last spring, sir, he wanted to ride the bookkeeper's horse, the one that lets no one mount it except its master. The horse won't be held, Ferdinand is enraged and strikes it in a fury—finally he outwits it by leaping into the saddle. The horse rears up, jumps to the side, kicks out, and strikes the youngest son of the coachman, who could not reach the safety of the stable door quickly enough. Then—then you should have seen Ferdinand! The bleeding, senseless child in his arms, he staggered toward me in the hall. His knees could scarcely carry him. I carried the boy into the next room and called for help. 'No use! No use!' he cried, weeping, 'dead! because of me!' He ran his hands convulsively through his hair and ran up the stairs. I hurried after him, as fast as I could go. He was just tearing the pistol from the wall, he struggled with me like a madman for possession of it. Only fear gave me the strength to tear it from him, and if men had not arrived who were capable of holding him, truly! he would have shattered his head against the wall. You see, this is how he is; it is so horrible when one considers that he has the best, most noble of hearts!"

"In the first moment of a feeling of responsibility—"

"Oh, no, no! In his case, it returns. The mortal danger of the child was his as well, as long as it lasted. He could not even bear the thought that the boy, formerly alert and comprehending, could sustain a blunting of his mental powers, as was originally feared. There were hours when the apprehensions of the doctor counted as a definite certainty to Ferdinand, and I know that I alone —"

She stopped suddenly, and with a glowing blush, dropped her eyes to the floor.

"Why," she continued in a softer voice, "why am I ashamed to speak of that which I can no longer hide? Yes, sir, I know, I *believe*, that at that time nothing gave him the courage to live except my solemn oath that I would not survive him."

Her tear-filled eyes were raised to heaven at these words. This sight and the tone of her voice moved me deeply. The charming creature was entrancing at this moment. If we had been alone I would have forgotten myself, would have embraced her, would have kissed away the falling teardrops from her cheeks. She appeared to have read this in my eyes, and turned shyly away. One glance at her father suppressed my excess of feeling. What a contrast! The man stood with his shoulders hunched and looked as though the talk had been of a low trade in which one was compelled to take the bad with the purchase of the good.

"Mr. Albus has such a peculiar temperament," he said with a coldness, with such a shriveled spirit, that I nearly had to laugh. "You, sir, will kindly excuse my daughter her vehemence; the young people have been attracted to each other for some time, and have had in recent weeks some cause to consider themselves betrothed."

Notwithstanding its tastelessness, this explanation affected me beneficially. It gave me a completely satisfactory insight into Ferdinand's puzzling utterances and his behavior of this morning, which had occasionally aroused my suspicions. Here were two temperaments of exceptional fieriness, two creatures who would, by all appearances, become one or perish together. Mariane's suspicion of the similarity of the two cases appeared to be all too well-founded. The tone with which Ferdinand on the previous evening had said of his pistol, "Oh, God, God! That was his death!" left me no more doubt that he ascribed to himself the responsibility for his brother's death, because he had torn the pistol too hastily from the holster and thus revealed it to the bandit, who was struggling with his victim and shot him down when he saw an armed man hurrying toward them.

During her desiccated father's dry remarks, Mariane had taken a seat once again upon the ottoman. I sat down next to her, took the hand resting beside her, and told her she could be completely at ease about Mr. Albus's present state of mind.

"Is it not possible for him to travel back to B... with us today?" she asked with urgent uneasiness.

"We should hear what the doctor has to say, my dear distressed friend."

"Oh yes, yes, sir," she said with a thankful handclasp, and two large tears rolled down from her glowing eyes.

I left the room forthwith to send for the doctor, and asked my sister to say a few words to the sick man to prepare him for the visit of his employer and the latter's daughter. Because this took place in the anteroom and I had left the door of the room from which I emerged half-open, Mr. Brand had heard these instructions. He came out and remarked that his servant had brought the requested clothing. I was glad of that, because I feared that Mariane would take fright at the blood-spattered vest which Ferdinand had been necessarily obliged to put on again. Brand's servant went to help Ferdinand change his clothes. Mr. Brand had meanwhile seated himself at the window and was reading the Hamburg newspapers which he found there! When my sister came in to inform us that Mr. Albus had changed his clothes, Mariane rose quickly, hurried to my sister, embraced her, pressed a kiss upon her forehead and said, softly, "This for his angel of mercy!" Mr. Brand rose with a degree of ill-will over the interruption of his reading, and followed behind when I led Mariane to the sick man's room. Ferdinand sat upon the sofa, started to rise as my mother received the strangers, but appeared not to trust the power of his knees, and spoke the words, "You came yourself?" with a look at Mariane which bared his entire soul. Hers appeared enlivening, affecting him like an electric current. Mr. Brand answered his question. "But of course, Mr. Albus, you know how little we can do without you in the business." Meanwhile Mariane bowed to my mother and — cleverly hiding her intention, I must say — quickly pressed my mother's hand to her lips before the surprised woman could prevent it.

CHAPTER V. *The Young Jewish Woman*

> If but the girl be healthy and devout
> Who thus has grown up here, before your eyes,
> Then still she is what in God's eyes she was.
> For is not then the whole of Christian faith
> Founded on Judaism?
> Lessing, *Nathan the Wise*, IV, 7

My sister remembered that she had already seen Mariane in B... Both women sat down to recall the when, where and how, and Mr. Brand sank down next to Ferdinand. He expressed his very great regret that such a valuable and industrious merchant as Mr. Heinrich Albus should have died so suddenly and in such a wretched fashion. He was especially sorry, he continued, that this misfortune should have occurred just now, because for financial reasons it would result in a delay of the desired union, which he, as a father, had never seen reason to obstruct. Completely aside from the great misfortune, however, he was very pleased to hear from a reputable source that the commendable probate courts had — completely unexpectedly — found the business dealings and the book-keeping of the departed man in a condition that was favorable beyond all expectations, although he, Brand, nearly had to fear that for just this reason he might lose the best worker in his office, etc. Into all this inopportune twaddle, during which Ferdinand's face registered first astonishment, then discomfort, and finally annoyance, Mr. Brand inserted many questions about business matters in Albus's keeping, and appeared to prepare himself with the carefulness of a merchant for the eventuality that the doctor would not give his permission for the sick man to travel.

This effort was unnecessary. The doctor came and found no objection to the short journey of a few miles, since Ferdinand's weakness was nothing more than the consequence of a long and lethargic unconsciousness. Mariane's face, which until then had not lost its expression of concern, beamed with joy. As soon as the doctor had withdrawn (very pleased, it seemed, with the fee which, after Ferdinand spoke a quiet word in Mr. Brand's ear, the latter handed him with due discretion), she suggested to her father that they depart. She did this with such undisguisable inner impatience that it was painful to me to obstruct her wishes. Albus needed first to take possession of his brother's effects, which he had deposited with me, and the release of same had to be documented. As the closest relative of the murdered man, he had to arrange for the disposal of the body. Additionally, the people whom I had sent that morning into the woods to hunt for Ferdinand's pocket pistol were not back. For my records this circumstance was somewhat important to me. After all, the man who made the report of murder was an armed man who could not give any information about where his deadly weapon, which he claimed to have used against the fleeing bandit, had gone. I asked the councillor to unharness the horses and take lunch with me. I only needed to mention that the purse and pocket-book of the victim contained the amount of 8000 talers to convince him of the necessity of a prompt and legally proper release. The sight of his beloved seemed to have restored physical strength to the sufferer. He followed us into the dining room on my sister's arm and would not choose his seat until Mariane had taken hers, in order to enjoy, by sitting opposite her, the feast for the eyes which her charms presented. The girl had interested me so much in her passion for Ferdinand that I took pleasure in observing the two lovers.

My observation did not appear to have escaped her, and she sought to divert my attention from Ferdinand through a conversation with her. Everything she said reflected so creditably upon her that she aroused in me the curiosity to discover how the daughter of such an uncaptivating father could have come into possession of so many intellectual virtues of precisely the kind that only tend to develop with a very good education and the daily company of superior persons. The presence of Mr. Brand allowed my curiosity no further question into this matter. But my sister accidentally enlightened me somewhat. She had heard of a Madame Brand in B... who had left behind her a reputation as an excellent pianist, and asked whether this person was a relative of the family. "My mother," answered Mariane, and with such a tone, with such a look! The purest child-hood love sounded in her voice and painted itself in her eyes, love to which the grave can erect no barrier, love which, through earthly separation, is more likely to gain depth than to lose it, and that hears every friendly remembrance by a third person with melancholy joy. My sister fell silent. Mr. Brand took up the conversation.

"It is true," he said, as dryly as always, "she played incredibly beautifully, and was also in general a wonderful woman. She passed away two years ago, and was from the lineage —" He faltered here suddenly with a kind of embarrass-ment.

A cheerful smile played upon Mariane's mouth. "Our family is Jewish, sir," she said to me.

"Used to be, used to be," corrected Mr. Brand.

"But no, dear father, the family is not of the faith. It was the work of my good — my unforgettable mother, that we became Christians; but she never denied that she was born a Jew."

"Well, now, it does not matter to enlightened people," said Mr. Brand. He directed the conversation to the topic of Heinrich's murderer once more, thank-ing heaven that at least the evildoer had not succeeded in the robbery, and finally turned to Ferdinand with the stupid question, "But was it not possible, dear Mr. Albus, to get there faster with your pistol and save your dear brother's life as well?"

Mariane started at these words and saw, with growing fear, their effect spreading across Ferdinand's face. He did not answer, but merely stared at Coun-cillor Brand and turned pale; his lips trembled, and he appeared to want to rise. He dropped his eyes, raised them then slowly to Mariane, and said with a gen-tle sigh, "What a question!" The girl looked beseechingly at me. I could not but understand her, and ended the meal.

The business of the release of Heinrich's pocket-book, purse, and watch was conducted with all possible consideration for Ferdinand's nervous state. There arrived meanwhile the unpleasant report that the search for the missing pocket-pistol had been fruitless. I could not allow Ferdinand to depart without asking him once more where he could have left it. Mariane was present. She appeared to fear that this circumstance could create a delay.

"I believe," he said, while looking at Mariane as though he hoped to read in her eyes what he could not find in his own brain, "yes, of course! One barrel was still loaded — on the bridge — I thought of you — it's clear to me, I flung it into the current, in order not to —"

"To commit suicide," added Mariane with a tone of reproach.

"That's how it is, sir, I remember clearly now; you can rely upon it."

The thing was in fact so likely that my criminalistic concerns vanished entirely. I limited myself to adding this new information in the margin of the statement without troubling Ferdinand for another signature.

At their departure, Mr. Brand asked me, with more earnestness than I expected of him, that I and mine should look upon his humble home as our own as often as we came to B...

"Oh, you must do that, my dear sir," said Mariane while giving me her lovely hand to receive my promise, "and you, dear lady, and you, my new sisterly friend! Or will you disdain the Christian Jewish girl?"

She was the last to step into the coach, after she whispered the words to the servant at the door of the carriage, "The picture in his room must go, before he enters it."

CHAPTER VI. *The Bandits*

The forest is our bedding-place, the moon our sun.
Schiller, *The Bandits*

The next few weeks passed, filled with distracting business matters. The murder had aroused fear in the vicinity. Yet the criminal police of the neighboring land were now forthcoming with that which they had denied me earlier: they offered the cooperation of a regiment of riflemen to purge the woods. With the help of our own few troops stationed in B... it was possible to surround the woods while the constabulary on both sides searched all the hiding places. On the first day a group of bandits was caught, spread thinly through the whole woods and numbering twenty-odd persons, some of whom had women and children with them. The ravines, caves, and earthen huts in which they lived left no doubt as to their primary occupation: poaching and the theft of livestock. We learned from the preliminary confessions of these nomads that they had many connections with scoundrels outside the woods, and several receivers of stolen goods were brought in from the neighboring villages and hamlets. The arrested persons were divided between the two states according to the jurisdiction in which each was apprehended.

I took part in this expedition in person, and I cannot deny that my decision was determined by a curiosity that was other than criminalistic. The officer who commanded the military detachment from B..., a young man of much social and cultural accomplishment, was familiar with the Brand household and spoke about the "entrancing Christian Jewish girl" as eagerly as I did. Her reputation was spotless and the business standing of her father was unquestioned. She was considered, if not a brilliant match, at least a very good one, and people had for some time now regarded Heinrich Albus as the lucky man whom Mr. Brand had selected for the occasion when Heinrich's silkwares business, opened a few years ago, should achieve the success which his industriousness, circumspection and thriftiness promised. But a year ago opinion had changed. At that time Ferdinand Albus returned from a two-year journey to North America, which he had undertaken as the employee of a large Hanseatic concern, and visited his brother in B..., where he had never been before. His stay lengthened beyond the usual confines of such a visit, and by means of Heinrich's energetic intercession Ferdinand not only joined Brand's business as an assistant, but also became the latter's resident guest. Since that time it was popularly believed in B... that Ferdinand was willing to serve the Biblical seven years to earn the beautiful Jewish girl, and that this plan had the consent of Heinrich, who had control of Ferdinand's modest inheritance from their parents. But since Heinrich's murder people were convinced that Mr. Brand would shorten the Old Testament service period for his daughter, since Ferdinand had unforeseeably become the heir to a fortune about the respectable size of which the results of probate had left no doubt.

The officer knew Ferdinand better than he had known Heinrich, and was of the opinion that the former would have been much better suited to the life of a soldier than a merchant. Ferdinand was full of fire and life, sat a horse well, was a good swimmer, dancer, ice-skater, and hunter, and reportedly also a good fencer because in his unusually fiery nature he always behaved like a man who is not afraid of a duel. His way of life was completely respectable and well regulated, his expenditures moderate, and if he entertained a passion for any of the amusements of young people, then it was for the least expensive of them all: the theater. It cost him nothing more than the price of a ticket since he did not enter into any relationships with the beauties of the theatrical world, but rather contented himself with the pleasure of the performances.

All of the features of this conversational portrait corresponded with the image of Ferdinand's character that I had made for myself, and I was happy for Mariane's sake, as she interested me too fervently for me to want to grant her to a man who would be unworthy of her ardent love.

CHAPTER VII. *Quiet Intimacies*

Rationality is impossible with two people in love.
Knigge

I could not resist the temptation to pay a visit to my new acquaintances when opportunity next led me to B... for a few days.

I was received like a friend, like a cherished relative, and the dry councillor himself fulfilled the literal meaning of his invitation to regard his house as my own by having my baggage brought into his courtyard from the hotel where I had alighted and placed in the most pleasant room of his house, all without my knowledge. It did not matter how I protested; Mariane was not to be opposed, and the more opportunity I found to hear from her about the positive sides of her beloved, Ferdinand, the more pleasant my stay became.

Reared from childhood in the merchant class, he possessed, it is true, no so-called scholarly or classical education; but he had read and reflected far beyond the limits within which the intellectual capacity of the merchant is customarily contained. His passion for theater-going had made him receptive to the effects of poetry and the fine arts, although at that time (circa 1816) the German stage had already begun to put true dramatic art second to that sensationalistic non-sense of every sort to which it yielded its place. Moreover, he had lived for a time in the great republic of the New World in which his uncle had made his home for several years, and he had brought back with him lively and vivid concepts of human rights and human dignity, of the freedom of the people and of conscience, of middle-class virtue and governmental justice, which made his views on European matters very interesting.

Mariane appeared to note with unspoken joy how much Ferdinand's intellect attracted me. There arose between us in a short time a kind of friendly relationship, in which my family was also included upon a further exchange of visits, and we soon enjoyed what one could call a close friendship.

As particularly regards my relationship to Albus, we were not entirely without a subject for intimacy, but it seemed rather unnecessary. The surprising impression that Mariane's physical attractions had made upon me had been replaced by the sympathy engendered in my heart by her moving passion for another, and by my entirely proper pleasure in her intellect and her temperament. Here, therefore, there was nothing to confide, and what should Ferdinand, for his part, have poured out upon the bosom of his new friend?

CHAPTER VIII. *The Young Lady's Commercial Venture*

Love finds a way.
Zedlitz (a comedy)

Spring came, my little village with its picturesque surroundings was an inviting destination for people, and I saw the lovers, according to rumor betrothed, in my home, albeit never unaccompanied by Mr. Brand or his Jewish relative, who was an educated and pleasant woman of forty-odd years and very welcome company to my mother. The continuing silence about the subject of the general rumor, the union of the two young people, began to surprise me. When I found myself in the garden one day with Mariane, unintentionally without witnesses, the correspondingly more intimate conversation drove me to the question, "Now, my beautiful friend, can one wish you happiness anytime soon?"

"I hope so," she said, not without some anxiety.

"You hope so? What do you mean?"

"May I bore you a little with the story of my small vexation?"

"Speak, Mariane dear."

"Now, you see, my weaker sex loves the abso — what does my republican call it?"

"Absolute power."

"Yes. I am probably absolute enough, in Ferdinand's heart, I think, but I cannot become the master of his entire soul. A rebel still rules there: the pain over his brother, a pain which I would like to call stubborn and capricious, and which confounds all my plans."

"After what I witnessed last autumn, the duration of that pain is not incomprehensible to me."

"And yet it is unnatural! — You never knew his brother?"

"No."

"Oh, there never were two more dissimilar characters than these brothers. Heinrich, almost ten years older, attractive, educated, sensible, but cold, dry, unsympathetic — in a word, every inch a merchant, like —"

She stopped short with a slight blush. "I know no similar character of the same age. My father may appear thus to you, but he was not always this way — he loved, he loves me; age, business, people with their self-serving deceit have caused him to develop a tough hide that only softens in rare moments. Heinrich Albus sought closer contact with my father because he helped his credit; he won my father's approval through the way he conducted business with him, and he did not fail to pay attention to his only daughter, who was the apple of her father's eye. Then Ferdinand comes to B..., moves into our house, thrills me with his ardent passion — enough of that, you can easily imagine all this for yourself; only you have no concept of the fierceness, of the impatience of his passion. And there was no solution to this! As my father's clerk he could not be my husband, and even if his inheritance had not been too small to permit him rapidly to become a partner of my father's, it was not available to him in fewer than three years; until that time it was in Heinrich's care by the power of a contract with Ferdinand's guardian. In spite of this I ventured to convince my father to accept a partnership for 12,000 talers; but Ferdinand could not convince his brother to release this amount three years before the expiration. Then Heinrich's sad fate overtakes him, Ferdinand becomes the master of a fortune four times that size, my father desires a business-partnership with him, and now —"

"What, my friend, Albus would be capable...?"

"Oh, no, no! His passion for me is still the same. There is no thought, no drop of blood, no nerve in him, about which I could not say with certainty that it is mine. His entire being is attached to me as steel is to a magnet. And yet he will not yield to my father's wishes. He has sold Heinrich's house, his furnishings, and his business, and wants to use nothing of the whole fortune save his inheritance from his parents, because he has convinced himself that he was the foremost cause of Heinrich's death."

"Upon what does he base this fantastic idea?"

"I do not know exactly myself; the web he weaves in his mind is so subtle that my memory can retain as little as my reason allows me to fathom. Heinrich wanted to go to M… to reach a compromise in the matter of an excessive demand made upon his pocket. Thrifty as he was, he wanted to go on foot; he asked Ferdinand to accompany him through the boundary woods and to bring his pocket-pistol. Ferdinand thought this unnecessary, and additionally he had neither bullets nor bullet-mold for it. Heinrich took the pistol to see whether he could find a suitable bullet-mold at the gunsmith's, and came back with two bullets that likely did not fit well, because I had to produce a small piece of strong linen before Ferdinand could load the weapon. That much I certainly know about the matter; what follows I deduced from isolated utterances of Ferdinand's. He had agreed to do Heinrich the favor of accompanying him in the quiet hope of persuading his brother to release his inheritance from his parents before the date of expiration. They speak about this in the woods, and Heinrich repeatedly pleads a shortage of funds, which Ferdinand does not want to believe. Ferdinand becomes heated and says loudly, 'No money? And yet you are carrying 8,000 talers in your pocket to M… to pay off a demand which is not pressing?' Just after these words Ferdinand claims to have heard a noise in the undergrowth as if a wild animal got up and ran away. Take note of that; if I am not mistaken it is the main thread in the web in his mind. After some minutes Ferdinand says, 'At the least it would be stupid of me to be good-natured enough to escort you and your money further through the woods.' Defiantly, he turns around. Shortly thereafter the assault occurs. Now you see, out of this he creates a crime. The aforementioned loud words were supposedly heard by a bandit hidden in the thickets or by the bandits' sentinels, and his turning around supposedly emboldened the villain to attempt the robbery. His running up with the pocket-pistol in his hand cost his brother his life; in the absence of this rashness Heinrich would only have been robbed, not shot; without the pocket-pistol the rashness would not have been possible; if he had not been so obsequious as to agree to accompany Heinrich the accident could never have taken place, and without the impatience of his passion for me he would never have been so obsequious. In this way he joins thread to thread. He regards even the fact that he had no bullets or bullet-mold as a sign of Providence to which he should have paid attention. Do you not think that such subtle detail in his self-torture borders on madness?"

"Not so completely, my friend; there is a great deal of probability in his suspicion that his loud words in the woods and his turning around could have given the hidden bandit the desire and the courage to attack."

"But what then underlies his refusal to make forthright use of his brother's estate, which he has inherited?"

"That is an exaggeration of his sensitive conscience. What does he think of doing with the remainder of his brother's fortune?"

"His uncle in Philadelphia is supposed to receive it, to use it in his business and keep it for an emergency — but what do I know? To tell the truth, I fear that he, always dissatisfied with Europe, as you know, has been quietly considering the thought of living in his beloved America after my father's death."

"Whither you admittedly would prefer not to follow him," I said, laughing.

"Oh, to the ends of the earth, my dear sir!" she said quickly, and with a sincerity of feeling which moved me to press her hand to my lips. "And yet I feel that Ferdinand's state of mind cannot be allowed to continue, and so I have availed myself of a quite audacious method to end it."

"An audacious one?"

"Well now, it is at least somewhat dangerous for his worldly possessions. I have — you will laugh, when you hear that a girl has been engaging in trade speculations; but you know that I am a Jewish girl by birth. Enough, I have brought my father to consider pursuing a business association with the uncle in Philadelphia, who is well-to-do, has a good reputation and is married, but is said to be still childless. Ferdinand has endorsed this idea eagerly, a thorough plan has been developed; and thereupon rests my hope, although I understand little of the plan."

"And the American?"

"We expect letters with every mail delivery. Meanwhile, could you disperse the phantoms in Ferdinand's mind? He recognizes and honors the superiority of your quiet intellect over his giddy, tempest-tossed soul. Oh, do this, dear sir! In doing so you brighten the future of a girl who admires you deeply, who loves you like a daughter." She had taken my hand in both of hers, and pressed it softly and with a soulful look to her heart.

CHAPTER IX. *The Power of the Senses*

> Not gentle breezes from the west
> Bore me forth to love's desire!
> No, I rode the wild storm's crest;
> flames that shot out from my breast
> stones would soften with their fire.
> Bürger, *The Solitary Woman's Epic Song*

On that same day I found an opportunity to speak to Albus alone.

"The suspicion," I said, "that your loud words in the woods could have revealed to the bandit that Heinrich was carrying a great deal of money, is probable, I will concede to you. Indeed, I will even allow it to be regarded as a certainty. What follows from this? Chance acquainted the bandit with the enticing circumstance, and even if it could be proved that without this chance the robbery would not have been attempted, your words still remain an accidental cause of the misfortune. You did not desire it, you did not foresee that it would take place, and so, like the marksman who killed a child hidden behind the target, it could have been brought about through your own actions without anyone's being able to blame you for it."

This appeared to make sense to him, and, to judge by the look which he turned upon me during the last of my words, to soothe him as well. This simple success caused me to go one step further; a step beyond Mariane's charge to me. What she had confided to me of Ferdinand's impetuous passion filled me with greater concern for her future than did his tendency to exaggerated self-blame. I therefore directed the discussion to the probable time of his marriage. He thought it very near. I remarked that a great distance lay between B... and Philadelphia, and that concerns on his uncle's part could perhaps oppose the formation of the partnership, concerns that could only be resolved by means of a lengthy correspondence or could even necessitate a journey. He appeared to be very disquieted by this prospect and admitted that this would make him very unhappy.

"Why, my dear Albus? What could trouble you about a brief delay? You live in Mariane's house, enjoy her company daily, the girl loves you so deeply, so purely, so exclusively; can you, while conscious of your advantages, yield to the worry of losing Mariane's heart?"

"My advantages? My pitifulness, you mean to say. Who am I, then, when compared to her? Do I still have an intellect? Does a soul still live in me? Am I still a human being, a creature endowed with reason, since I first saw her? I feel like an animal, like a base, lascivious, obscene animal that she must be ashamed to love, whose mute speech she must be ashamed to understand."

"You are fair to Mariane," I replied, "but unfair to yourself. What you feel you regard as a crude carnal desire, unworthy of its object, but therein lies the proof that you have grasped the essence of Mariane's spirit and that your soul loves the girl as intensely as your senses desire her."

"That is true!" he cried, his hand upon his breast, "I feel that, I know that; but can she know it? Can I tell her that, can I allow her to see into my heart?"

I was amazed at the mighty battle of the intellectual and sensual natures in the breast of this man. I knew nothing to say to him except the platitude that possession of her would temper his ardor.

"Of course, of course!" he cried out, "and for exactly this reason — this intoxication of my imagination will only last until the reality of our union, and then my soul will right itself, my mind throw off its fetters, and I will again be the one I was, worthy of her heart, happy, and able to make her happy."

Thus — I thought to myself— thus loves a man who is in the fullest youthful power of body and soul. Thus do women want to be loved. The fiery girl had made a choice which can only succeed where there is a healthy heart and a sound spirit. And she appeared to know that so well that it would have been superfluous to tell her what I had heard.

CHAPTER X. *The North American Partner*

To you, oh Gods, belongs the merchant.
Schiller

The letters from Philadelphia had arrived. Their contents could not be more auspicious; they brought with them the signed partnership contract. Mr. Brand invited us to a family party, the formal engagement of the lovers, to which we should be witness. The wedding was set for a mere three weeks later. How bewitching Mariane was in the transfiguration of her inner happiness!

"Now, my dear confidant," she whispered in my ear while squeezing my hand, "now everything is as I wish it to be; you have swept the ugly cobwebs completely from his mind."

Indeed, Ferdinand appeared to be a completely different person. The certainty of the fulfillment of his wishes appeared already to have wreaked in him that which he had heretofore expected of its presence: the subordination of passion to the scepter of reason, the "righting of his soul," as he had called it in that conversation. The serenity of his mind was apparent with every word, visible in every expression; and when he joked with Mariane, who was accustomed to calling him her republican, that she would sooner or later have to set sail with him for the new world in order personally to explain to his uncle the true goal of the partnership plan which she had invented, then this took place on both sides in such a fashion that I suspected that the thought of living in the youthful, flourishing republic sometime in the future might already have been seriously discussed.

CHAPTER XI. *The Murder*

"No, murder's too damn short a word;
The act will stretch out to eternity."
Marduff in *King Yngurd*, V, 2

The evening before the wedding festivities (the day before, I should actually say) had arrived. Mariane had informed my sister that we should not expect to return to our own four walls again in fewer than three days, and that we should prepare ourselves for a considerable ball at which no one was allowed to be merely an onlooker. I was arranging some files in my office which could be needed in my absence, and my sister was sorting through my drawers to gather together the individual pieces of my rarely-used formal dress. The hooves of a horse at the door drew her to the window.

"Good God, what could this mean?" she asked. "Albus has just arrived."

I hurried to her at the window. My servant had hold of the reins of the lone horse; it was bathed in sweat and flecked with foam. Not without fearful hesitation I opened the door to greet the comer.

"Ferdinand," I cried, "why are you here? What brings you to us, and today of all days?"

"That which first brought me into this room: the murder."

"For God's sake," cried Juliane, "what has happened? Albus!"

"Albus!" I repeated in the same startled way.

"Albus?" he said, with a scornful smile coloring his features: "*Cain*, you should say!"

Juliane gave vent to a cry of horror. She hurried from the room and closed the door, which had been left open.

"What sort of strange relapse is this?" I said. "And of all the days! Speak! You are in the presence of a friend."

"That you cannot be anymore," he answered firmly: "You are my judge. It is fratricide that I freely confess to you. Not caused, but committed, of my own free will. Not my hasty speech, but this, my hand, is Heinrich's murderer. I demand of your office that which is mine by right: death."

I was stunned by the expression of truth with which he spoke these words. And yet my entire soul strove to disbelieve what must surely plunge Mariane into the deepest misery.

"Albus," I said, after I had, with difficulty, gained some composure, "the friend must be convinced if he is to give way to the judge. An unsought confession, an uncoerced accusation of oneself of a capital crime is not the same as proof thereof. You have presented yourself to the judge; now give clear and certain answers to his questions. What has come between you and your bride?"

"What has come between the sinner and the goddess? The unexpiated crime."

"Does Mariane know this?"

"I have confessed it to her."

"When?"

"Yesterday evening."

"Why did you confess it to her?"

He stared at me rigidly a few moments. "It was high time; two days later and the saint would have been soiled by a murderer."

"Madman!" I cried. "What have you done? How did Mariane bear this fright? Is she still alive? Will she live?"

"She will; the pure are strong."

"Does she believe in your crime?"

"Can she doubt it? She wanted to doubt it; indeed, she sank down upon her knees with a plain and pitiful 'No.' But I could not lie, could not play this horrible role anymore. So she rose from the floor, stood before me like a goddess, and severity and gentleness were joined in her face. 'I will cry for you, Ferdinand,' she said, 'but I will not see you again upon earth.'"

My fear for the unfortunate girl ebbed. "Does she know," I asked, "before whom you now stand? Is she aware of your decision?"

He thought a moment. "She cannot be in doubt of it," he answered, "and I have informed her father of it in writing."

"It is horrible!" I sighed, in anticipation of all of the miseries which threatened me in the handling of this case. "It is impossible, Albus, I cannot conceive of it! You said that you shot your brother willfully?"

"Yes."

"With malice aforethought, with planned and considered intent?"

"What?" he cried in astonishment. "Does it not amount to the same thing?"

"No, no!" I cried, invigorated with new hope. "Tell me! Exactly and down to the smallest detail!"

This he did, frequently interrupted by my questions. I shall narrate the episode as a whole.

Chapter XII. *The Altercation*

"Desist from hurling such sharp words."
Aeschylus in *Prometheus Bound*

Up to the words that Ferdinand had spoken to Heinrich in the woods, and which he believed had made a bandit aware of the good booty to be had from Heinrich, everything was in accord with that which I had already heard from Mariane. Ferdinand truly had heard the noise in the thicket, and, anticipating an attack, had drawn the pistol and cocked it. He held it thus in his hand, and the interrupted conversation began anew as they traveled further. The more stubbornly Heinrich insisted upon his contractual rights, the more heated Ferdinand became.

"But what do you want with the money now?" the former said. "Nothing presses you; I have arranged a good position for you, your wages are more than you need; establishing yourself at your age is utter foolishness; you still have a great deal to learn here, and for three more years."

"Well, then you must know," said Ferdinand. "I am in love."

"You are? Sincerely?"

"How else? With my whole being!"

"Is that so? And with whom then, pray tell?"

"Mariane."

"My, my! And she?"

"What do you care about it? It is enough that I hope to be happy if you deal in a brotherly, compassionate fashion, and release the small advance."

"Yes, esteemed brother, that makes the issue even more ticklish, since — to offer candor for candor — I have not myself entirely given up that thought and that hope."

Ferdinand felt as if lightning had struck him. Jealousy flared up.

"You will do that on the spot! Not a step further! You will swear an oath — by your hope of heaven — never to think such a thing again! Or as truly as God exists! As truly as I love! A bullet — today or tomorrow — upon the slightest suspicion — I will send *this* bullet through your brain!"

"Madman!" screams Heinrich, shoves Ferdinand away, and threatens to bare his sword cane. Ferdinand, to forestall his own danger and blind to that of his opponent, strikes out with the pistol against the latter's hand; it discharges, Heinrich cries out and collapses gasping.

One will notice that this testimony agrees most exactly with the condition of the body, even if the circumstances had also left room for doubt. Heinrich would have had to take the cane in his left hand in order to expose its blade, and it was on the left side that the bullet had penetrated his body and the shot singed his clothes.

Ferdinand stands stunned for a few moments; but Heinrich still twitches.

"Save yourself—*yourself*, Ferdinand," he stammers. "Over there —*there*— a bandit — not *you*— hurry! Our honor — our name — go report this — go — go!"

Those were, as well as Ferdinand had remembered them, the last words of his brother, who, clear-headed as he was, wanted to indicate to Ferdinand a means by which he could avoid the suspicion and the scandal of a killing.

Ferdinand naturally could not say how long it took before he became receptive to the thought of using this means. He remained on his knees next to the dead man, stunned by pain. When consciousness returned to him fully, he took up the weapon, which had only released the contents of one barrel, and thought to end his torture. At that moment it was as if he heard Mariane's voice in his ear, as if he heard the words of the oath which she had sworn after the accident of the coachman's child: not to survive his suicide. It was a question not of his life, but of Mariane's, and in a stubborn battle the power of despair was overcome by the omniscience of love. He took upon himself and studied the role which the dying man had shown him, and the reader has seen with what effort he played it for nearly a year.

CHAPTER XIII. *The Interrogation*

"The best explanation of what a person intended to do
comes from that person himself."
Erichson in *King Yngurd*, I, 5

However great Ferdinand's culpability was, since he had struck at Heinrich's hand with a loaded and cocked gun, still it appeared to me to be conclusive that he could not be regarded as a deliberate murderer. So that this could also be clearer to him who passed judgment upon Ferdinand, I believed that I would have to convince the perpetrator himself before I legally interrogated him. But that was absolutely impossible.

"Even if I did not have the intent to kill Heinrich when I struck him; nonetheless I had the will to do so when I held the weapon to his forehead. If he had not pushed me away, if he had let but one single word more fall about his intentions toward Mariane, I would have pulled the trigger, that is certain. Accordingly, I killed him of my own will."

All of my attempts to convince him that not merely his will mattered, but also its immediate causal connection with the deadly course of events, were useless, whether that was because his reason was not practiced enough to grasp such concepts or because he desired death with his usual passion.

Meanwhile, however, I did succeed during the actual examination in preventing him from accusing himself of a clear intent to murder. I asked the question whether he had had the will to kill his brother with the blow from the weapon.

He denied this and added, "I struck at his hand so that he could not draw the blade; even a child understands that."

"Did you not think that the weapon could discharge and kill him?"

"I thought about nothing; the weapon could just as easily have been a rolling pin."

Rarely has the reluctance of a suspect to answer the question laid before him caused the inquisitor so much joy as I felt in that moment. I almost saw Ferdinand's life secure. In any case, his answers, together with the confession that he had freely made, entitled me to spare him the handcuffs, and I thought I was risking nothing when I gave him as a prison the room in which he had spent the night after the deed. To guard Ferdinand I chose for this and the following day four of the most reasonable men of the village and I provided him with reading as well as writing materials.

CHAPTER XIV. *The Lady for the Defense*

"Thus thou must the burden bear
Of the crime thou didst commit.
Every step thou now doest take,
Makes it harder to submit
Life and soul to black despair."
Hugo in *The Guilt*

I passed the night sleeplessly, and with the break of day I hurried to B... In order to be there all the more quickly I mounted Ferdinand's horse and gave orders that my carriage should follow me to bring me back. From his window the councillor saw me dismount, and a glimpse of the horse relieved him of any doubt that Albus had carried out the course of action which he had set down in writing, and had presented himself as a criminal to me in my official capacity. Pale and with tear-swollen eyes, his head and hands trembling with weakness, the councillor came toward me with Ferdinand's letter in his hand.

"Oh, Mr. von L... ," he said, "what a house of misery you enter!"

I could speak only a few words of comfort to him, because I felt myself drawn, impatiently, to Mariane. As I opened the door she had already left the sofa upon which the myrtle wreath was lying which should have adorned her lovely hair today; and stood in the middle of the room.

"Welcome, wedding guest!" she said in a voice that pierced all my nerves.

I could not speak, she read my feelings in my eyes, appeared to want to show me her composure in her own, but in the next moment threw herself, loudly sobbing, upon my chest.

"It is true," she said, as she righted herself slowly again. "Tears bring relief. Come, sit down with me, tell me everything that I am allowed to know about the horrible deed."

"You may know everything, dear Mariane, but as I believed you to be informed in detail of the circumstances, I am that much less prepared for a recital of them."

She shook her head in denial and stared rigidly at the floor. I asked her to tell me instead what could have driven Ferdinand so suddenly to a confession.

"Guilt," she said.

"Naturally, but that was present since the deed."

"But not the tragedy of that name," she replied.

And thus it actually was. Although not new anymore to the German stage, the content of this drama was completely unknown to Ferdinand until two days ago. The playboard of B... announced it "for the first time," and Ferdinand had little trouble persuading Mariane to see the performance with him. One can imagine the impression which this tragedy and especially the role of Hugo — a guest appearance by one of the greatest tragic actors of Germany — must have made upon Ferdinand. Mariane did not realize the depth of his impression until the conclusion of the third act, at which time Ferdinand repeated aloud the catch-word of the actor, "*scaffold*," crying out, giving voice to his inner horror, and, as everyone looked quickly toward the place from which the strange sound had come, stumbled senselessly from the box.

Mariane hurries after him. Suspecting that the guilt that still torments him could be greater than he has hitherto admitted, she beseeches him with all the power of her fear. He remains silent for a long time. Finally he says, "You yourself just heard it, just saw it. It is Oerindur, before whom you stand, it is Cain! I — I shot my brother."

She stands there, destroyed. She falls down before him and entreats him to recant the horrible thing he has just said. Thereupon he explains to her with the firmness of a clear inner insight the intolerability of his burden, that he wishes to save her Elvira's disgrace, and that instead of climbing into the bridal bed he will mount the scaffold.

Here she closed the description of this scene. After a while she raised her eyes — not without shyness — to mine, and asked, in a melancholy fashion, "Tell me, dear sir, does one execute people here by de — de — does one decapitate, with an ax?"

"No, unfortunate girl," I replied. "God willing, it will not come to that."

These words worked upon her spirit with all the power of a joyful surprise.

"What? It will not, you said? You said that? His judge?" Her half-opened lips trembled in anticipation of my answer, and her eyes hung upon my lips.

"I uttered a hope, dear Mariane, but a hope which I do not harbor without foundation. Much is missing that would implicate Albus to the same degree as this Hugo."

She rose. "Oh, for God's sake, speak! If he is not so — if my heart — if I did not have to despise him — Oh, Jesus! The bliss could kill me!"

With urgent brevity, I gave her a description of the essentials of the unfortunate course of events.

"You see, my dear," I continued, "he is not a deliberate murderer. A surge of emotion and a carelessness — admittedly an enormous one — are his offenses. I do not want to conceal from you that there could be difficulties in making the involuntary nature of his killing comprehensible to the judicial scholars who will pass sentence upon Ferdinand; they keep to the coarsest outlines of the external facts and to the dead letter of the law. Nevertheless, if he is well defended —"

"Who will defend him?" she interrupted me hastily.

"That is still uncertain. I have come mainly to seek here a man whom I trust —"

"I want to defend him!" she cried out, with a tone and a look of inspiration. I was scarcely able to suppress the urge to press her to my bosom.

"Magnificent, heavenly creature! Yes, by God you would! You would be moving, would suppress all doubt, fetter conviction; you would be victorious if you could speak for him to a jury that is allowed to bring a heart with it into the fearful rooms of that court. But in Germany? He must be defended in writing, on dead white paper, before shriveled souls, before ice-cold judges who rule upon the written record."

She dropped her eyes, ashamed. A sigh escaped her breast. "Oh, I am a fool! Oh, dear, dear sir! Just rescue his life! I can bear to lose him, but I cannot bear the picture of his bloody and disgraceful death."

I assured her that I had come to B... to request the best defense lawyer in the land to take up Ferdinand's defense; and took my leave of her with the feeling that I ought not to see her again, at least for the immediate future. I had escaped the power of her physical charms, but the beauty of her soul, the wonderful mixture of feminine tenderness and masculine power in her spirit, endangered the peace of my heart.

Chapter XV. *The Counsel for the Defense*

> If he can really split a hair,
> He's just the man to not despair;
> If he can merely cut askew,
> He's only good to barber you.
> The Author

Doctor Rebhahn in B... was, in my opinion, the right man to fight a victorious battle for Ferdinand's life against the usual obtuseness of the periwigged company who would rule upon the record. Not that I knew him personally, but I had read many of his arguments for the defense. They had been conceived with such knowledge of the law, understanding of human nature, acuity, emotion and eloquence that I had formed the highest opinion of the inner substance and worth of this man.

I went to see him. I had imagined he would be a man in his middle years, with the captivating and imposing figure of an orator. Nothing could be less true. Small, gaunt, not exactly humpbacked but noticeably misshapen, a pointed nose the color of burgundy, clever and penetrating gray eyes under shaggy brows, more powder than hair on his head, and, in appearance as well as in dress looking as if he had been close to fifty at the turn of the century. He received me among his papers as a craftsman is wont to receive his customers in his workshop. After I had told him my name and position he tipped over a chair upon which a mountain of documents had lain and offered it to me to sit upon with the request to state my errand without preamble or digression. As soon as I had mentioned the name Albus he interrupted me.

"Have already heard of the *casu . Fratricidium* , freely confessed under strange conditions, the day before his wedding! The rumor has been circulating since this morning through all of B..., since Councillor Brand hastily cancelled the wedding and lost his *countenance* to such a degree that he allowed the reason to become known among his servants. You, dear sir, are, I hear, known in that worthy home?"

I answered in the affirmative, and added that I sympathized most intensely with the misfortune of this family, and hoped to lessen it if I could move the most competent attorney of the area to take upon himself the defense of the prisoner.

"Oh, my dear sir, please! Yes yes! the beautiful Jewish girl is well suited to the task of arousing lively sympathy, all right. Her father ought to be concerned about that. I do not deny that I have already secretly wished a little to get my hands on this remarkable case."

"Doctor," I said, allowing my gaze to survey the numerous piles of documents, "you appear to be overburdened by business. Perhaps you have a few young and clever beginners to help you?"

"Not at all. I myself am the man, most honored sir. I claim no work that comes from other pens, and take upon myself no more than I can master. *Excipe* the defenses! That is my main work, everything else must wait."

The servant brought wine and a small meal. I stood up, announced that I was pressed for time, and asked merely to know whether he would prefer to read the files in the courthouse or wished them to be sent to him.

"Please take a glass of Tokay wine with me. Files? Hm! They won't be thick, and the best document is always the person of the accused. I will therefore go there myself. Since you are interested in the matter, you can meanwhile share your private view of it."

I gave him the general content of the interrogation. At the beginning he listened with a clever wariness, as if it mattered less to him to hear about the case than to see through my inner self, and I put it down to the wine, to which he addressed himself energetically, that his eyes gradually lost this unpleasant expression and took on a lively fire. I was mistaken about the effect of the wine.

"Magnificent case!" he cried out. "A borderline between intent and chance, deed and accident, like the blade of a razor."

"Unfortunately, doctor!"

"Doesn't matter, doesn't matter; we could sharpen the bread knives of the knights of the Round Table with God's help. When do you expect to be home again?"

"Today."

"I shall turn up tomorrow, provided that the accused is in agreement with the choice—"

"I assure you of that; he is completely indifferent about his defense."

CHAPTER XVI. *The Verdict*

"They cannot tell what's meant, what's accident."
Alf in *King Yngurd*, V, 12

Rebhahn came, spoke to the prisoner, took the files away with him, and eight days later I had in my hands the written defense, which as a jurist I admired and which filled me with new hope.

Thin files enjoy a kind of prerogative over thick ones in the halls of the judges: they are read sooner. Within a month's time the verdict was handed down; but what a product!

"Whereas it may appear to be the case (this was approximately the quintessence of its content), that the defendant — because he accompanied his brother, who was carrying a sizable sum of money, into the woods for the supposed reason of protecting him from bandits, and for this reason took with him a loaded pocket-pistol, but thereupon desired money from his brother for the establishment of his own business, and then complained bitterly about the fact that his brother wanted to take this money to M... instead of paying it to him, and whereas, on the occasion of his brother's continued refusal, drew the pocket-pistol and threatened to send the bullet contained therein through his brother's brain, and whereas then, as the threatened man, in order to defend himself, reached for the sword-cane he had with him, the defendant struck at him with the pocket-pistol in such a way that it discharged and killed his brother, whereupon the defendant, when the wounded man was dead, took to himself the latter's bag of gold, pocket-book and watch — whereas such is the case, therefore might the defendant be regarded as a murderous thief and for this be sentenced to the punishment of the wheel; however, because the defendant neither admitted, nor can it be established with certainty from his actions since the time of the deed, that he intended to keep the objects which he took from the dead man and which he has given up to the court as such, and also because the intent of robbery could, to a certain degree, be disproved by the fact that the defendant, had he succeeded with the murder and the subsequent clever hypocritical concealment of the identity of the perpetrator, would in any case have received as the closest intestate heir the entire fortune of the murdered man, and consequently it could only be ascertained from the documents, that the defendant, for the sake of future advantage, had secretly deprived said brother of his life and had sought to assign the deed to an unknown person; whereupon, however, with regard to the murder of a blood relative and other pertinent circumstances which increase the suitability of the death penalty, not merely the defendant's freely made confession, stemming from penitence, but especially the circumstance that the defendant really was entitled to demand from the murdered man the sum which he sought, should be taken into consideration — etc., etc., etc.; therefore, if the defendant continues to persist in his confession of this capital crime, he shall be

sentenced and punished from life to death with the ax, and the costs of this judgment shall be taken from his fortune — etc."

To whatever degree the punishment that was pronounced was in accordance
with the law, the reasons given for the decision were not in accordance with common sense. When they were made public, Albus listened to them with astonishment, with indignation, finally with such visible wrath that I anticipated a
vehement outburst of his deeply wounded moral sensitivity. But as soon as he
heard the punishment to which he had been sentenced, the storm in his head
quieted suddenly and his face became cheerful.

"That is just," he said, "that is the justice which I can demand, because I
deserve it. But great God, what kind of people are those! Did they first have to
make me into a devil in their minds in order to pave the way for my reconciliation with God?"

He would hear nothing of a second defense. When I had persuaded him of
the indispensability of the thing, he said coldly, "Well, if it must be, then Mr.
Rebhahn can write it; I only ask for permission not to see him again; I found
him repulsive."

"And yet he is the only man who is perhaps still capable of saving you."

Proudly he opened his mouth. "I *am* saved; he wants to see me damned
again, damned to my former pain."

CHAPTER XVII. *The Long Delay*

You don't try all at once to know,
Whene'er the snow melts, it will show.
Goethe

Dr. Rebhahn laughed over the verdict. "One must admit," he said, "that
the gentlemen of the court have purchased their grounds for doubt devilishly
cheaply. They could just as well have doubted whether Albus ought to be burned
at the stake because he had introduced fire by means of the spark from the pocket-
pistol. That would then have made the rebuttal, which was supposed to supply
the grounds for the decision, all the easier. Best of all would have been: Where
fire is not usable, one reaches for iron, as Hippocrates said, or Salenus, or God
knows which old physician."

"But how do you plan to reverse the matter now?"

"First of all, I'll try to prolong the thing; I'll hoodwink the examining magistrate, with your permission. I can keep things in a state of confusion for a while,
but *interim aliquid fit*." (="In the meantime something else could happen.")

Indeed he did delay with the second written defense, and finally brought
forth the objection, formerly only superficially treated, that a mistake had been

made in the investigation: the facts of the matter were not completely ascertained, nothing had been done to produce the tool with which the manslaughter was supposed to have been committed. Yet this was necessary if there was any possibility of finding it, because the weapon could provide grounds for a defense as easily as an autopsy could. He demanded a search in the river. Naturally it resulted in nothing; how does one find a pocket-pistol again on the bottom of a current a fathom deep?

"The search was not careful enough," he maintained, "it must be repeated." One will note that he had created a vicious circle which I could not let him use as he pleased. I made a report to the government. Here his legal argument, supported by the letter of the law, had made such inroads that there was distress about how the objection could be thrust aside. A chance situation helped unexpectedly. The Department of Road Construction had just decided to raze the wooden bridge, which sustained yearly damage from ice-drifts, and build a stone bridge in its place. For this purpose, during the construction of the foundation of the bridge, the entire stream was to be deflected by means of damming and the digging of two temporary canals that could take the flow during low water, in order to empty out the entire portion of the river bed in which construction was to take place. One was consequently of the opinion that Dr. Rebhahn (against whom it was occasionally pleasurable to retaliate on account of his tiresome acuity) could not demand a more careful search for the pocket-pistol than would be possible with this opportunity. It would take place, and if one did not find the weapon it must then be regarded as undiscoverable.

CHAPTER XVIII. *The Blue Beans*

"Caspar, I'll kill you. Tell me, what kind of bullet was it?"
Max in *The Marksman*

Rebhahn was triumphant. That has bought us a delay of a couple of years, he thought. But the autumn and the mild winter were so dry that already in the middle of December the interim canals were opened, and soon the ground below the new bridge had dried out and was laid bare. To Rebhahn's great annoyance, the pocket pistol was found. Albus recognized it as his. His initials, F. A., were engraved on it. It was presented to Dr. Rebhahn in court. Peevishly he turned it this way and that in his hand. Everything fitted Albus's confession perfectly. The right barrel discharged, the left cocked and still loaded, as revealed by the priming powder, which had become a solid mass. After he had carefully unscrewed the flint so that it would be impossible to fire accidentally, he examined the loaded barrel.

"Thunderation," he said, "if that isn't mud in there, then it's a messed-up, misfired shot. Let's coax that out of there."

The forester of the town, to whom we immediately adjourned, and who was equipped with the necessary instruments of a gunsmith, took upon himself the removal of the breech-screw in our presence. He found the usual charge of gunpowder, but — two bullets instead of one.

"Good Lord," cried Rebhahn, "what's that? If there are two blue beans in that barrel, what in the name of a thousand devils — what was in the other?"

I was struck by the phenomenon myself. According to Mariane's story no bullets were originally available, and Heinrich had obtained only two of them from the gunsmith in B... The thought ran through my mind that one can often make a mistake when loading a double-barrelled weapon if one does not load powder into both barrels one immediately after the other, and put both bullets into the muzzle right away; because if one turns the weapon in the hand, as can easily happen unthinkingly, for example while conversing, then the right barrel becomes the left, and both will be improperly loaded.

"Correct, correct!" said Rebhahn: "It's clear, the right barrel was loaded with moonlight!"

"But where did the bullet in Heinrich's breast come from?"

"What? A bullet? A bullet from the corpse? Is it there?"[4]

"Of course."

"Quick, quick! Come! The bullet, the third bullet!"

He scraped the individual pieces of the disassembled pocket-pistol together hastily, stuck the smaller ones in his pocket, and hurried, holding the barrels in his hand, out of the forester's house into the street and, without pausing, to the courthouse.

I could not catch up to him before he was in the courtroom. He stood before the court clerk, who had just fetched the little box sealed with the court seal in which the bullet *quaestionis* was to be found.

"The bullet, the bullet!" he cried impatiently, stamping his feet while the court clerk appeared to doubt whether he was allowed to break the seal. "Quickly, open the box. The magistrate will attest that the seal is unbroken."

I did this, as impatient myself as Rebhahn. He held the barrels of the gun upright with a trembling hand. I tried the bullet, and it was — too big. There was no doubt that it must have weighed twice as much as this caliber pocket-pistol could take.

"Now — now — now?" said Rebhahn, chortling with pleasure. "The devil himself should come and try to stick that in there! Even he couldn't make it come out over here, still as round as a ball — it's pretty obvious."

---

[4][Müllner's footnote]: That Rebhahn only asked about it now was a grave mistake on his part. The size of the bullet would have awakened doubt in him from the very beginning. This doubt would, admittedly, not have occurred to him without the bullet, since the confession was already on hand.

"It is obvious," I said, "but incomprehensible!"

"What, sir? That this bullet here could not have been in this pocket-pistol there, even the most blockheaded tribunal councillor will have to understand! Hands down! Document the *novum*, the new evidence, in *optima forma*! Albus is innocent!"

"But his confession"—

"Is a lie or a mistake."

There was in fact no other possible explanation but one of these. The former made it advisable to attempt to surprise the self-admitted criminal in order to discover the truth. I had him brought before me after the weapon was reassembled.

"Albus, a circumstance has arisen about which you must make a statement."—I had the court clerk read him the record of his confession.—"That is word for word your confession; do you insist upon it?"

"Yes."

"That is the pocket-pistol which you have recognized as your own, as the instrument of the killing. Do you insist upon this?"

"Yes."

"In this box was kept the bullet that killed your brother, and which was found in his breast. I myself saw it removed, received it from the hand of the surgeon, placed it into this box and affixed the seal. Here it is."

"Well?" he asked with annoyance. "Should I maintain that it — is made of lead?"

"No, not that; but I must ask that you load it one more time, before my eyes, into this pocket-pistol."

"Are you mocking me? You, who are otherwise so compassionate?"

"It is merely a pedantic form of the judicial process. Try it!"

He set the bullet upon the muzzle and stopped short. "That is not —" He looked at me and Dr. Rebhahn in turn, his mouth twisted in scorn, he threw the bullet and weapon upon the table and said to Rebhahn, "You devil's advocate! You want to test me as your master does the Lord! You want to gain honor with your work, you want to deceive the court, you have changed the bullets like a conjurer."

I assured him of the absolute impossibility of that, I swore the truth of my words by our earlier friendship and "as truly as Mariane loves you."

He caught his breath at these words, his chest rose and sank like waves in a storm, his eyes became fixed, he clutched his forehead and rubbed it anxiously; he was in the condition of a man who doubts his consciousness, who doubts the soundness of his mind.

"If that — God in heaven! if— if— but it is not possible — not thinkable!"

"Who knows? How many bullets did you have when you loaded the pocket-pistol?"

"Two."

"Only two?"

"Heinrich brought no more."

"Well then, Albus, in this one, undischarged barrel we found both bullets."

"Oh, Lord Jesus!" he cried. "My head, my head!"

With this he dropped his head upon the table, but soon straightened up vehemently, cast his eyes to the ceiling and said: "I see nothing — nothing! The devil is after my soul, he has blinded me with glowing steel."

CHAPTER XIX. *The Bullet Seed*

"The Marksman" bears of madness news
The happy listener to amuse;
Who's truly mad, believes the ruse.
The Author

A shudder ran through me when I looked in his eyes. If all the signs did not deceive me, then he was mad. My unhappy idea of tearing apart by surprise his confession of a falsified self-accusation may have cost him his powers of reason, because the accusation was not falsified — of this there could scarcely be any doubt anymore — but rather based upon an incomprehensible self-deception. I had the doctor brought, he shook his head thoughtfully, and unfortunately it was clear all too soon that he had had good reason to do so.

Ferdinand believed that the devil, who would not tolerate his reconciliation with God, was trying to deceive him into thinking that he had not sinned, and took for this purpose the forms of all sorts of friends and acquaintances.

If any of us could succeed in communicating with him, it was Juliane with whom he most liked to speak, and to whom he would even listen without annoyance when she struck this chord. Once she even believed she had reached her goal, but then he began to cry, and said softly, "So young, so beautiful, such a heavenly soul, and yet possessed by the devil for my sake!"

In contrast, there was an almost comical scene when Rebhahn, armed with all the weapons of logic, also marched against Ferdinand's fixation. As soon as the latter recognized the former's intent, he struck the same attitude and appeared to summon up the entire remainder of his mental powers for a disputation with Rebhahn.

"You maintain that I am innocent; define my innocence for me! Of what does it consist, piece by piece?"

"It's the whole thing, my dear Mr. Albus; you imagine that you have killed your brother by a shot that was fired through your carelessness. That is, however, impossible, because the barrel that discharged was loaded with a blank, and the bullet which was found in his breast is too big for the caliber of the weapon.

"Even loaded with a blank!" he said sarcastically. "Hunters can do all kinds of things of which your philosophy cannot dream. Have you never heard of bullet seeds?"

"No."

"That should surprise me, I would have bet that you were already familiar with them. Just think, the seed looks black, like gunpowder, but it is really a bullet seed, is sowed in the barrel, and grows in there. See, don't I know the arts of hell?"

"But my dear Mr. Albus, the bullet was too big for the barrel, and cannot have come out of it."

"Ha, ha, ha! That's the twist; it swells up when it emerges into the air, and you swear that it is a different bullet."

"That is a mad notion, Mr. Albus," said Rebhahn angrily, because he thought he had been ridiculed.

"Not half as mad as your jurisprudence. If one person holds his pistol to the bosom of another, and it discharges before he pulls the trigger, and the other is dead, the lawyer demonstrates: the one did not want to pull the trigger, *ergo*, he did not fatally shoot the other. But man has a conscience, and that conscience is not a lawyer."

"That is of no concern anymore," Rebhahn replied. "Law and common sense both demand for the concept of manslaughter that the actions of the one and the instrument that he used for it bring about the death of the other. That is not the case here. You can have as many twinges of conscience as you like about your anger, your attack, your shot — that is no business of mine — but law proclaims that you are not the person who brought about your brother's death, and your weapon not the cause of it."

That appeared to bring about an effect upon Ferdinand's powers of comprehension that also activated his temperament. He fell silent some seconds, and then said with a sigh, "Ha! if someone could only explain to me how else he died!"

"It is as clear as the sun," Rebhahn responded. "The circumstances permit of no other assumption; the proven facts force human reason to the conviction that another shot, fired simultaneously with the contents of your weapon, perhaps from a significant distance, propelled the larger bullet into the breast of your brother. Could not one of the poachers at exactly this moment have missed the game that was his target?"

Albus started, his hand closed, he stood up and strode quickly across the room with his lips pressed tightly together. "He is clever!" he said to himself, and turning to me, he continued. "But he cannot catch me; he is a stupid devil; he should have taken on a better form this time. I recognized him right away in this one."

The stubbornness of his madness left nothing else to do but to leave the madness undisturbed, and to wait and see whether nature and time would free him of it.

CHAPTER XX. *The Popgun*

"'In jurisprudence there's no sense to find.'
I cannot criticize this state of mind:
I know just what this study's all about.
All laws and codes drag on and on.
Just like some terrible disease;
They are passed from every father to his son,
and gently move where'er they please.
Reason yields to nonsense —"
                    Mephistopheles in Goethe's *Faust*

Rebhahn now submitted the second written defense, and I hurried even more with the report since I expected a verdict which would free the unhappy man completely from the self-accusation of manslaughter. Not in the least!

"While it might not be completely unthinkable according to the known circumstances — the judges opined — that Heinrich Albus could have been killed by the shot — whether intentional or accidental — of a third person; still, since the prisoner insists upon his confession, and since another perpetrator or causal agent of the resultant manslaughter has not been identified; then Ferdinand Albus should be confined to a prison or work-house up until the time of his complete vindication, according to the law."[5]

Since the condition of mental confusion in which Albus continued to be found did not permit the verdict to be made known to him, it was revealed to Dr. Rebhahn as the counsel for the defense.

"Oh, the devil take you!" he cried out. "Soon you will lay down the principle that no one may be acknowledged to be innocent until he produces the guilty party. I almost wish that I were the man Albus believes me to be, in order to be able to sniff out the fellow who fired the cursed mystical bullet."

He had scarcely spoken these words when the postal messenger brought a package from a court in the neighboring state. The official sent me a certified copy of a file document with the remark that he had to believe, after everything he had heard from the rumors of the unusual case against young Albus, that the document would shed some light on that dark matter. Therein enclosed, specially packed, were a gold signet ring with the letters H. A. on either side of a staff of Mercury resting upon an anchor, and a rifle of such diminutive size that one would almost have regarded it as Lilliputian. The barrel was scarcely eight inches long, and had rifling grooves cut close together like the sort of pistol which

[5][Müllner's footnote]: This verdict is almost more characteristic than the first one, and I believe I am able to avoid all misunderstanding through the assurance that it did not come from the assessor's court in Leipzig. Saxon legal scholars will readily note that the entire case could not very well have taken place in the kingdom of Saxony. This case is the product of a German area which has, for the last quarter century, so changed its form that it may be regarded as altogether gone.

has a range beyond that of the ordinary pistol, occasionally even up to a distance of 150 paces. It appeared to have been made from such a pistol because the short stock was attached and could be unscrewed. Apparently a poacher's rifle. Both objects had in fact been found in the possession of a thief who had been taken into custody in the boundary woods after Heinrich's murder. He called himself Curly, and the investigation of him had quickly revealed that he had earlier belonged to a robber band from the other side of the Rhine, had been captured, convicted of several murders, condemned to death, and had escaped from prison and associated himself with the poachers and livestock-thieves of the boundary woods. According to his assurance, he had had the intention of bettering his life, because he knew that here one had to take a grave oath not to kill anyone except in the case of pressing danger to one's own life. He claimed to have kept that oath punctiliously; until the utterance of the instructing counsel that the sentence which he incurred for his earlier murders, and which had already been pronounced on the other side of the Rhine, could not be commuted, moved him to the confession that he had indeed once broken the oath, shortly before his most recent capture, for which the captain of the band himself was actually responsible because the latter had given him a weapon which was half an arm's length in size and yet was supposed to be able to shoot a distance of two hundred paces. He lies in the bushes near the path with this "popgun," sees two gentlemen go by, and hears that the one says to the other, "Why are you carrying 8000 talers to M... ?" This tempts Curly to practice his earlier, freer craft once more, or at least to see whether he can obtain some of the 8000 talers by means of threats. But he notices that one of the gentlemen has a double-barreled pistol in his hand, and so gets up and merely follows the travelers from a distance. It is not long before they stand still, the one dances around the other, and it occurs to the highwayman: you should see whether the captain has lied, whether the popgun really does shoot that far. He takes aim, shoots and —"just then the one doubles over." The other — he thinks — will now take to his heels; but what next! He stands still, like a lantern-post, and then kneels next to the other one and doesn't move from that spot for an hour. Finally "he staggers off," the highwayman slithers up, looks through the pockets of the dead man but finds them empty, and has to be satisfied with a ring that he pulls — not without some difficulty — from the dead man's finger.

No one will doubt any longer that it was the ring of Heinrich Albus, which Ferdinand might have noticed was gone if his reunion with the corpse had not robbed him of his senses. The mystic bullet (as Rebhahn has just called it) fitted perfectly in the highwayman's popgun, and upon closer examination even the impressions of the rifling were visible upon it.

"Now," cried Dr. Rebhahn, "now even the madman himself will have to comprehend that he is innocent!" He wanted to go to him on the spot.

"Will he believe it if he hears it from the devil?" I asked.

"You're right. He must hear it from someone who looks better than I do."

Who would be better for this purpose than Mariane?

CHAPTER XXI. *The Doctor of the Psyche*

"Therefore, as physician I surrender the patient,
If you will not come to give him this potion."
Benvolio in *The Albanian Woman*

In order to tear herself away from her grief, the strong-minded girl had seized upon a means which one admittedly cannot recommend to weak souls, simply because they are too weak to make use of it. She had occupied herself with learning the English language (the choice explains itself, because Ferdinand loved it) and had absorbed so much of it, was already so accustomed to thinking in this language, that she spoke English to me more than once at the beginning of our conversation. She had heard of the discovery of the murder weapon in the river, of the puzzling bullet, of the new verdict, and also of Ferdinand's madness; but she regarded the last as a fancy of Rebhahn's, as the so-called temporary insanity by means of which lawyers often seek to free defendants from their sentences.

I described briefly for her the way things were — that is, Ferdinand's mental state — and acquainted her with the discovery of the real perpetrator, and told her that I had not revealed this to him, because I believed that the news would have a salutory effect upon his brain if it came from her lips.

"If all my earlier observations do not deceive me," I added, "then you have such a decided power over his entire nervous system that I almost want to believe in a magnetic rapport between you two."

What joy in her eyes! What a trembling of ecstasy in her voice as she answered me. "Oh, God, yes, yes, dear sir! I wish to — no, I *shall* rescue him! I have power over his spirit, over his heart — his conscience alone is stronger than my love."

She took a coat and hat, and hurried with me to her father, to whom she explained in hurried words that she had to accompany me to Z… this minute, because Ferdinand was truly mad, and she would bring him to his senses. He found nothing to object to in this impetuousness since I confirmed the substance of her words, and a few minutes later I was sitting with her in the carriage.

CHAPTER XXII. *The Lady Reads the Record*

You're strong by nature, save yourself from death!
The crisis is decisive.
The Albanian Woman, II, 5

Anybody would understand that the goal of the short journey was the only subject of conversation. She questioned me about the history of his madness down to the smallest detail, developed thereafter the plan for her own approach, and at the same time dictated to me my own role.

I was to prepare the mentally disturbed man for her visit. As I entered he was reading Pope's "An Essay on Man," which Juliane had given him, and looked annoyed at the interruption.

"I was in B... again, dear Albus."

"Well?"

"I also saw Mariane for a few minutes."

He looked at me with a trace of disquiet in his expression, and answered, "I see her all the time."

"But as far as I remember you have not spoken of her since your stay here."

"For exactly that reason."

"All the more earnestly did she speak of you."

He took a few steps away from me. "Is she still — is she still beautiful?" he asked, turning back to me.

"She certainly is, despite the grief which she carries in her bosom."

He stared fixedly at me, stepped close to me again, stretched out his hand, let it glide down my right arm as if he could discover something by the feel of it, and then cried out, "Ha! Do not deny it! Mariane is here, I feel that she is near."

"So she is, Ferdinand; she wants to speak with you, she has something important to tell you; summon all the powers of your mind to understand it."

I gave the prearranged signal with the bell. He stood silent and trembling. I was afraid of the risky scene to come. Mariane came in quietly. While she shut the door behind her, Ferdinand covered his face with his hands. But soon he let them drop again. Mariane stood before him, spoke his name in a most moving chord of tenderness, and with the words, "Oh! my angel!" he sank down at her feet.

She raised him up; he opened his trembling lips to speak.

"Don't say anything, Ferdinand dear, not now! I see what you feel, and feel that it is inexpressible. Poor dear, how much you have suffered! How pale you have become! Let us sit down. Give me your hand. Feel the quiet beat of my heart until yours keeps pace with mine."

He did not appear to understand what was happening to him; confused about himself, his eyes sought light in mine. "Where am I, then? Are you not the — am I no longer covered with blood, no longer the fratricide — Hugo?"

"No, no," said Mariane, as she wrapped her arms around him and pressed him to her breast, "you are mine, my Ferdinand, my husband! You are free of all guilt, you were free when I fled from you as if you were a murderer. The horrible puzzle has been solved, your bloodguilt was a self-deception, a cleverly hidden lie of hell; your confession was a mistake, as forgivable as it was dreadful. Do you doubt it? Here (she stretched out her hand, in which she held the rolled-up document containing the bandit's confession), here I hold the truth, the irrefutable truth. You are innocent, the real murderer has been discovered!"

Albus leaned back away from her, and in his eyes, which remained fixed upon her, was revealed an inner battle between love and pain that made me hold my breath.

"And you, too? You, too, Mariane?— Ha, tempter! Tempter!— Come in any form you wish, only not in this one! not in this one!"

"Oh, my Ferdinand! If there is a spark of human reason left in you, then do not rob me of mine. Rave, kill me, tear me to pieces! But do not make me insane!"

These tones of deepest pain appeared to penetrate into his mind. "No," he said: "it is impossible, that is not the tempter! He has deceived you, but you are Mariane!"

"Will you be reasonable, my Ferdinand? Will you listen to me?"

"Speak! Speak!"

She snatched up the paper, which had fallen onto the sofa next to her, rolled it quickly in the opposite direction in order to straighten it out, told him with urgent words what the forest bandit had reported, and read him then his own account of the unholy deed, literally as the court reporter had written it down. But with what expression, with what tones that compelled belief! Certainly a court record has never before been read in such a fashion.

When she had finished, she looked at him like the victor in a battle. "Now, Albus," she said, "what do you think? Who was the murdered man? From whose finger did the murderer steal this ring?" (She had put it on her middle finger in reverse and held her hand out flat with the seal in front of his eyes.)

"It is Heinrich's ring!" he cried out. "It is certain, it is as clear as your eye; Curly shot him! Oh, my God, and he died deluded in the same way I was. He believed me to be his murderer!"

"Not that, either, dear Albus," I inserted. "Certainly not! Remember his last words! Did he not say: 'There — there — the bandit!' I would wager my life that he saw the perpetrator, and that it was this that he wanted to tell you."

He sprang up. "It's so, as truly as there's a God, it's so! Mariane, I am inno-cent! Not innocent, I have committed a great misdeed, have toyed with a weapon like a madman; but God has been merciful, I am not a murderer, no blood, no brother's blood clings to my hands. Oh, Mariane, my good angel, my rescuer from the tortures of conscience."

He threw himself upon her breast. "My good Ferdinand!" she said, crying softly. There were no words for my joy. Ferdinand turned to me. "Mr. von L..., my friend, I can say again, I have committed a misdeed; you are a legal scholar, what punishment awaits me?"

"None, I hope."

"That would not be just; I am prepared for it; but not a disgraceful, a dis-honorable one — that would not affect me alone."

I tried to make clear to him the impossibility of that; but I had not entirely understood him. He had not thought of a legally dishonorable (infamous) punishment, but rather of one which demeans one in the eyes of the public: cleared of the charges or not, the masses tend to regard with doubt a man over whose head the executioner's ax has hovered, whether or not the damning or exonerating judges have made a mistake. Albus seemed to feel this, and spoke of it with increasing anxiety.

Mariane heard our conversation with a gentle smile on her face. Finally she stepped up to us, took Ferdinand's hand, and said in English: "Be calm, my beloved! my republican! If the prejudices of Europeans burden us, the Atlantic Ocean is not bigger for my love than it is for my hand on the world map: the width of a hand."

How shall I describe the expression of surprise, the astonishment, the ecstasy on Ferdinand's face. For the first time he heard from the mouth of his beloved the language of the land for whose shores he had not ceased to long since he left them; and he had of necessity to recognize, in the object upon which she had spent her time and her industry during the separation from him, the greatness and inextinguishability of her love.

"Heavenly creature!" he cried in the same language, and pressed her to his breast, "how have I, as intractable and raving as I have been, deserved this heart?" Punish me, you judges, or exonerate me, think ill or well of me, you people; there is a happiness upon earth of which you cannot rob me."

Chapter XXIII. *The Devil in Person*

> If only you can bring your heart to court,
> Your mind will see the law does not fall short.
> The Author

He was acquitted completely, and in such a way that even Dr. Rebhahn, who generally did not rate the "periwigged company" very highly, was forced to admit that the one who had worked out the verdict had to be a good man, a many-sided man; *id est*, the sort of person in whom the heart as well as the brain is in the right spot. And indeed, when one read the reasons for this verdict one could scarcely doubt that the author had had the intention of acquitting the defendant not merely of the charges against him but also of the accusations he brought against himself and of those of public opinion.

"Of the crime," it said, "of which Albus accused himself, there is nothing left but an unconsidered act of passion, which the state is not entitled to punish since it did harm to no one other than the doer himself. Nor can he even be burdened with the costs of the investigation: because even if he alone brought about the investigation by means of an unfounded confession, still the misapprehension from which the confession arose was unavoidable; that is, was such as he would, under the circumstances, have necessarily had to consider the truth until his defender and the investigating magistrate succeeded in bringing the hidden truth, unknown even to the defendant, to light."

Of course, Albus was no longer my prisoner, but rather only Mariane's, by the time this statement was made known. Two weeks later the lovers were wed, publicly and with such a press of persons around them, half of them curiosity-seekers and the other half sympathizers, such as never had been seen in B.... The wedding celebration and the "real ball" took place as well, and distinguished themselves by the presence, as a guest, of the devil in person, for in this way did Mariane refer to Dr. Rebhahn, whom, in his own form, her crazed beloved had once regarded as the devil incarnate.

One month later the young couple left for Hamburg, and set sail for Philadelphia. Mariane is now the mother of two vigorous boys and a daughter who promises to resemble her in both body and soul.

"We are happy," she writes to me on the 12th of August 1826, "still as happy as we became through your efforts and those of the devil in person. My republican, my intractable beloved, has not wasted the lessons of his misfortune. His uncle and his uncle's wife love us, and our children are theirs."

Councillor Brand, although without probable hope of seeing his daughter again upon this earth, comforts both his mercantile heart with the sums which his American partner helps him earn, and his fatherly heart (which, indeed, is not to be despised) with the thought that the growing riches of the aging Philadelphian will one day be the inheritance of his family line. He has also not given up the hope of living until such time as his grandsons shall make their first journey to Germany to learn the German mercantile trade on the spot.

Since I have just thought of Mariane's most recent letter, I see no reason why I should not also quote from the postscript, which, as one knows, is seldom missing from a woman's letter. She writes, "Sometimes I really wish that our story could be made known in Germany, I mean printed; it could be useful to many an unruly lover. Now I know that you don't waste your time with such things: but I believe that if you narrated the main events to the author of the tragedy which could easily have cost my Albus his head, he would understand how to go about it. I read once in a newspaper here that he had written another tragedy, called *Albana*. Now, my name is Albus, and my Fritz (my oldest child) insists that is wrong, I actually ought to call myself Alba. So he will probably do it."

CHAPTER XXIV. *The Dear Sir*

"What? This was truth, that we just read?—"
Dear ladies, you are asking me too much.
Ask of your heart if it be such:
"The heart oft feels what to the mind is dead."
Zacharias Werner[6]

It has been done, and, I hope, in such a fashion that Alba will be satisfied when this novella reaches Philadelphia. But she will have me to thank less than her "dear sir," who has not left me much to do with respect to describing her. There are — I can say this without flattery — there are presently in Europe few women and young ladies of her caliber. That is my postscript.

Müllner

[6]Zacharias Werner, 1768–1823, Prussian civil servant turned priest; friend of, among others, E.T.A. Hoffman, Mme. de Staël, and St. Klemens Hofbauer; author primarily of tragic plays but also prose, poetry, and speeches. The source of this verse is unknown.

Otto Ludwig Emil Freiherr von Puttkammer (1802–1875)

Little is known about Emil von Puttkammer. He was born in the Prussian-Schleswig town of Reichenbach in 1802 and studied law and philosophy in Breslau. He entered civil service, rising eventually to become a privy councillor in Potsdam, where he lived at the time of his death in 1875.

Puttkammer wrote using the pseudonym Otto Ludwig. This has frequently resulted in the mistaken attribution of his work to his far more famous contemporary, the well-known writer and dramatist Otto Ludwig (1813–1865). Puttkammer wrote more than one crime novella, suggesting that his interest in mystery fiction was not entirely incidental. The work we have included here is the 1839 story *Der Tote von St. Annas Kapelle* (*The Dead Man of St. Anne's Chapel*), which first appeared in the *Urania Taschenbuch auf das Jahr 1840*, published in Leipzig in 1839; a translated and severely edited English version followed in *Blackwood's Edinburgh Magazine* in May 1840. Also extant is a crime novella called *Reden oder Schweigen* (*Speak or Be Silent*), published in Leipzig in 1842 (F. A. Brockhaus) and again as part of *Urania Taschenbuch auf das Jahr 1843*: a search of the *Urania* series might well uncover further Puttkammer works.

We have included *The Dead Man of St. Anne's Chapel* because it demonstrates very effectively the degree to which the analysis of physical clues of a crime had emerged by the 1830s as the logical focus of a narrative of detection. The plot has a few Romantic overtones, but the story as a whole is an early example of the courtroom drama type of detective story, and provides a fascinating view of judicial procedure and priorities in certain parts of mid-nineteenth-century Germany.

The Dead Man of St. Anne's Chapel

by Otto Ludwig
Emil Freiherr von Puttkammer

Upon a prominent outcropping of the wooded mountain ridge that cuts through the outermost province of a German kingdom stands a small chapel dedicated to the service of St. Anne. Except for her feast day, on which countless pilgrims stream to her miraculous image, the chapel is seldom visited, and then mostly only by country folk who do reverence in passing. The heavily wooded heights, lacking a clear vista of anything, do not even offer a worthwhile destination for the walks taken by the guests of the nearby mineral spas, among which friendly Hilgenberg takes first place.

In the early hours of August 26, 1816, a farmer from one of the outlying villages of the valley walked the narrow footpath to the chapel. His little son ran ahead of him. A short distance before the chapel, the little boy turned to his father breathlessly and tried, with confused and frightened shouts, to pull him forward. The astonished father hurried after his son, and his first glance, as he reached the open space in front of the chapel, fell upon a corpse. The lifeless body of a well-featured young man lay upon the steps of the little church, smeared with blood, half undressed, wearing only a shirt, long, light-colored Nanking trousers, and boots with spurs. On the right hand of the dead man, which lay upon the upper torso, there gleamed a heavy gold signet ring.

The father sent the small boy back to the nearest village to report, having decided to guard the "quiet man" faithfully. It struck him that there were very few traces of blood in the vicinity of the corpse. If a murder had taken place, it could scarcely have been committed at this spot. Faint and obviously effaced footprints pointed sideways into the brush where the Raubstein, a steeply ascending, fairly high mountain peak, rises. The ruins of a watchtower lie there, destroyed long ago, old, weather-beaten stone, avoided by the common folk as haunted: reason enough for the farmer to leave all further investigation until the justice of the peace of the district had appeared, accompanied by the physician, the surgeon, and the authorities of the nearest villages. There was even the train of curious hangers-on that such scenes always tend to produce.

The corpse was inspected. Resuscitation was unthinkable; traces of beginning decomposition were already visible on the exposed body parts. Soon the experts discovered the cause of death. Under the dead man's shirt was a wide, brightly colored silk bandage, apparently a fragment of a woman's shawl, carefully knotted around the torso. Under it, on the left side of the chest, lay a second cloth, wadded into a ball and glued firmly to the body by dried blood. This cloth covered a deep, broad stab wound. It had penetrated directly into the heart, as the autopsy shortly revealed, and had brought the unfortunate man a death as unavoidable as it was instantaneous. The nature of the wound indicated a long, double-bladed tool, probably a knife. Moreover, the dead man's stomach and intestines betrayed that he had died immediately after the enjoyment of a considerable amount of strong wine, perhaps even while drunk.

While the autopsy was being performed, some of the onlookers had, upon hearing the remarks of the farmer, already climbed the Raubstein in the silence. Soon the report came down to the judge that a murder must have taken place in the ruins there. Judge, doctors, and village authorities went to the site. The appearance of things indicated strongly that it had been the scene of a bloody deed. Blood coated the gravel-strewn floor of the round ruin, and clung to the stones round about. On the floor were the remains of a recently held meal—crusts of bread, fruit peels, and finally the bottom of a smashed bottle holding the dregs of a sweet, heavy wine.

With effort, the traces of the footprints that the farmer had already noticed were also discovered, leading from the ruins down to the open space in front of the chapel. But it was difficult to differentiate them from the footprints of the curious who had already trod that path before the arrival of the authorities. More visible were the traces of human feet in another direction, leading away from the chapel, in broken twigs and trampled underbrush through the thicket surrounding the ruin. Here, not far from the stonework, was found a second loose strip of the colorful silk fabric, and deeper in the bushes, hanging in a low shrub, a long ladies' glove of Danish leather, delicately worked and brand new, but soiled with dark spots that the doctor recognized as blood. Tensely attentive and not without anxiety about coming upon further disquieting discoveries, the authorities followed the path indicated by the breakage in the underbrush. Even so, nothing more was found. The trail was lost in the trampled path that leads down to Hilgenberg.

In the hope that someone would recognize the dead man, no one turned away the growing throngs of the curious. In vain: as twilight fell, he was brought to his last resting place, which he would find in the graveyard of the nearest church village, Hoffstede.

On the following day, the owner of a nearby forest tavern came to see the judge. The tavern keeper had seen the dead man, already lying in his coffin, in Hoffstede. He testified that he recognized him as a guest who had spent the night before August 24th in his tavern and had left it early on the morning of the following day. He had not asked his guest for a name, a profession, where he had come from or where he was going. In his simplicity, the tavern keeper opined that the gentleman was without doubt a lieutenant from the foreign troops quartered in the area, since—he added naively—"he came wearing boots with spurs even though he was on foot, that's why, and my wife said lieutenants were always like that, they even went to bed with boots and spurs on."

With such inadequate information, the judge had to be content with asking the tavern keeper for the most exact possible description of the clothes in which he had seen the stranger and, beyond that, any possessions he had noticed. The tavern keeper mentioned a gold watch with a chain and key, a red pocketbook and a green silk "double" money bag, which the traveler had entrusted to him for safekeeping when he went to bed, and had retrieved early the next morning. Then there were *two* rings that the gentleman had kept, one of which was a signet ring; the second had been a thin band. The signet ring of the dead man, which had only been removed with the aid of the surgeon's knife, owing to its having become deeply imbedded in the flesh of the finger, was immediately recognized by the tavern keeper as the signet ring he had mentioned.

The investigation, brought no further forward by this information, was now transferred from the justice of the peace to the chief prosecutor of the superior provincial court, which at that time had its seat in Hainburg, a lively middle-sized town.

Meanwhile, because of the witnesses at the scene of the crime, the case had become notorious and the object of lively interest, but in the mouths of the numerous, mostly only imperfectly informed disseminators, there were soon admixed so many alien, arbitrary additions to the official facts that the attention of the authorities was led ever more astray. Thus, acting upon unverified finger-pointing, the police looked for information about the person of the dead man almost exclusively among the circles of the spa guests of the nearby mineral baths.

All the rumors only had the result of confusing rather than clarifying the incident. Even the publication in the newspaper of a description of the deceased, using information that had been gleaned from the examination of the body, brought, initially, no results.

Finally, in November, the chief prosecutor received a letter from the chief of police of the district capital of K***. A Mr. von Breisach, allegedly born in the province ***, who had retired and lived privately for quite a while there, had often, it was said, undertaken trips of several days into the mountains; and from one of these trips, at the end of August, he had not come back. His landlady, concerned at his absence, had already gone to the police in September, seeking advice, but the latter found no reason at that time to involve themselves in her private business. Now, their attention alerted by the public notices, they questioned the woman more exactly, and according to her report the dead man and "Mr. von Breisach" appeared to be one and the same. The woman was sent to Hainburg; with her appeared also a disabled soldier, who had served Mr. von Breisach in K***. When he saw the well-preserved clothing of the dead man, the soldier recognized the boots with certainty as the same ones he had often had in his hands in the course of his duties.

The witnesses also claimed to recognize the missing man in every aspect of the description of him; voluntarily they mentioned the gold watch and *both* rings that Mr. von Breisach had always worn, and although they had never examined these treasures precisely, the signet ring, laid before them, still appeared to be the right one. They described the second ring, matching the statement of the forest tavern keeper, as a simple band, formed, they added, like a *wedding ring*.

The body could not be shown to them after such a long time had elapsed; we should also add that none of the later witnesses saw it either.

According to the statement of his landlady and several other persons questioned in K***, Mr. von Breisach had led a withdrawn but not very praiseworthy life. There was talk of contact with questionable individuals from the personnel of the theater there; especially, of an intimate relationship with a dancer. The relationship supposedly sustained a sudden breach, but no one knew exactly how or when, or where the dancer, who had left the theater, had gone.

As promising as these discoveries originally seemed, all the less did they actually bear fruit. Who was this Mr. von Breisach? The name was completely unknown in the province, it was not contained in any register of noble families consulted for guidance; even the coat of arms on the signet ring did not seem familiar to any of the collectors and experts to whom it was shown.

These puzzles, mocking the efforts of the courts and the police, were solved by chance. There was talk at a private gathering of the name "von Breisach," which had occupied the authorities to such an extent, as the public knew. But while all present were in agreement that a family of this name did not exist in German lands, an ex-diplomat, a seasoned heraldist and genealogist, remarked that perhaps there was merely an error in the spelling. He, who knew of nearly all the noble houses in Germany, was familiar with a family "von Preussach," and he himself had the coat of arms of the count of this lineage.

The counselor of the provincial court, to whom had been allocated the office of the instructing judge in the unresolved investigation, and who had heard through a friend of the diplomat's remark, lost no time in approaching the heraldist about the coat of arms in question. Flattered by the importance attached to his statement, the heraldist brought the coat of arms to light, and behold, except for the expanded ornamentation of the count's title, it showed the same figure as the ring of the dead man. The heraldist then opened his well-annotated encyclopedia of the nobility, and under the correct letter there was the family von Preussach listed with all its branches and possessions.

One of these branches had settled in the province of ***, and as we know, the man who had disappeared from K*** was also supposed to have come from there.

The chief prosecutor began an immediate correspondence with the government of this province, and shortly there arrived a written statement from one Ferdinand von Preussach. He identified himself as the *second* son of the aged Baron Anselm von Preussach, owner of an entailed estate in ***. The *older* son, Hermann, had departed from the country two years ago and, for some time now, had left his family with no knowledge of his whereabouts.

"Everything suggests," wrote Ferdinand von Preussach, "that the dead man is my brother Hermann. It is of extraordinary importance to the family to obtain certainty about this. Baron Hermann was the heir to the familial estate according to the law of primogeniture, and after him I myself am heir, since there are no living male offspring from my brother's dissolved marriage, merely a single daughter. I will present myself to the authorities in person and offer everything that can help throw light upon this sad event."

Ferdinand arrived in Hainburg in January 1817. He read through the files of the investigation attentively, examined the ring and uttered his certain conviction: the dead man was Hermann, his brother. He approached the court with the request to provide him with an authoritative certificate to this effect, one that would make possible his succession to the entailed estate; his father's life, weakened by old age, would not last much longer.

As little as the court doubted Ferdinand's testimony, it still could not be denied that the word of the person most closely involved would not satisfy the demands of civil law for the issuance of an official death certificate. Ferdinand understood this; he had heard as much from legal experts elsewhere.

Thus he was even more eager to hasten the course of the investigation into the origin of the bloody deed, in order indirectly to bring about certainty in the identity of the victim.

The court recognized that it was less the impulse of brotherly love than an interest in the estate's fortune that fired Ferdinand's eagerness, but it promised him all legal assistance and advised him to choose legal counsel from among the lawyers of the tribunal. They also advised that even if more definite clues yielded the guilty party, he should still appear in a civil capacity (private plaintiff). Ferdinand took this advice.

Lawyer Senkenberg, his chosen counsel,—it is to him we owe the most essential facts of this narrative—was a man of rare circumspection and industry. A native of the district and having the widest variety of connections, he was extraordinarily well suited to further his client's interest through his knowledge of places and persons. Beyond that, the motives for his eagerness were the importance of the case and the auspicious monetary situation of his client.

Since he found nothing immediate to do in Hainburg, Ferdinand traveled to K***, the last place where his brother had lived. After certain difficulties were quickly dispensed with, the assets of the missing man were returned from their earlier confiscation and inventoried in Ferdinand's presence. With efficient industry Ferdinand looked through all the papers that might shed light upon his brother's final fate; not a single leaflet escaped his attention. Then a sheet in letter format came into his hands; the address had been torn off, but the content seemed significant. It contained the following lines, written in a fine hand, which we reproduce literally in their characteristic orthography:

"Je vous accorde cette entrevue, pourvu qu'elle Soye décisive. Vos mennaçes ne pourront jamais m'épouvanter, jé saurrais me défendre moyennant les armes, lesquelles me pret-

teront l'honneur et la vertue. Voici ma dernière. La coursbondance segrette ne peut se continuer.
    Bl. ce 21 Juill.   A.[1]

Preussach directed that a legal file be assembled pertaining to the finding of the letter, and turned both file and letter over to the instructing judge. He did not find here the support that he sought for his firmly grounded view that the letter had some connection with the mysterious events, and for this reason he candidly explained to the chief prosecutor, in a comprehensive document, what he thought of the object of the investigation and the way it had been managed thus far.

"The court," he said, "has pursued up to now only the preconceived idea of a robbery. I have never wanted to believe that. I make bold to say that whatever gives the appearance of a robbery is purely pretence or the work of a third hand, and not of the person who brought death to the unfortunate man. *That* hand, the murderer's hand,—I'm sure I'm not deceiving myself—was a *woman's*. In the police reports there are several places that state that at the time in question, a woman was seen in the vicinity of the chapel; the justice of the peace found fragments of a shawl and a woman's glove at the scene of the crime. This data was merely collected in order to search for a second person, a victim threatened with robbery and death, and when such a person was not found, the matter was entirely dropped.

"What if the woman was the murderer? The handwriting of the letter from July 21 is decidedly feminine. The letter tells of a decisive meeting; fine! the meeting took place, there by the chapel; it became decisive, fatally decisive for the unfortunate man.

"I do not wish to throw suspicion upon any innocent person, but I must give voice to something that no stranger can know as well as I, Hermann's brother. Sensuousness, unchecked passion was a prominent feature in the character of my otherwise estimable brother. This was the reason for the dissolution of his short marriage; his excesses, when he yielded to them freely, later led him into entanglements that are too often solved only with blood. There was talk in K*** of his contact with a ballet dancer who disappeared from that place at almost the same time he did. One ought to ask the informants of this rumor about the wanderings of a woman in the vicinity of the crime."

The chief prosecutor considered that some of the reprimands voiced here were not without foundation. The authorities looked more closely at the relevant old police reports and brought the following events to light by questioning certain persons, who were quickly made known to them.

The events referred to the 24th of August, the day on which the deceased

---

[1]"I will allow you this interview, provided that it will be decisive. Your threats will never frighten me—I will be able to defend myself by means of weapons that will restore my honor and virtue. This is my last [letter]. This secret correspondence cannot continue.
    Bl., July 21   A."

left the forest tavern in the early morning. This day was particularly remembered by the witnesses as the name day of a beloved princess of the ruling house, who lived in the area. The people were accustomed to celebrating in the evening with bonfires upon the surrounding heights.

A twenty-year-old but mentally deficient boy from the Swiss colony in the mountains climbed the Raubstein that morning looking for wood for the bonfire. The sun was already quite high when the boy saw a pair ambling close to him in the bushes: a man who looked like a fine hunter and a girl in a brightly colored dress with a straw hat and a parasol. The boy was not able to describe the clothes more closely; as became evident, he could not differentiate between colors.

The pair backed away into the bushes upon seeing the witness, as if frightened. After a good while the boy saw them again, high above him, very near the Raubstein. "The man," thus were the witness's words, "seemed to scuffle with the girl." The gestures he used to explain this expression suggested hand-to-hand fighting. In the process of staring up at them, the watcher slipped and slid down a stretch on the steep incline. By the time he picked himself up and looked upward again, the pair had disappeared.

That was all that laborious questioning could glean from the mentally deficient young man. The statements of the barber-surgeon from Schlingen and his wife were more substantive. Schlingen is a colony of a few houses adjoining the most outlying, scattered residences of Hilgenberg.

Late in the afternoon, the couple reported, a woman arrives in elegant dress, tall, slim "delicate and charming of face, but pale and worn-out," with dark, curly hair. She asks the barber to dress a wound that she shows him, a wound in the palm of her right hand, which she had kept hidden till then with a bloody white cloth. The barber discovers a wide but shallow cut, bandages and wraps it, and at the woman's request the barber's wife provides a clean cloth. For this the woman presses a ducat into the wife's hand, says goodbye hastily, and goes away.

The couple, astonished and rather curious, watch the hurrying woman leave. At the garden gate an old man in the dress of the mountain woodcutters meets her; the woman leaves with him along the footpath to Hilgenberg. It is not long before the old man returns the same way at a hurried pace. The barber's wife speaks to him and asks him whether he knows the lady. "What? Lady?" the old man replies, brusquely. "God knows her!" and therewith he went on his way.

A neighbor, who had, unseen, watched the woman in conversation with her escort before she went into the barber's surgery, told the barber and his wife wondrous things afterward about that conversation. Crying agitatedly, the woman spoke of her fear and anxiety, but the old man is supposed to have said the clearly audible words: "God, father in heaven! Go home and to bed! Crying won't bring him back to life! You've nothing to fear from me! I swear by my salvation that I'll be as quiet as the grave."

The barber's wife was the only one who could remember a few things about the lady's clothing. She mentioned a green silk dress, and black, veil-like scarf, a straw hat with flowers, and a parasol made of thin silk.

The neighbor, who was also quickly interviewed, confirmed what the couple had already stated; he could not say more than that.

Preussach was very satisfied with the contents of the interviews. "We're beginning to see the light!" he told Senkenberg. "The glove is an important piece of evidence. It's clear that the wounded lady lost it; it's for the right hand. We'll also find that hand!"

The energetic Mr. Senkenberg urged the police anew. He obtained a description of the missing dancer; it conformed, as such descriptions do, fairly exactly to that of the image sketched by the barber and his wife, and finally there was success in discovering the whereabouts of the runaway woman. But in the interrogation, which the authorities of the place kindly undertook upon the mere basis of Senkenberg's request, the suspect provided an unquestionable alibi. Her identification and papers were in perfect order: by the middle of July she had left K*** and had not been back in that region since that time.

Senkenberg did not allow himself to be frightened off by the failure of this effort. If it wasn't this woman, if could be another. Soon the agents of the police had traced another individual far below the dancer in morality, a so-called harp virtuosa. We'll call her Cecilia, for she had many names. For some time now she had given up her art, which she had practiced in K***, where she was counted among the most popular courtesans; the story was that her right hand was lame. That appeared questionable. In addition, she was tall, stately, and brunette—enough for the searching eye of the police. Cecilia roamed the country with a gambler of ill-repute who was himself under official surveillance; Senkenberg's request to have her interrogated was therefore fulfilled without difficulty.

This interrogation, in the main as fruitless as many earlier ones, turned out to be remarkable because it brought to light a circumstance that had hitherto evaded the legal eye, obvious though it was. After several questions that resulted in no certain agreement or disagreement, but which revealed the virtuosa to be a person requiring decisive handling, Senkenberg insisted on one last test: namely, whether the glove they had preserved fit her hand. Cecilia, not altogether dissatisfied to have cause to show her extremely pretty round arm to an attentive set of male eyes, met this request without concern and set about the task with the niceties of a lady of the world, but in vain—the glove was much too narrow for her hand. There was only the fear of recovering that important *corpus delicti* undamaged. In the careful process, the glove was turned inside out, and with surprise one saw underneath the edge a name stamped there: *Wilh: T. . ffe.* The letters in the middle of the name were printed illegibly.

It goes without saying that Cecilia was released in peace and everyone's attention turned to the half-deciphered name. Now, it was quickly conjectured that the name was not that of the owner, but of the maker; but even so that could lead to further discoveries. At the direction of the chief prosecutor the glove was turned over to a trusted official of the court's police in order for him to question glove dealers carefully for a closer explanation of the stamp.

Soon afterward a new and wondrous report arrived at court. The feast of St. Anne drew near, and according to the old custom, the priest in Hoffstede, as caretaker of St. Anne's chapel, took down the alms box kept there, to take in the donations from the previous year and make room in the box for the hopefully more generous gifts from the pilgrimage day. This time, the box sheltered an unexpected find. A green bag lay in it, damp and mildewed as if it had lain there a long time. It was well filled with silver pieces, and there were even some gold pieces mixed in. A piece of parchment had been attached to the bag; upon it was written, with pencil and in deliberately disguised handwriting in large, clumsy strokes: "Give the dead man a Catholic burial. God will reward you."

The priest turned everything over to the court. The statement of the forest tavern keeper came to mind; the man was sent for, and he assured them: the money bag of his guest that night had looked just like this one.

Meanwhile Preussach had received letters from home that caused him to place the operation of the investigation completely in Senkenberg's hands. Decisive steps finally had to be taken to clear up the civil consequences of Hermann's death, because the old baron was daily tottering visibly closer to his grave. Ferdinand was advised to travel to the capital in person, because at the seat of the central government one could more easily hope for exemptions from certain formalities, exemptions that seemed an insuperable hurdle at the provincial level. Additionally, Hermann's former wife, who lived with her parents in the capital, had never been informed of the event so closely concerning her. Necessary in any case according to the demands of propriety, such information became even more unavoidable because according to the divorce decree, upon his death Hermann's wife and daughter would come into possession of a capital settlement, provided by the successor to the title, instead of the yearly pension they had received up to now. A meeting on the part of the Preussachs with the family of Hermann's former wife might, finally, gain the not insignificant support of her father, old Colonel von Siegsfeld; it was well known that the elderly gentleman was still highly regarded at court as a consequence of his outstanding service.

This first renewal of relations with a family with whom there had been no contact since the divorce—it had been almost three years—was no pleasant step for Ferdinand, however. He had never been friendly with his sister-in-law, and the pride of the Preussach house had been sorely wounded at the colonel's unyielding disposition, which had at one time emphatically rejected Hermann's serious attempts to obtain the forgiveness of his offended spouse. But there was no other way, and in August 1817 Ferdinand departed for the distant capital.

Soon after arriving he had himself announced at the home of Colonel von Siegsfeld. The colonel and his wife—their daughter, Albertine, was out—received the unexpected visitor with a coldness that allowed him to feel how estranged they were. But Ferdinand's initial explanatory words sufficed to change their behavior even as the message increased their surprise. The upright character of the colonel and his wife's delicate feelings caused them to receive the news with all the sympathy that suppresses any hostile impulse in noble and educated people. *Only life bears hate—death reconciles.* The colonel promised Mr. von Preussach all the assistance at his disposal, and Preussach, completely satisfied, was just about to take his leave when Albertine's carriage rolled up. He could not avoid staying, but he gladly complied with Mrs. von Siegfeld's request to keep silent for the moment about the horrible event, since she reserved for herself the right to tell Albertine in a way that would spare her.

Albertine walked in. For one moment she stopped short at the sight of Ferdinand von Preussach, who went toward her with a deferential greeting; then, shuddering in sudden recognition as if in the grip of a strong fever, she went pale, staggered, and disappeared into the next room without a word of greeting. Her mother followed her. Preussach felt deeply wounded by this brusque and ruthless expression of a dislike that he had, it is true, always shared and returned, but which should not have been displayed so openly, according to his sensibilities. Disconcerted and wordless he stood across from the colonel. The old man rescued him from the embarrassing situation, gave him his hand as if saying goodbye, and said, "We'll need to see each other frequently; let's consider and carry out calmly as men what we will need to do." He emphasized noticeably the words "calmly" and "as men," and Preussach thought he understood therein, to his satisfaction, a criticism of the so recently displayed proof of *feminine* susceptibility.

At this point Ferdinand left. On the third day, the colonel paid him a reciprocal visit. The old gentleman reported what he had discovered about this family matter. It was not auspicious. With respect to the succession to the estate, it was said, there were only two possibilities: either a formal authentication of Hermann's death would have to be presented, or the missing man had to be publicly summoned and then declared dead; but the declaration could only take place after the lapse of the legal period of several years. If the old baron were to die during this time, the estate would be placed in guardianship, and everything would remain in this provisional arrangement until the missing man was legally declared dead—measures which would certainly seem to the Preussachs to be extremely embarrassing and repressive of any free disposition of the estate.

During the conversation, Preussach learned that Albertine had been informed of the death and it had shaken her more deeply than the colonel appeared to think proper.

In September, Preussach received a letter from Senkenberg.

"I have a unique new piece of information to report in our sad investigation," the lawyer wrote. "The glove we have has found its mate, the left. It matches the blood-spattered right one as one twin matches another. Even the stamp is the same, only more clearly printed. The family name is *Tieffe*. The name is meaningless, regarded generally as the name of the firm, but it led to what I want briefly to describe to you.

"During his inquiries, the police agent, whose mission was decided while you were still here, goes to see one of the local milliners, Madame Lax, who has a customer with her at the time, the wife of the tax commissioner, Mr. Zeltwach. This lady involves herself in the conversation, inspects the proffered glove, and incidentally pumps the official for information: is this about an important theft, etc. The man says yes, but must also have mentioned me; enough, a few days ago Mrs. Zeltwach is announced to me and hands over the aforementioned left glove.

"I ask her, 'Where did you get it?' and discover the following:

"Mrs. Zeltwach is acquainted with the family of the reformed minister in Blumenrode, three hours from here. Recently she paid them a visit with her daughters, and during a fashion discussion among the young ladies the second daughter of the minister coincidentally pulls out this glove; they all joke about the name Wilhelmine Tieffe. Mrs. Zeltwach notices the name, thinks of the police inquiries and becomes concerned. The minister's daughter states that she has it from the chambermaid of a lady who visited the local manorial family during the summer of the year before, but she never had the other glove. Mrs. Zeltwach takes the minister to one side, speaks to him urgently, and thus the glove comes into her hand and now mine.

"This happened the day before yesterday. Today the minister appears—his name is Rauch—together with his daughter, Adelheid. Both are worried and afraid of inconvenience due to the purported theft story. I entreat the young lady to tell me exactly how she came to have the glove. She freely describes what Mrs. Zeltwach already stated; that she has the glove through a third party. A young widow from the capital, a Mrs. von Süssfeld, paid a long visit to the family at the manor (Baron von Kettler). Adelheid often played music with the lady; she became more closely acquainted with the lady's maid, an educated person of good family. She helped the maid a little at the time of their departure; in a dressing case among cast-off things this single, new glove turned up. The maid did not think it worth taking with them, *because the second was missing*, and Adelheid jokingly took possession of it as a memento, as she said.

"I would be inclined to believe the story, especially since Miss Rauch is a young lady of good repute and I know of nothing even remotely hinting at a connection at any time between your unfortunate brother and Blumenrode. It merely strikes me that at the end of the apocryphal letter from K*** there stand a *Bl.* and an *A.*

"But—strangely—the maid *quaestioni* supposedly has the first name *Agathe*, and her last name is *Roger*. Again an A and a French name! She is supposed to be tall and slender (Adelheid is neither). I was not able to discover anything else about the lady, except that she is a young widow, as mentioned, her circumstances are excellent, and she is even received at court.

"I have refrained from taking any further steps, even more so since the Kettler family in Blumenrode is very well regarded and consequently extremely reserved and sensitive.

"You, baron, have often demonstrated in this sad case a perspicuity that I readily acknowledge. You are in possession of reports about your brother's last days with which I am perhaps not completely familiar. It is possible that you will see a connection where, for me, the threads are missing. I place everything in your hands and await your further instructions."

Preussach laid the long report aside with a fair amount of indifference. *O quantum in rebus inane!* he thought. How could that clever Senkenberg place such value on this discovery! The stamp was only the trademark of the manufacturer: how many products with this mark could be circulating in the world, and how many resemble each other!

He wanted to share this thought with the lawyer, but the question of succession, which now consumed his attention entirely, took him again to the Siegsfeld house. Mrs. von Siegsfeld was alone. The conversation turned to Hermann's death. With sympathy the elderly lady heard the story of the discovery of the corpse, of the long uncertainty about the identity of the dead man, and the coincidental revelation that came later.

"So then," she asked, "your brother is probably also buried in strange soil, there, where his life so sadly ended?"

"Yes," came the answer. "He is lying in the churchyard of the village Hoffstede, not far from the Hilgenberg spa."

"Not far from Hilgenberg? God, if Albertine suspected that! How close she was, even then, to the scene of that horrible deed!"

"What? Was your daughter in Hilgenberg then?"

"She was in the area, paying a visit to Baron Kettler's family. Their estate is called Blumenrode. From there Albertine often went to Hilgenberg. I know that friendly spot very well too, from my own youth."

"So the estate is called—"

"Blumenrode! It's just three hours from Hilgenberg."

"Blumenrode!" repeated Preussach pensively. A thought rose within him, a thought he didn't want to acknowledge. Albertine!—a third *A*, and this one appeared to be the right one! He noticed that his distraction had become evident to Mrs. von Siegsfeld, and took his leave as soon as an appropriate reason presented itself.

He read Senkenberg's letter again and everything seemed clear. The letter from July 21, the glove—were from Albertine. *She* was the wounded lady at the barber's surgery, the description he remembered so well from the witnesses fit *her* exactly. Mrs. von Süssfeld, a young widow—now he also knew how to interpret this. It suited the beautiful, vain lady better, he thought, to show herself to less well-known acquaintances in the alluring guise of a young widow instead of the doubtful position of a divorcée, a position which gave rise to questions prompted by curiosity. Süssfeld—the name was deformed, as had already happened to the name of another actor in this drama. Siegsfeld is the correct name! He knew that the colonel, in the first flush of hatred toward the house of Preussach, wanted to lay claim to Albertine's family name for her, but the petition was not approved, since both parties were Catholic and the sacrament of marriage could not, therefore, be completely dissolved. But in her private life, Albertine was frequently called Mrs. von Siegsfeld, even in the capital. Now Albertine's curious behavior at their first meeting was clear to him too. The fear of discovery, he told himself, was what so suddenly overwhelmed her and made her forget her otherwise so composed bearing.

Day and night he considered the plan that could bring him most quickly to his goal; as he saw the matter, he had to assure himself of such proofs against his sister-in-law as would make the court feel compelled to take formal steps.

Finally he decided to seek a meeting with Albertine herself. He trusted his guiding angel, which would lead him down the surest path at the right moment.

After a few days he paid another call to the Siegsfeld house. He found only the ladies at home; only later did the colonel join them. Preussach directed the conversation to Hermann's death, which had, by now, also been discussed in Albertine's presence. He told of the investigation still in progress, keeping an eye on Albertine, who listened attentively but apparently dispassionately.

Suddenly he turned to his sister-in-law. "I recently heard, madam, that you are acquainted with Baron Kettler's family in Blumenrode?"

Albertine answered affirmatively.

"So perhaps you also know the daughter of the reformed minister there?"

"The minister has several daughters."

"I mean the second; her name is Adelheid."

"Yes, I know her. What about her?"

Preussach hesitated, somewhat embarrassed. Silently he longed for the keenness that Senkenberg had, in his praise, ascribed to him; for his part he felt how difficult it was to find the right approach.

"I would like," he began, "to hear more about this girl. She is involved in the investigation in a most unique way. The police have made discoveries... "

"For God's sake!" Albertine cried out. "The poor unfortunate girl! She is innocent, completely innocent!"

She trembled as she spoke these words; all the blood had drained from her cheeks. Her mother rushed to her, fearing she would faint. With visible effort Albertine regained her composure.

"Oh, mother!" she cried. "Is it possible? I must go there, I must, I can save the unfortunate girl!"

Mrs. von Siegsfeld rang the bell, a servant appeared, and Albertine was led to her room. Just then the colonel came in; he stopped in front of Preussach without speaking. "Another scene, just like the recent one!" he said dully, staring into space.

Preussach took his hand and said, "You will damn me, colonel, but by God—"

"No," the old man interrupted him, "I don't accuse you of anything; you have no knowledge of such sensitive spirits. I only have one other request for the duration of your stay: avoid scenes of this sort. What has already happened is enough."

"Yes indeed, it's enough," said Preussach with unconscious double meaning. "My presence here also serves nothing. I leave you, colonel, and regret the disturbance I have caused you; I regret it more than you might believe!" He fell silent then, so as not to say too much.

He left the house. But now he found neither rest nor peace in the capital. What further proof do we need? he asked himself. The girl is innocent; Albertine wants to vouch for this. Who can say that except the person who knows the true guilty party?

He wrote to Senkenberg: "You praise my keenness because I deduced a woman's hand from a woman's glove. Here is more. You found the other glove, I found *the hand*! Cease every pursuit of the minister's daughter; there can be absolutely no more uproar in Blumenrode. I can't say more than that in writing. I'll be with you in a week at most."

Then Albertine declared her intention of going to Hainburg personally and rescuing the unfortunate girl. Her own testimony and that of the house of Kettler would suffice, she thought. A written statement, as her mother had suggested at first, seemed to her to be insufficient. Her mother had convinced herself of that and would accompany her on the long journey despite the lateness of the season.

Preussach eagerly supported the ladies in the decision they made. Nothing could have fit his plan better. He regarded Albertine as more easily reachable by the prosecution once she was already in the jurisdiction of the investigating court than if she had to be torn from the protecting paternal home by means of the long and formal path of requisition. Additionally, the norms of French criminal procedure were valid in the provinces, while in some areas, including this one, the German process of interrogation held sway. So all the advice he gave the ladies had this goal. He advised them to apply to the chief prosecutor only in writing at first, and to ask in very general terms for clarification without mentioning right away the person whose vindication they intended.

Senkenberg was more than a little astonished when he heard the oral report of his employer. To be sure, he had also quietly inquired more closely about the "young widow," but he was unable to imagine Hermann's former wife by that designation, since her family name had never been made known to him. After he had promised Ferdinand, who was on the way to K***, that he would inquire more closely, he was able to inform him, in brief, as follows:

"I obtained reports about the so-called Mrs. von Siegsfeld through a girl from the castle at Blumenrode who appears to be connected in an important way to the incidents about which we have statements from the Swiss boy and the people from Schlingen. You remember that the day when your deceased brother left the forest tavern, the twenty-fourth of August, was a Saturday. The noble families in this area have a custom of gathering on Saturdays in Hilgenberg; on the day in question the Kettler family was not there, *but Mrs. von Siegsfeld was.* She joined the Countess von Koss from Langnitz and her daughters, and the maid from the castle at Blumenrode went along to wait upon her. In Hilgenberg Mrs. von Siegsfeld was called away from her party, and did not return until evening. What happened during these hours of absence? That's the question! The residents of Blumenrode and Langnitz *could* tell us a lot, but *will* they?

"Should I apply for a formal interview? I trust myself to justify such an application legally, but your sister-in-law would admittedly be very compromised as a result, and perhaps you must consider this."

"I have no considerations beyond those demanded by the interests of my family. I want to and will pursue the guilty party where and as I find him. But I will undertake the inquiries in Blumenrode and Langnitz myself. You will not hold it against me if I say that the court is skeptical and formal, and its steps revolve in the narrow path of its code. I can take suitable secondary paths as they are offered to me by need and the opportunity of the moment."

"You're not wrong there," Senkenberg replied. "Work ahead of the examining judge. But—allow me a few hints about the terrain on which you'll be operating. The name von Preussach is not unknown in Blumenrode; in the castle at least they are very familiar with the family situation of your sister-in-law, who is a close friend of the Kettlers. This demands caution. You'll have more success in Langnitz. The estate is for sale by the countess. Many potential customers have already made themselves known—a useful introduction! Discover anything you can about the amusements that Saturday; pay attention to every detail. If the information about the wound is correct, it could hardly have escaped the ladies at Langnitz; it must have been spoken of somehow. At least you will be able to learn whether Mrs. von Siegsfeld was dressed on that day the way the barber's wife describes. Ladies have a good memory for that sort of thing. Make a note of everything you can find out."

So much for the lawyer. Now we'll see how his client knew enough to take these hints and use them.

In Blumenrode he noticed that he was received, just as Senkenberg had conjectured, with such marked coldness and formality that investigating the family was unthinkable. They simply could not comprehend the meaning of his visit, and gave him to understand this very clearly. Despairing of the family, Preussach tried his luck in the servants' quarters. But the baron's family discovered this and was extremely displeased; Preussach had to leave without having accomplished much if he did not want to betray himself.

It was different in Langnitz. The countess, informed that a foreign cavalier had taken an interest in the estate and had greatly praised its well-ordered administration, courteously received the welcome admirer of her saleable property as soon as Baron von Preussach was announced. The local minister, who served in one and the same person as both the counselor of conscience and the legal advisor for the lady of the castle, took a very particular liking to the strange gentleman; in short, the traveler in haste became a guest of many days at the parsonage and a daily visitor at the castle. The countess mother was full of conversation, the three daughters of the countess, Aurelie, Mathilde and Betty, were pure life and fire.

At their first luncheon, Preussach had drawn the critical trip to Hilgenberg, with all its details, into the scope of the conversation. On that morning, the ladies explained, Mrs. von Siegsfeld had been called away and received, from a girl dressed like a peasant, a letter that she gave to the countess to read. It was an invitation from a friend who was originally from the far north—Poland or Russia; the name was clearly remembered: Mrs. von Seehausen. Somehow she had heard of Albertine's presence and urgently requested a visit. Upon the countess's encouragement, Albertine decided to accept the invitation, and asked that they not wait for her at lunch; the ladies, on the other hand, asked that she not feel compelled to hurry such a happy reunion, etc. So, in great haste she collected her hat and shawl—

"And doubtless her parasol?" Preussach interjected, jokingly.

That too, to be sure! was the answer. After all, it was a long way; Mrs. von Seehausen supposedly lived in upper Hilgenberg (the heights of the village). The servant went with her.

It was almost dark, and the lamps had been lit in the salon, when Mrs. von Siegsfeld returned. Only the countess and her daughters were still there. Mrs. von Siegsfeld was very overheated and exhausted; her eyes were red-rimmed from crying and she answered their sympathetic questions with a moving tale of the sad fate of her friend and how her leave-taking from her had been very painful.

Adroitly Preussach diverted the conversation to the "shawl and hat and parasol" again, and understood how to entice a closer description of them from the ladies, who were in their element here. The clues he had received from the barber's wife helped him; he confirmed them completely, but in the more comprehensible terminology of high society; the black "veil-like" shawl was an *écharpe* of patterned silk lace.

The dress alone afforded the ladies great rumination and consultation. Their inquisitor threw out the remark that he had his suspicions, namely of a green silk dress. The ladies looked at each other, smiling. The conversation interested them, and Preussach allowed the cryptic remark to slip that it would become obvious to them why he was inquiring so industriously.

"Well," said the countess. "I remember well a green silk coat that Mrs. von Siegsfeld often wore. Whether she wore it on that day..."

"No!" Aurelie interrupted hastily, "not on *that* day. I remember definitely, she wore a dress with short sleeves, because she was wearing *long gloves!*"

Preussach listened attentively.

"Oh, yes, that's right!" cried the chorus, laughing. "That was when she made the peculiar exchange!"

Preussach had difficulty hiding his fearful tension behind the mask of pleasantry.

"Oh, if I might only be allowed to pry deeper into this secret!" he said, bending gallantly toward Aurelie. "The long gloves appear to harbor an extremely alluring memory for you."

"Don't deceive yourself," Aurelie countered. "Just a trifle, a fashion caprice of your beautiful friend."

The countess intervened with a reproachful tone. "The best thing is to tell the silly story. Who knows what Baron Preussach must suspect!"

Aurelie took up the tale with coquettish pathos. "Well, then, listen! It was a beautiful summer morning, etc., as we—Mama and two little daughters, Betty wasn't there—picked up Mrs. Albertine from Blumenrode. The Kettlers were prevented from coming and had entrusted their charming guest to us. We were late, so we didn't get out, but rather waited for our charge in the carriage. Incidentally, she let us wait long enough, for her toilet couldn't be rushed. Finally she appeared and got in, and a lady's maid from Blumenrode climbed onto the coachman's seat. Albertine never traveled without a servant, not even for an hour. The usual compliments had been exchanged, and our coachman was spurring the horses on, when Albertine dropped her fine white kid glove, and oh! fate, coarse and cold, threw it under the hooves of our horses. To that glove fell the lot of beautiful things on this earth. A substitute had to be provided. The lady's maid flew into the castle, and brought another pair, but—*Danish*.

"Mrs. von Siegsfeld was indignant. She was completely insistent upon having white gloves. The Danish gloves, which furthermore were brand new and very elegant, were only reprieved by our approval, which we gave so that we could finally leave. But underway she complained again and again how badly attended she was, since her own maid was sick and the rural substitute wasn't at all to her liking. So that was the second set of gloves. In the evening, when Mrs. von Siegsfeld came back from her northern friend, my first glance fell upon her gloves. She had white ones on again. Mama and I didn't say anything about it; her moving story about her friend had infected us with melancholy, too. But Mathilde, who had been out of the room, went over to Mrs. von Siegsfeld when she came in, and looked at her, smiling.

"Somewhat embarrassed, Albertine asked, 'Why are you looking at me like that, countess?'

"'I'm admiring your persistence,' said Mathilde. 'For good or for ill, then, you wanted to begin and end your day in white kid gloves.'

"'Oh, one can't speak of persistence this time,' Mrs. von Siegsfeld responded. 'In the confusion of parting I made an unintended exchange and only noticed the mistake too late.' And then she explained that at her friend's there had been a young lady, the white gloves probably belonged to her, and she said other similar things. Mathilde had her own opinion about it."

"But certainly a very clever one!" Preussach said, turning to Mathilde. "The exchange did not appear to make sense to you?"

"Admittedly not!" Mathilde smiled. "I thought the confusion must have been very great, and the advantage in it was clearly the other lady's, for the third set was not an improvement: the white gloves were of extremely common fabrication, large and clumsy."

Preussach thought of the wounded, bandaged hand. He had to try to over-hear something more about that. But here he met only astonished denial. Nobody knew, nobody suspected that Mrs. von Siegsfeld had brought home a wound; unless it had been, as Mathilde roguishly added, an invisible one, in her heart.

Preussach broke off. He had learned enough, more than he could have hoped. He would leave the rest to the examining judge.

He remained in Langnitz only as long as the mask he had donned required of him. When he left, both sides courteously voiced and received the wish that they might see each other again; the unsuspecting ladies had it granted only too soon.

Preussach wrote out all his notes, into which we have dipped here, with literal fidelity, and sent them to Senkenberg. He was not idle on the way home from Langnitz to K***. He took the detour through Hilgenberg, and at the police station there he inquired about Mrs. von Seehausen. Obligingly the police looked up the lists of the spa guests: the name was nowhere to be found. At Preussach's lively insistence, a door-to-door inquiry was conducted in the upper reaches of Hilgenberg, but nobody knew of a Mrs. von Seehausen.

Now Senkenberg could not put it off any longer. He worked up an exhaustive petition in which he emphasized the many coinciding circumstances which appeared to reveal the participation of the divorced Mrs. von Siegsfeld in the death of her former husband, or at least an accessory presence at it; he mentioned her arrival in the area of the court's jurisdiction, to be expected any day now, and applied for the speedy examination of the witnesses to the circumstances of Hermann's death. At the time he turned over this petition to the chief prosecutor, Preussach formally applied to the court as the plaintiff in a civil action.

He ventured to explain this deed, for which he named his sister-in-law as the culprit or at least an accessory, as arising from the wish for a more independent situation, which the already mentioned capital settlement would provide her, in contrast to the pension she had received before.

In the capital, he said, he had definitely learned that with her inclination toward lavishness, Albertine had never managed on her yearly pension, however considerable it was; indeed, she was deeply in debt. From this point of view he also justified the private interest of the Preussach family in the investigation, because through her participation in Hermann's death, of whatever sort that might be, the accused had forfeited the remuneration promised to her.

It remains to be seen what fate this admittedly very far-fetched exposition would have met before the court if it had had to be decided all by itself. But chance connected this presentation together with another, from which a glimmer of suspicion began to dawn upon the court, a glimmer still so weak that only Senkenberg's petition gave it definite direction. Albertine had arrived in Hainburg and, following Preussach's advice, had asked in a letter addressed to the chief prosecutor for an audience with the official who was in charge of the investigation into the death of her former husband. She had learned that in this matter a person was suspected, whom she, the writer, felt obligated as well as able to vindicate.

This last point was incomprehensible to the chief prosecutor; quite naturally, since the court had not yet thought of any proceeding against the minister's daughter. He showed the letter to the instructing judge and suggested that the latter question the supplicant more closely about this point. A word in the otherwise well-composed letter struck the judge: the word "correspondance"; it contained the same spelling mistake ("coursbondance") that appeared in the apocryphal letter from K***. He took up that sheet of paper, compared the strokes in the French word, and found a distinct similarity! He showed the two writings to experts, and to them was added the parchment sheet from the alms box. The writing experts declared that no definite judgment could be made about the parchment with the disguised handwriting, but the other two could be regarded with fair certainty as the product of one and the same hand. The instructing judge betook himself to Langnitz in person and thoroughly questioned the countesses about everything they had so innocently described to Preussach. One can imagine the ladies' amazement as they became aware of the fateful intent of this examination.

Interrogations were held in Blumenrode, too. The manorial family was away, but all the statements necessary to confirm the Senkenberg petition were gathered in the parsonage and among the servants at the castle. The maid who had accompanied the outing to Hilgenberg on August 24, 1816, was examined most carefully. Her statement revealed essentially nothing new; on the contrary, she claimed to know from hearsay, as the subject of the lady's wound arose, that Mrs. von Siegsfeld supposedly burned herself on one hand while sealing a letter. The maid had not seen the injury herself.

Thus prepared, the instructing judge waited for the appointed date upon which Mrs. von Preussach was supposed to provide a more detailed explanation of the purpose of her letter. She appeared in the company of her mother.

Adroitly, the judge arranged the questioning so that Albertine was induced to speak her mind about various events of the previous summer that touched on the investigation at hand.

Albertine's answers were definite, short, and well thought-out; but a certain effort never to say more than the question required became conspicuous.

Thus the matter proceeded for a time, when Albertine's glance, already uneasier, fell upon the recording clerk, who sat some distance from the judge, looked at him frequently, and, following the judge's every motion, had put the whole conversation down on paper. Albertine asked whether that was her statement being taken down there. The judge answered affirmatively. "Then I have been misunderstood!" she declared. "My wish was not for a legal questioning, only for a private conference about a matter of such a delicate nature that I could only hint at it in my letter and even now do not want to surrender to formal proceedings."

The judge answered courteously but definitely: a written record of the meeting was unavoidable, but the content would be read aloud to her.

Mrs. von Preussach fell silent for a while, then asked whether she would be required to swear to her statement. That would depend on the circumstances, responded the judge, according to the nature of the statement; in any case, testimony had to be sworn. There was another pause. Then she said, "I think I have been deceived about the necessity of my presence here. I know little of the course of this investigation, but persons who represented themselves to be well-informed told me of suspicion against an innocent, defenseless creature, whom I felt called upon to vindicate. But there is no mention of this, as I now hear; I can see no reason for staying any longer."

The judge was somewhat embarrassed, as he himself admitted in a note in the clerk's record, about how to move the interview forward without precipitously revealing the actual intent of his questioning. He kept to Albertine's last words and asked,

"Who is the person you speak of?"

Albertine hesitated with her answer and looked at her mother. The colonel's wife stepped in. "We have no reason to hold back what we know only third-hand. Baron Ferdinand von Preussach is the informant, and the person whom he described to us as a suspect is a Miss Rauch, the daughter of the reformed minister in Blumenrode. We know nothing of the reasons for the suspicion."

"Is that it?" The judge turned to Albertine. "So you wanted to clear Miss Rauch of suspicion?"

"Yes," said Albertine, "provided, namely, that a suspicion really did prevail, a possibility that I, meanwhile, find incomprehensible."

"And how do you account for your opinion of the impossibility of this?"

"I know for a fact that Miss Rauch never knew my deceased spouse, indeed, never saw him."

To the judge this was a longed-for point of connection with which to further the interview. Prudently, he did not touch on the suspicion and asked only for more certain proofs of the last and most decisive claim, that Adelheid Rauch had never known the dead Baron Preussach. In the course of the conversation, as if incidentally, he let the following question slip out:

"When was the last time you saw and spoke to your deceased spouse?"

Albertine was somewhat taken aback, but she answered thoughtfully and with dignity:

"In deference to my parents' desires I was allowed neither to see Mr. von Preussach nor to speak to him since our divorce."

"And you have deferred to this parental desire without exception?"

"Only my parents could have permitted exceptions, and I believed and still believe that I must justify myself only to them!"

The colonel's wife rose and uttered very decisively her wish that the interview be ended. Whatever Albertine had to state had been stated; the family at Blumenrode would be able to confirm her testimony, and if the court wished any other information from her daughter, she would gladly be available before her return home, which would likely be delayed by some days due to visits in the neighborhood.

The judge had to accede.

On the same day the results of the proceeding were discussed in the council chambers of the court. It was decided that the accused should appear anew; she should be questioned politely but firmly about her experiences on the 24th of August, and at the same time the Swiss youth and the barber-surgeon couple from Schlingen, together with their neighbor, should also be summoned.

The intent was to show Mrs. von Preussach to the others without her being aware of it; if they recognized in her the lady from the 24th of August, then a formal confrontation could be held, and if necessary the departure of the accused from Hainburg could be stopped by means of a temporary warrant for her arrest.

The date was set. This course of action was decisive for Albertine's fate. The regular judge, prevented by illness from appearing, had found a substitute in a younger member of the court, and this representative took up the matter with the fiery eagerness of a beginner who aspired, in hasty revelation of the concealed facts of the matter, to deliver a brilliant example.

Albertine appeared again in the company of her mother. But the latter was asked from the outset to step into a separate room. This audacity was distasteful to both ladies; however, they had to comply, inasmuch as the judge cited court regulations.

As soon as he saw himself alone with Albertine, the young official began with the customary request for very precise, truthful speech and answers. He then brought up the day in question, and explained all the particulars that made that day remarkable: it was a Saturday, the day of the weekly reunion in Hilgenberg, the princess's name day. Albertine remembered these facts; of her own accord she said that that had been her last visit in Hilgenberg.

The judge then demanded an exhaustive account of what she had encountered on that day, from morning to evening. Albertine said nothing. She said nothing even when warned repeatedly. She became ever more frightened and anxious; the official pressed harder and harder. He mentioned that the Countess von Koss and her daughters had already been questioned.

Albertine grew pale. "What does that mean?" she asked, the question dying away. "What does the countess's testimony have to do with me?"

"The Countess von Koss," said the judge, "states that you left her company early and did not return until late. Where were you in the meantime?"

"I do not understand the sense and purpose of these questions!"

"The judge poses his questions on the basis of his office. He needs only to press for answers. You owe these answers for your own vindication!"

Albertine rose from her place. "Vindication?" she said. "I stand here, then, to vindicate myself? God in heaven, of what am I accused? Who is my accuser?"

"There is no talk yet of an accusation!" was the judge's response. "But it is up to me to demand answers. I repeat the question in the name of the king: *where were you during this time?*"

With solemn dignity Albertine moved to face the official. "You remind me of the king! Fine! You know, my father bled for this king, my brothers died a hero's death for him. I know what I owe the king's name. I have been torn from those who are my natural protectors; I have been pressed with questions whose purpose I do not comprehend and cannot answer. Well, then! I will invent no answers; such an outrage is beneath my dignity. But I can and will be silent. From now on my mouth will be closed and no power on earth will unseal it. Deal according to your law. That is my last word."

She sank back down upon her chair and broke into tears. The judge was not able to bring her to say more. He had to be content with noting the strangely ominous words literally, and betook himself therewith into the next room, where the witnesses waited who had been called. The Swiss youth, the barber's wife and the neighbor had come; the barber himself had died earlier in the year. In his simplicity, the youth did not understand what was wanted of him and had to be dismissed. But the barber's wife, who had observed the whole stormy interview through the glass panel in the middle door and had heard every word, declared without hesitation in answer to the judge's question:

"Yes, it's the lady from back then. It would be impossible not to recognize such a beautiful creature. Walk, manner, speech—everything matches!"

The neighbor did not trust himself to recognize her.

The judge took the step of confrontation. Albertine sat, in deep thought, in the same spot in which she had been left. She started when the court personnel walked in with the witness, but her glance fell coldly and with no familiarity upon the face of the elderly woman.

The judge charged her: "This woman assures us that she saw you on that often-mentioned August day, wounded, in her home in Schlingen. The husband of this woman, the barber-surgeon there, bound your wound."

The elderly woman also tried to make herself known through a few friendly words. Albertine bent her head; no word came from her lips, but her tears flowed without stopping. By the end, the witness was crying with her, but she held to her statement. The episode ended there.

The young judge had a difficult task to perform. He had to impart the news to the unfortunate mother, after she had waited for hours, that her daughter could not accompany her. One can imagine how the colonel's wife received this message!

The judge feared even more distressing scenes with Albertine. But he was wrong: he found her in a state of calm incomprehensible to him. She received the news of her formal arrest without excitement, and when she discovered that her mother had been taken home, she said with resignation:

"Good, it's better that way. God will strengthen her, so that she can take the blow. I do not want to see my family again—a dark power separates me from them."

The arrest was carried out with with all the consideration that courts of the French judicial system always show the merely "accused" (*prévenu*). The prisoner enjoyed respectable, indeed attentive treatment. She was allowed the necessary servants; and upon the advice of the doctor who was sent to her in the first flush of concern about the consequences of this unexpected turn of events, she was even allowed to have books and music of her own choosing. However, the prisoner's quarters were subject to a strict prohibition against the outside world, a measure that was particularly painful for her mother.

The situation of this matron became truly desperate when letters from the colonel arrived, who ardently insisted upon the return of his family and could not explain their long absence to himself. The colonel's wife did not know what to do. She was a complete stranger in Hainburg. Finally she decided to remain in Hainburg for the present, where she had taken rooms in an inn, and to respond to her husband's urgent reminders to come home by putting him off with excuses. She could not bring herself to reveal the truth to him, as far as she herself knew it.

Preussach did not hesitate to ascribe to Albertine the guilt of autonomous cooperation in the murder. He was inexhaustible in providing reasons for this allegation; the wound appeared to him to be the most important, the most compelling argument. Not completely trusting that the testimony of the barber's wife would suffice to convince the judge, he insisted upon an ocular inspection; in his opinion the injury could not be healed without a trace after barely fifteen months. Senkenberg, ever gallant, made him aware of the indelicacy of this procedure; the spouse of one's brother, he said, likely had a right to greater consideration than the individuals under suspicion prior to her. Preussach merely replied: "The old Athenians were not ill-advised in having their Areopagus speak justice only in deepest darkness; I wager that the sight of our opponent has not been without effect on the delicacy of my legal friend."

He brought his request personally to the attention of the court; it was considered unavoidable in order to assure that the evidence was exhaustive.

With deep indignation but without refusing, Albertine surrendered her hand to the scrutiny of sworn surgeons. Opinion wavered. One of the surgeons claimed to see no sign of any injury from that time; another declared that there was, indeed, a slight, more palpable than visible depth in the surface of the hand, running parallel to the upper crease in the palm, which one could well regard as the trace of an old, superficial and well-healed cut; a third finally agreed with the first that he could see and feel—nothing.

At that time the instructing judge opened the hearing again in Blumenrode, since the manorial family had returned. None of the von Kettlers knew of the wound. They remembered that Mrs. von Siegsfeld—more correctly, Mrs. von Preussach—was unwell during an unspecifiable period of her visit, and had remained in her room for several days. The family physician, whom the judge encountered coincidentally at the castle, also recalled the indisposition of the visiting lady; he claimed to have found her, however, not actually ill, just worn out and in a depressed state of mind.

Miss Hedwig von Kettler, the oldest daughter of the house, brought up incidentally a circumstance that the judge regarded as worth noting. Mrs. von Preussach had left Blumenrode at the beginning of September 1816, although she had intended earlier to stay until October. Letters from home had brought about her decision to depart early, it was said.

Some time afterward, Hedwig had written her and had mentioned in passing, among other things that had happened recently, that a robbed and horribly murdered officer had been found in the mountains. In Albertine's answer, which the young lady produced, there was the passage:

> So even in your beautiful mountains there are dreadful robberies and murders? The unfortunate officer! It wasn't one of your chivalrous admirers from France, was it? Heaven save us! Do write me, if you learn more of this. Don't forget.

In a later letter from Albertine from January of 1817, there was in a postscript:

> Have you heard no more of the murder in the mountains?

The words were underlined.

At the time that the judge was presiding over these examinations, a schoolteacher came forward, a musician respected in the area, and turned in a page that, as he expressed it, he "could not withhold from the eye of the judge according to certain reports going around." He had found it a long time ago in a musical score that he had lent Mrs. von Siegsfeld during her stay at the castle and had gotten back after her departure.

It was, to all appearances, the incomplete draft of a letter with the following content:

> I respect the convictions from which your warning stems, but my decision is firm. I will see him. Circumstances upon which the peace of my life depends must be decided. For this reason I have put all reservations aside. I have no fear. A. knows me. He knows that in decisive moments the weakness of my sex—

On the empty part of the page there were a few other meaningless words and syllables, the way someone scribbles while trying out a new quill. The letter was unmistakably from the now satisfactorily familiar hand of Mrs. von Preussach.

Armed with all the gathered knowledge, the instructing judge began examining the arrested woman anew. We scarcely need mention that it was the regular judge; his zealous substitute had stepped down after that one interrogation.

It is a peculiarity of French criminal procedure, separating it sharply from the old German trial of inquisition, that while the latter always aims toward a confession, the former stands aloof from all such striving and takes as its task the conviction of the accused. The principle is based on an honorable feeling of justice: human nature opposes a self-accusation that guides the sword of justice down upon its own neck; denial or silence is the natural defense of the accused. The judge fights against these with the weapons of proofs. Thus equality is produced in the dispute. The voice of society, the true *vox populi*, given voice through the mouth of the jury, decides between plaintiff and accused who is victorious, who is defeated.

The interrogation proceedings that we have seen illuminate the authority of this principle in a lively fashion. The judge, for his part, puts before us openly and ruthlessly the accusatory circumstances and obligatory questions about every issue pertaining to the crime. Where an answer is denied, the denial is quietly noted; there is never further pressure and imputation.

And the accused? She persists in her firm and impenetrable silence. Her constantly repeated explanation is:

"I do not want to tarnish my conscience with a lie, it is burdened enough without this. But no one shall tear the truth from me!"

The letter given up by the schoolteacher in Blumenrode appeared to affect the prisoner very strongly. It was obvious that she had not suspected that this paper was in the hands of the court.

The judge reminded the prisoner repeatedly of her right to produce evidence to vindicate herself. Her constant reply was, "I cannot show such evidence. I may not intentionally lift the veil that covers this calamitous incident. As far as this matter has now developed, I will say no word on my behalf; and if the voice of the judge pronounced death or eternal imprisonment, I would receive the verdict without objection. To the world I am dead, I can only find peace in the dungeon or the grave."

She also decisively rejected the opportunity to choose a defense lawyer.

Things were in this state when the files went to the appeals court of the province, which had to decide whether to relegate the case to the status of formal accusation. In line with his client's instructions, Senkenberg had also added a judicial exposition, which carefully compiled everything that could justify a charge of spousal murder.

The court's decision was interlocutory. Before relegation to the status of formal accusation, light still needed to be shed upon some points, the most important of which we will describe here:

First, the moral character, the lifestyle and the disposition of the divorced Mrs. von Preussach were to be determined as precisely as possible and exhibited.

Second, one should investigate more closely the basis for Ferdinand von Preussach's claim that the spouse of the deceased had a clear interest in his death with reference to certain economic embarrassments. Third, the sentiments she cherished toward the dead man needed to be probed more than they had been; and to this end and fourth, a useful means would be furnished by the confiscation from the parental home of all her papers and correspondence, which were to be turned over to a reliable police officer who had been well informed in this matter via the files on the case. This officer was also to take note of any other suspicious effects and to consult with the authorities there.

At the end there was also the note, "Moreover, the influence of the private plaintiff, Ferdinand von Preussach, upon the procurement of evidence (which influence the court observes with displeasure), is to be limited as much as possible."

These instructions, which bore witness in equal degrees to the judgmental keenness and the impartiality of the higher court, were faithfully followed by the provincial court. Unfortunately, they led to the saddest consequences for the family of the prisoner.

Provided with the authorization of the local authorities, the police representative appeared unexpectedly at Colonel von Siegsfeld's house to discharge his commission. The elderly man, completely unfamiliar with the proceedings in Hainburg, was frightened to death, and soon a horrible suspicion dawned about the cause of his family's delayed homecoming. With rigid resignation he himself opened his daughter's rooms to the official and directed the latter to perform his duty.

The laments of the humbled father were poured out more loudly now in a letter to his wife. He implored her to return home without delay if she wanted to see him still alive, for the blow had struck fatally a man grown gray in honor and renown. The frightened wife, torn between her duties as a wife and as a mother, had to make the decision to leave her daughter.

Up to this point, Albertine had pleadingly rejected any meeting with her mother. But now, with the moment of parting imminent, she must have been unable to resist any longer the call of the maternal voice. The circumstance we will shortly describe permits us to conclude that the judge's well-meaning indulgence allowed one last private meeting in Mrs. von Siegsfeld's lodgings.

On the day after Mrs. von Siegsfeld's departure the report was heard in the city, and soon brought to the attention of the court, that a traveling private tutor who had lodged in the same inn as Mrs. von Siegsfeld, and whose room had been separated from her parlor only by a door, had, as an unseen witness to the conversation of the two ladies, heard words that appeared to him to be extremely strange. Under curious questioning he had communicated them to the innkeepers, who passed them along to the court since the eavesdropper himself was no more to be found.

The ladies had conducted their conversation in French, but their listener, who knew French, had understood every word. According to his tale, the older lady had said to the younger one: "Unfortunate girl! I realize that you are not unconnected with Armand's death!"

And the younger one responded, crying hard, "Mother! God knows what happened. I may not speak; I will perish in misery, but I will be silent!"

Let us now hear what the police deputy brought with him to Hainburg.

In Agathe Roger, Albertine's former and very close servant, the clever man had found an informed tool for the difficult business of the examination and sorting of such abundant furnishings as those found in the residence of the accused. This was precisely the Agathe Roger whom we know from the preacher's daughter's story. She had become a respected housewife in the meantime: soon after her return from Blumenrode she had married the Siegsfeld children's former teacher, who was now the headmaster of a school in a town not far from the capital.

The cupboard that contained the correspondence also held Albertine's jewelry and adornments. The former lady's maid lost no time in looking through these treasures once confided to her care, to see whether everything was as it had been before. Thus an unusually wrapped package came into her hands: it contained a gold watch with a chain and a wedding band.

"Ah!" Agathe cried out, moved, at the sight of these pieces. "That is the late Baron Hermann's watch, which he always wore, and this is his wedding ring! My dear lady gave him the watch when they were still engaged. No doubt he had to return them both after the divorce. Not even I knew that!"

But the police officer, well versed in the contents of the police files, had other ideas altogether and eagerly took the treacherous treasures into custody.

There were no letters that could shed brighter light on the relationship between the spouses after their divorce. In Albertine's correspondence with third parties, however, there was information that had previously been unknown to the files and even to Ferdinand von Preussach, that industrious reconnoiterer—Albertine had received some marriage proposals. We will hear more about these from Agathe.

Extremely favorable were the many official as well as private statements that the official had collected pertaining to Albertine's character and moral habits. She was praised for having a noble pride happily paired with affability and beneficence, extraordinary intellectual gifts and an exceptional education, and for showing boundless devotion and obedience toward her worthy parents and exemplary care in the upbringing of her own daughter. Only one accusation was generally directed toward her, and this concerned her exaggerated preference for outward splendor and expensive amusements, among which her passion for music appeared to play the starring role. Even the otherwise highly laudatory confidential report of the office of the chief of police in the capital noted this. It said:

> *In the interests of the truth the fact should not be withheld that the Baroness von Preussach did not observe all the necessary orderliness in her financial affairs, because*

she was often sued and even threatened with executive measures due to her not inconsiderable debts.

Among the numerous bundles of bills—which added up steeply—for fashion and toilet articles, there were many with the name "Wilhelmine Tieffe," which had earlier been the cause of so many inquiries, and Agathe stated that this Wilhelmine Tieffe was the proprietress of a fashion and dressmaking shop in the capital, a business much frequented by her employer.

It is time now to let Agathe speak, herself.

"I have known Mrs. von Preussach," Agathe said, in her statement, "from the earliest days of her childhood; indeed, I grew up with her, so to speak, although she is quite a few years younger than I am. My mother was already in service to Mrs. von Siegsfeld, the colonel's wife, when she was still unmarried and a lady in waiting at the court of the late electoral princess of ***. My father, who had a small business, died, and my mother, as a widow, often came to help in the colonel's house. As a child, I played with the two young masters in the von Siegsfeld family, who died during the war as officers. They were my age: Miss Albertine, as I said, was younger. She was brought up well, but also very pretentiously: her mother appeared to be grooming her for court. At sixteen she was presented at court and took part in the assemblies, which were brilliant affairs here at that time.

"The young lady was admired by the whole world and deserved it: she was really as beautiful as an angel then. At that time, Mr. von Preussach came to the capital; he had served as an officer with our young masters and was still in the military. A very attractive man, a daring and elegant rider and nimble dancer. He soon became an admirer of the beautiful young lady, who was particularly taken by his voice, a wonderful tenor. I have often heard people praise it who understand such things: this voice was perhaps unique in Germany. The young lady was passionate about music and she herself sang beautifully and artfully; in short, music was the secret bond that united the hearts of that dear pair. Herr von Preussach was not a bad match, destined as he was to inherit his father's large estate, and our young lady had no fortune to speak of. The bridegroom gave up his military service, although our colonel was not completely in favor of this, given the continually warlike state of things. Nevertheless, the baron had earned his spurs in the campaign of 1809. His resignation was granted. The wedding was in the spring of 1811; the bride was not yet seventeen and Mr. von Preussach was about twenty-six. For that summer, the pair lived on an estate which the family von Preussach had vacated for the son, and it was then that the young mistress suggested that I accompany her. She was used to me; I was, as it were, on intimate terms with her toilet and fashion needs, which were very important to her. My mother looked with favor upon the advantageous position, and so I went with her.

"In the beginning, the couple lived splendidly and happily. The old

Preussachs, who were a frail pair, bent over backward for their beautiful daughter-in-law, and the master's half-sisters, two fading, grim spinsters, at least put on a pleasant face. Baron Ferdinand, the younger brother, was at the university then.

"Every day we called on people and received visitors. Everyone paid homage to the charming young wife, but for all her youth and her pleasure-seeking there was still something so imposing that Baron Hermann found no cause for suspicion or worry.

"It's just too bad that Mrs. von Preussach, the spoiled darling of the court and the big city, knew at most only how to extract the poetic side of country life, but she had not the faintest idea of the demands—even upon ladies of the upper classes—that an extensive estate makes, or of the cares that it brings. The master wasn't at all inexperienced with managing an estate, but it was not in his nature to give his wife encouragement and guidance. The estate income would have been completely sufficient with greater thriftiness, but as it was there were soon shortages in every hole and corner. At the beginning Mama von Preussach helped out; she had a significant personal income and Hermann was her favorite child. But that began to annoy the other siblings when it happened too often, especially Baron Ferdinand, who had meanwhile returned home and was fairly painstaking in matters of money. If the estate went to Hermann, he and his sisters could only hope for an inheritance from their mother's money, and it wasn't unreasonable that they didn't like to see it whittled away, particularly by Hermann, who was already so favored by fortune. That was the first source of the disagreement that began to spread more widely throughout the family and, in those bad times, found more and more fuel in the baroness's continued extravagance. It's true, she kept a wardrobe which many a princess would envy her, and what she thoughtlessly flung away would have kept a couple of good families respectably clothed.

"The problem grew when young master Alfred was born, who was followed in a year by little Konstanze. The children had a French wet nurse, and later also a governess, which was not an easy thing to achieve in the province. Every winter they went to his parents in the capital and kept a large apartment there with servants and carriages, and thus frittered away more than too much from the future estate.

"Meanwhile, as long as there was peace between the two, everything was fine. Hermann took his wife's part to such a degree that he fell out with his siblings; the parents were insignificant and completely subject to their favorite son.

"But unfortunately even marital peace suffered a blow, and it was the dear departed master's fault. Heaven only knows how it happened—he really loved the young mistress and she was in a period of the most glorious bloom of youth—but enough, she discovered a scandalous unfaithfulness, doubly injurious to her because the object was one of her maids. Their happiness was gone, because Mrs. von Preussach could not see any way to understand this; she herself prized marital fidelity and dignity very highly. She left suddenly with me and the children and went to her parents, a step which disconcerted the Preussachs very much. Hermann himself, with his mother, came after her. There were fierce scenes, but nevertheless the old love, especially the love of the children, was victorious; Mrs. von Preussach, who feared that her son would be taken from her in the event of divorce, agreed to a reconciliation, which admittedly could not bring about a closer relationship between Hermann and his in-laws. Hermann, feeling his guilt, lived only for his wife, and avoided his siblings entirely in order to give her a certain satisfaction, so that everything seemed to take a turn for the better.

"Then little Alfred died, and this death affected the young mother in the most horrible fashion. She had exerted herself excessively in caring for the child, and after the funeral she fell into a brain fever. The doctors sent her to a spa to regain her strength. Baron von Preussach could not go with her, because his brother was traveling again and their old father had become quite childish. The baroness's mother accompanied her, as did I.

"After their departure, the evil spirit must have come over the baron again; the relationship with the bad maid started up anew and had serious consequences. I don't know who revealed her husband's lapse to the young mistress; in short, we did not return to the estate, but rather went to her parental home. No remonstrance on the part of the Preussachs had any effect; the formal divorce was pursued to the degree that our church allows it. The colonel brought all his influence to bear; the judgment came quickly and was extremely disadvantageous for the guilty party. The Preussachs had to make great sacrifices, for the divorced lady was allowed to keep her daughter with her and both were granted a substantial yearly allowance.

"Only now could the Preussachs tell that their fortune had suffered many a blow during the short duration of the marriage. However, it was too late. Hermann paid little attention to money or the estate, he regretted only the loss of his wife, whom he fundamentally truly loved. The wench who was the cause of all this turmoil died in childbed together with her child. Hermann offered up everything to obtain forgiveness; his parents, who would gladly have had the marriage continue because of the great sacrifices they had made, also made attempts to smooth things over, but the colonel was unyielding. The young wife— I know this for a fact—was secretly still devoted to her husband; I have every reason to suspect that at first she received letters from him and answered them. But the old colonel even protested against this, and she honored her father too highly to have ever denied him her obedience. And thus it has remained to this day. We heard nothing more from the Preussachs. Mrs. von Siegsfeld—that's what she called herself now—was rather taciturn with me in this respect. Otherwise she talked to me about this and that, but she scarcely mentioned her husband's name after she herself had outwardly put it aside. I only heard incidentally from a third party that Hermann had gone into the wide world, having fallen out with his family altogether; supposedly he swore that he would not come back before he inherited the estate and title, and then all who would place themselves between him and his wife should tremble before him. The old Baroness von Preussach had died during this time, I must note, and Hermann had wrung his maternal inheritance from his family and gone away with it.

"Mrs. von Siegsfeld, my employer, remained, with little Konstanze, permanently with her parents, except for the few months in the summer of 1816 that she spent with friends in the *** mountains. It was Baron von Kettler's family; the estate is called Blumenrode. I accompanied her on that journey, but fell ill in Blumenrode and was therefore with her very little toward the end of that visit, and did not accompany her on the trip home; I did not return to the capital until October.

"After I returned from Blumenrode I stayed in service to my lady until Christmas. Soon after that I was married to my husband, who had received the headmastership in his home town. I have only seen the von Siegsfeld family once or twice since my marriage; but toward me and my husband they have continued to be very kind and affable."

This court, informed by means of an exhaustive missive about the points at issue in the Hainburg investigation, had taken advantage of the opportunity to put some other particular questions to Agathe. This was prompted by a casual remark of the witness's husband, who, as Albertine's former teacher, was mindful of her outstanding intellectual and emotional dispositions, but also of an unpraiseworthy quality, her flaring temper. Agathe confirmed this and could give supporting examples from recent years.

"It is true," she said, "Mrs. von Preussach was heated and easily angered to a fever pitch. In the grip of rage she is not herself and is capable of excesses about which she has often felt the bitterest regret afterwards, as truly good-hearted as she is. This happened to her especially when something attacked her pride and her very keen sense of honor. Thus I remember—we were still at the von Preussach estate—that the master once put together a hunting party in which several ladies also rode out. He had gotten it into his head that his wife would ride out too, and had provided an expensive dress and beautiful accoutrements. But he didn't know the baroness very well in that respect! She found it highly offensive for a lady to allow herself to be seen on horseback, and was extremely indignant about this presumption. The master, who did not want to be compromised in front of his guests, became vehement and began to threaten her; in short, the argument ended with the young baroness, in the most horrible state of excitement, seizing his hunting knife and threatening murder and manslaughter. Whether she meant her life or his I don't remember anymore, but the master gave in and nothing came of the hunting party.

"Even toward her own servants she often forgot herself in anger. On the estate there was a girl, admittedly a clumsy, stupid thing, who spoiled something once, while helping Mrs. von Preussach dress. My dear lady got into such a rage that she threw a flower vase at the girl's head. The poor thing lay there for a long time as if she were dead. There was a horrible uproar; the girl's parents, rebellious people, wanted to sue. The old country judge, who was a good man, interceded, and the matter was hushed up.

"It even happened to me, whom she treated more like a paid companion than a lady's maid: she often boxed my ears so severely when she was heated that she herself was sorry for it, afterwards, and she sometimes came to ask forgiveness with tears in her eyes."

So much for Agathe, now the headmaster's wife. We will encounter her again.

The appeals court had, in the admonition we mentioned before, given the Hainburg tribunal the task of making every effort in the investigation of two persons, namely the girl who led Mrs. von Preussach that day from the gathering in Hilgenberg to her alleged friend, and the old woodcutter, the man who accompanied the wounded lady. Happily, the maid was found, due to the untiring efforts of the police. She was now in service to a tradesman in the market town of Möllheim, not far from K***.

The instructing judge took down the important statement, which was as follows:

"Two years ago I was in service to a shoemaker in Hilgenberg, who had a little house there. A civil servant's widow, Madame Veitel, actually a resident of Möllheim, had rented the front part of the house for the summer months and sublet the rooms again to spa guests. That summer there were rooms standing empty. One day—it was already almost autumn—she called me to her and asked whether I would run an errand for her. I was willing, put on some neat clothes, and went to her rooms. A young gentleman was there, to whom Madame was very polite. Then she led me outside the door to the room and gave me a sealed letter; I was supposed to take it to the assembly rooms of the spa and give it to a noblewoman there, into her own hands. I have forgotten the name of that noblewoman, and would not know it again if I heard it. There were many fine people in the assembly rooms, old and young; I asked for my party and they indicated a lady to me that I would have thought was a young miss from her appearance, but she was the right one. She read the letter, talked a little more with the other people, and then got ready to come with me. Madame Veitel had already told me that I would have to guide the lady. She told me to walk ahead of her, and followed me at such a rapid pace that we got to our destination fairly quickly. Scarcely a word was said underway. Madame Veitel was already in the front hall to receive the lady, thanked me, and let me go. I do not know what happened after that. I never saw the gentleman anymore. Later I heard from my own employer that a gentleman and a lady had gone walking through the back garden in the direction of the mountain; but I cannot say whether they were the persons I am to speak of here.

"I did not look especially closely at the lady, since I walked in front of her. I can only state that her complexion was beautifully white and pink, and she was very tightly laced; her waist was extraordinarily fine and slim in proportion to her rather tall stature. As to her clothing I only remember that she wore a silk dress of a bright color—I really don't remember any more which color—and a straw hat with flowers.

"The gentleman was, as I said, still young, also tall and slim and had a brownish complexion. He had on a short green jacket and very tight leather trousers. He wore spurs on his short boots."

Using the directions the girl provided, the house in Hilgenberg where Mrs. Veitel had lived was found easily. The owners no longer remembered the gentleman and lady and their walk through the garden; on the other hand they were sure that a Mrs. von Seehausen had never lived in their house, indeed, that the name was completely unfamiliar to them. The widow Veitel had recently died, as an inquiry in Möllheim revealed.

The old man was and remained undiscovered; the police had no basis on which to develop a positive line of inquiry.

The court of appeals now proclaimed, by means of a quickly announced final finding, that the accused was to be remanded and formally charged. The public proceeding was to take place at the next assizes in the Hainburg judicial district, and the accused, in order to satisfy legal form, was to have a defender officially assigned to her. But this became unnecessary. An old lawyer, devoted to the von Siegsfelds and attached to the highest appeals court (the supreme central court in the capital) appeared. He requested acceptance as counsel for the defense and received it. With loyal zeal the stout-hearted defender studied the already very swollen files and conferred then with his charge, undisturbed by other eyes. But the presentation of the defense, which we will communicate to the reader in good time, shows that his client proved herself no more candid with him than she was toward the judges.

The time for the court sessions drew near, and the Preussach case was the first on the roster. The interest in the case, the alluring personality of the defendant and even the number of witnesses and the respected social positions of some of them gave the trial a certain distinction and lured an unusual number of onlookers. A total of thirty-four witnesses were called, among them the manorial families of Blumenrode and Langnitz; from Blumenrode also the preacher's family and the schoolmaster. Even Agathe Roger, now the headmaster's wife, had not avoided the long journey and, assured that all her expenses would be reimbursed, had appeared in Hainburg.

The bench at the assizes had been taken over by one of the oldest counselors in the court of appeals, and the function of state attorney by chief prosecutor Schömberg, a man of significant reputation, the highest official of the public ministry of the province.

The opening of the sessions fell in the first days of June 1818. At eight in the morning the galleries were opened to the public and were overflowing within a quarter-hour. The narrator of this story was present for the entire duration of the proceedings with the exception of one day; what follows is therefore the report of an eye- and ear-witness.

Toward nine o'clock the presiding judge ordered that the defendant be led in. All eyes turned toward the door through which she would come. Albertine appeared, led by her lawyer, a venerable and still sturdy old man. A woman of respectable appearance accompanied Albertine to her seat and then took her place, somewhat removed, in the room. This was the servant allotted to her. As we later learned, even her physician was there during all the proceedings.

She was beautiful indeed, this defendant—consummately beautiful. The rosy color of an earlier day, which some of the witnesses had praised, had admittedly faded; marble paleness adorned that nobly formed countenance, but it appeared expressive and full of meaning that way. The clothing of the defendant was as simple as it was respectable; today, as on all the days that followed, she wore a black silk gown, a hat with a veil spilling down of the same color, and as her only jewelry merely a fine gold chain that held her watch fast to her waist. Her entire appearance proved that even in her present, more confining imprisonment she enjoyed all the comforts that social position and upbringing had made necessary for her.

The impression that this pleasing appearance made on the public was unmistakably positive. After her, the plaintiff, Ferdinand von Preussach, was the object of the greatest attention, but it was visibly less benevolent. His otherwise so well-featured face showed a repellent mobility that over the course of the trial often increased to the point of grotesqueness. Some of the witnesses avoided him assiduously; he ignored this with a nobleman's indifference. Most of the witnesses sat with serious and dejected expressions; several of the ladies—we will meet them later by name—dissolved into tears. The strongest contrast to them was provided by a single person, who attracted attention unpleasantly by her unconstrained, even bold manner; this was Agathe, now the headmaster's wife. Over the novelty of the drama of a public court proceeding she appeared to have forgotten its portentous tendency.

The presiding judge, a man of imposing exterior, approached the defendant. She rose and answered the usual questions about name, marital state and residence with a voice that was soft and barely audible to the onlookers. There followed the calling of the defense attorney, the reminders of the duties of his office and the solemn swearing-in of the jury. Finally an officer of the court stepped before the great council table, and, after the presiding judge had demanded the close attention of the defendant, read the judgment of the court of appeals that remanded her case to this court, and then the statement of accusation that had been worked out by the public prosecutor.

After a pithy sketch of the peculiarity of the case, which lacked both a proper eyewitness to the deed and any statement whatsoever from the accused, the file began with an enumeration of the results of the objective facts of the case, in which the reports about the deceased, the type of killing, the location, and the time all had their place.

The prosecutor offered the following statements as more or less proved, enough, at least, to convince the judges: Baron Hermann von Preussach lost his life in a violent fashion by means of a stab in the heart from a sharp, cutting instrument, probably a knife. The definitely and instantaneously fatal wound was the work of another's hand, so that one could speak of a killing in the legal sense. The originally contemplated suspicion of a robbery-murder had been rejected completely.

Although it had not been discovered exactly to the hour, the time of the killing fell without doubt during the day of August 24, 1816, the day on which the unfortunate man had been seen alive early in the morning. The location of the killing was to be regarded without hesitation as the ruins above the St. Anne's chapel that are called the Raubstein; only from there was the lifeless body moved to the chapel.

Next, the prosecutor busied himself with the subjective circumstances, or the perpetration. He developed the indications that led the court first to the traces of a female individual, and then finally to the person of the divorced spouse of the dead man.

It was certain, he said, that a secret correspondence had taken place between the estranged spouses, from K*** on his part and from Blumenrode on hers. The goal and object of it had been an equally secret meeting at a third place; this meeting had had its beginning on August 24th in the rooms of the widow Veitel in Hilgenberg, and had continued upon the Raubstein.

After this time, Hermann had not been seen alive again, but the defendant had been seen wounded, bleeding, in fear and flight, in the surprising company of a low-bred man; this man had made utterances about whose sense and meaning there could be no doubt. The defendant had maintained a pervasive silence about the events of those hours toward her companions in Hilgenberg—whom she even deceived by means of invented statements toward her hosts in Blumenrode and toward her servants. She hid her wound and accelerated conspicuously her departure from Blumenrode, but inquired about the dead man with continuing fearfulness in her letters from home. Her behavior at the time of Ferdinand's first appearance, during the pretense of suspicion of the minister's daughter, and during the court interrogations was likewise considered. Finally, the conversation overheard by the traveler in the inn and—especially important— the possession of the dead man's watch and his wedding ring were emphasized.

"From all these circumstances," the prosecutor concluded these observations, "we must come to the unavoidable conviction uttered even by the mother of the defendant in these words, according to the testimony of that listener:

"'Unfortunate girl! You are not unconnected with Armand's death!'

"We must assert, as proven fact, the *accessory guilt*, the *presence* at the deed, of the defendant in the killing of her husband."

The prosecutor then turned to those circumstances that show, according to the language of the law, "the inner disposition," that is, the motivations for the deed. With impartiality he rejected here the often-mentioned insinuations of the civil plaintiff. He dismissed the thought of a premeditated attack upon the life of the husband. He expounded: however much the self-inflicted devastation of her finances might suffice to reproach the accused, still the generally positive testimony about her morality had to provide strong protection against every conjecture of such a base sort as that.

Thus the prosecutor finally came to the development of his own notion of the deed, and he described it as follows:

"The killing was the work of a sudden passion that welled up in the stress of fear and the belief that self-defense was necessary."

The arguments for this point of view were derived with care and not without keenness from the available correspondence and witness statements. Hermann's intent was clearly directed at a reunion with his wife, he had given vent to his feelings in threats—the nature of which was admittedly unknown, but they were surely not undangerous ones, since third parties had warned Albertine. Against these threats she had set her own pride and her trust in the weapons of honor and virtue; with this confidence she had agreed to the secret meeting. Hermann might have expressed himself more ruthlessly with his threatening intrusion during that lonely rendezvous; perhaps he wouldn't have scorned physical violence, removal by force. The most respectable witnesses held him capable of using such means to gain his end, especially in the extremely drunken state in which he was found, according to the autopsy.

"If we summarize all these circumstances," said the prosecutor, "then what remained obscured at the beginning is satisfactorily explained. The weak woman, recognizing too late the inadequacy of her invisible weapons, which she trusted in proud certainty, struggles for more useful weapons; a knife, used during the meal they shared, is at hand; a great rage: she points it at the breast of her husband and the deed—is done!

"We may only remind the court of the examples of outbreaks of wild rage that the accused's trusted servant and companion of youth describes and is prepared to affirm publicly; they are examples in which merely a fortunate circumstance averted the same sad consequences of haste that we have here before us.

"And how," asked the prosecutor at the end of his document, "how does the accused respond to the striking evidence developed here? Does she call witnesses to disprove the accusation? Does she elaborate on that which is still obscured? Does she at least try to weaken the evidence? No! She is silent. She is unable to deny the power of the evidence. Her silence has convicted the accused in our eyes; she has spoken—silently—her verdict herself!"

The presiding judge turned again to the defendant. "You are free to make any reply. We will take it down; express yourself without shyness or reservation. There is still time to break your silence. If you should have evidence to present, we will also grant you the necessary time."

Albertine tried to respond, but her voice failed her. She did not appear to be able to steel herself to speak publicly. She spent a long time in quiet conversation with her lawyer. The latter then announced, "My client wishes to await the end of the proceeding; I retain the right to put the best possible interpretation on this decision."

The state prosecutor recapitulated then, in an independent, compressed statement, the most salient points of the accusation, and had the list of witnesses who would be called to testify read out. The testimonies then began.

The witnesses of that day addressed only the facts of the inquest and the recognition of the dead man's possessions by those who had known or seen him living. At three o'clock that afternoon the proceedings were adjourned.

The next day's continuation brought, among other things, the experts' elucidations of the available handwriting; it was these proceedings that the narrator was unable to attend.

For the public, meanwhile, the case had become the object of general commentary and nearly the only point upon which the day's conversation turned.

The third session gathered such a large group of spectators as was never seen here before. This time there were particularly many ladies in the galleries, even from the best circles; the gathering resembled a theater auditorium before a performance.

Today there were witnesses scheduled whose testimony made closer reference to the accused herself. The questioning of the Countesses von Koss aroused particular interest. They provided an unpleasant denunciation of the civil plaintiff. The mother allowed a few remarks to fall, apparently unintentionally, about the way in which Mr. von Preussach had insinuated himself at Langnitz and gained the trust of the ladies. The counsel for the accused eagerly took note of this and demanded more information. He made reference to the court of appeals' stated denunciation of Preussach's unauthorized meddling in the duties of the investigating magistrate.

Even more surprising was the testimony of the old barber surgeon's widow. She who had so decisively claimed to recognize in the accused the wounded woman of August 24th now expressed herself uncertainly, was embarrassed, and finally said, amid tears and sighs, "May God, before whom I will certainly shortly stand, be merciful to me: I cannot say for sure that this lady here is the lady from that time."

The presiding judge showed the old lady her written statement, but she held to her words: "I believe she is the same one, but I cannot definitely say so." Then she added, "Just imagine: the light was already dim in our parlor and the whole business with the bandage didn't last long enough to say three Lord's Prayers!"

The defender noted that to press the witness further would be to do violence to her conscience. The modification of her earlier and daring claim did her honor.

Preussach stepped forward with the greatest of indignation. Senkenberg tried without success to hold him back.

"It almost seems," said Preussach, "as if the public proceedings only have the goal of completely nullifying the painstaking investigation conducted by the instructing judge!"

The president called him to order with very serious words.

The second witness from Schlingen, the barber's neighbor, merely repeated his previous statement. He had only seen the unknown lady fleetingly, and did not observe her face at all; it would be impossible after such a long time to say anything definite.

The defender asked to be permitted a word with the jury, and was granted it.

"The most important points of the accusation," he said, "are based on the presumption that the wounded lady in Schlingen and the accused are one person. There is now not a single witness present to support this assumption; therewith any conclusion that follows from this assumption must also be discarded, even more since none of the experts has dared to claim with certainty the existence, at that time, of a wound, and no member of the von Kettler family or the servants, Albertine's daily table companions and those around her, ever perceived a wound, which would have been downright impossible to hide completely."

The court decided to question Mr. von Kettler and his family right away about the nature of their domestic interactions with Albertine, since they were shortly to be called anyhow. The baron, his wife, two grown daughters and a fifteen-year-old son appeared one after the other. Very little that was satisfying could be had from their careful, restrained statements. Nobody seemed to know when and for how long Mrs. von Preussach had been unwell; but during this time, they stated, she did indeed dine alone in her room and not, as usual, with the family.

Agathe, herself unable to work at the time in question, had already stated earlier that she knew absolutely nothing of any wound.

The Kettler family physician was to be questioned during the following session, since, due to the late hour, he could no longer be reached.

This fourth session introduced even livelier debate than the earlier ones. The questioning of Agathe, now the rector's wife, began the day. We have already mentioned the bold and resolute way in which she presented herself. Today she was truly offensive. She strayed far beyond the bounds of the question in every answer she gave, most of the time in such a stupidly impertinent manner that she made the audience laugh more than once.

First the torn strips of fabric found next to and in the vicinity of the body were laid before her, along with the familiar, much-discussed gloves. The rector's wife regarded everything with an affected importance. Then she said, tersely and boldly, "What should I say about these rags? Are they supposed to belong to my lady? There can be no question of that!"

The presiding judge said, "These strips were thought to be part of a woman's shawl that was torn to pieces; do you not recognize them?"

The witness answered, "Whatever the scraps are, they have nothing to do with my lady."

The presiding judge: "How are you able to say this so certainly?"

The witness: "How? I certainly would know that! My dear lady would never have worn such gaudy, tasteless colors. Where I live not even a cook wears such a shawl anymore."

The defender requested that the jury take note of this disavowal of the shawl.

The witness continued: "Believe me, I speak what is true according to my conscience. The Danish gloves, for example; they belong to her ladyship, that's for sure!"

The presiding judge: "And upon what do you base your assurance?"

The witness replied, "Now, there I can help you. These gloves are from Madame Tieffe; my lady always had them by the dozen, long and short, however they came. Her ladyship had an uncommon love of Danish gloves because they smell nice and preserve the hands. She often said, in a *scherzando* fashion, 'I have only three passions: music, Viennese cake, and Danish gloves.'"

The audience broke into resounding laughter. The witness looked up, indignant. "I find that rather unseemly; I'm speaking according to my conscience."

The presiding judge reproached the audience for the disturbance and tried to keep the witness to the point. The story about the preacher's daughter came up. After some thought, Agathe confirmed the story in details that, once again, strayed endlessly. In the course of the questioning, episodes were mentioned that the witness had described to the court in the capital as proof of her mistress's sudden bouts of rage. She added more to these, and she did not spare the courtroom, which was already in a mood to laugh, the ominous ear-boxing story.

Meanwhile, Dr. Bestelmeyer, the Kettler family physician, had been announced, and was introduced immediately since he had requested that they finish with him quickly.

He produced his record book and indicated from it that he had seen Mrs. von Siegsfeld on Monday, the 26th of August 1816 for the first time, and on Thursday August 29th for the second and last time. He had also noted that all she complained of was weakness and exhaustion as the consequence of an arduous walk; he had only prescribed strengthening medicine to refresh her and put some life into her.

The presiding judge asked, "Did the patient uncover or have visible a wound on her right hand?"

"She definitely did not show me one, nor was one visible," answered the doctor.

"But doubtless you felt your patient's pulse?"

"To be sure, and for that reason I say that she never allowed me to see a wound whose existence I can as little affirm as deny. Like many ladies of high society, Mrs. von Siegsfeld always wore gloves, even in her room. I remember quite well that on that occasion also, as I took her pulse—I cannot say whether it was the left or right hand—I did not see her hand uncovered. Rather, she pulled her glove away as much as was necessary. I already told this to the instructing judge when I was questioned in Blumenrode."

The chief prosecutor took up the discussion. "It is disturbing that the instructing judge nowhere mentioned the doctor's remark in his records. It is extremely important. From this habit of the accused, which indeed many ladies of the higher classes have, we can fully explain how the wound and the bandage could have gone unnoticed by Mr. von Kettler and his family. I propose that we re-question the von Kettler family with particular attention to the circumstance just noted."

The defending attorney broke in, "I must solemnly protest such bold conclusions. All honor to the doctor's word; it may be regarded as a general habit that vain and idle ladies of high society, who lay their fine hands in their laps from morning till night, force themselves constantly into the tiresome constraint of gloves. But I cannot allow this to apply to my client. She knows how to keep herself busy, works delicately with scissors and needle, likes to play music—and all these activities can only be carried out with a bare and free hand. Moreover, we speak here of the closest and most confidential contact among the residents of the house. One may well receive a doctor in a complete toilet, to which gloves may properly belong, but certainly in family circles a lady gladly sheds that uncomfortable covering. Her indisposition and her keeping to her room were also not of many weeks' duration, but a bandage would have been."

Preussach also asked to speak.

"The defender will allow me a rejoinder," he said with a sardonic smile. "For domestic activities, the ladies make use of so-called *mitons*; these are gloves which completely cover the hand but leave the fingers free and thus do not hinder any activity. The lady of whom we speak once belonged to my family; my testimony is not, therefore, completely without value. I can only confirm the doctor's observation with respect to the aforementioned lady."

"I thank Mr. von Preussach for the edification," responded the defender evenly, "but allow myself the criticism that the baron is here as the plaintiff, not as a witness. This fact has unfortunately been forgotten too often during this trial."

The presiding judge brought an end to the piqued exchange of words.

Then it was Agathe's turn again. The current line of questioning fell within her sphere of influence. With her quick decisiveness she said, "That is completely correct. Her ladyship set tremendous store by her beautiful hands. She always wore gloves; she even wore them to bed. Her Mama had accustomed her to that from the time she was a child."

The defender made quick work of this petty discussion. "Well, then," he said with annoyance. "I must let it stand that my client was always gloved, sleeping as well as waking. I would have preferred that she had never made the acquaintance of these articles; she has had a rare misfortune with them. We have had to listen to debates that truly have taken on something of their material: one could call them 'leathery!'"

This moody and unexpected turn caused such general laughter that it infected even some of the most prominent men of the court. And with that the proceedings took on a new direction.

At the end of the session, another point came under discussion that held the attention of the listeners to a high degree. Agathe volunteered information of her own accord; her conscience, she said, had brought her once more before the judge's bench.

She asked, "May I be silent about things that I am not expressly questioned about?"

The president asked, in turn, "What things do you mean?"

The witness answered, "Oh, my Jesus, I mean about the wound that there's so much talk of!"

"Do you know something about the wound? You were specifically questioned about that!"

"No, upon my soul! I have no knowledge of it. But—a kind of suspicion. If the bloody dress had anything to do with the wound!"

Preussach approached with a look of the most burning curiosity. Even the defender was disquieted.

The witness approached the accused. "For God's sake, for Jesus'! Forgive me, your ladyship! I'm talking you into misfortune, but my oath is sacred!"

The presiding judge interrupted this most uncustomary speech. "What about the bloody dress?" he asked.

The witness allowed a stream of tears to flow, which was finally followed by a long story. The content was, in brief, this:

Mrs. von Preussach owned a colorful, green- and purple-checked silk dress during the time of her stay in Blumenrode. It was called her "Scottish" dress. She liked to wear it, for she found it becoming. Shortly before leaving Blumenrode, Agathe examined her mistress's wardrobe and found spots in that dress that looked to her like blood. Perplexed, she informed her mistress. The latter recoils, becomes embarrassed, and says, dismissively, "*Ah, vous êtes folle!*" Agathe then brought the dress for her mistress to see herself. Anxiously Mrs. von Preussach turned away and cried out, "Take it away! Tear the dress apart! You can keep it!" The servant, astonished and suspicious that some misfortune had occurred, put the dress to one side and later reworked it into a close-fitting jacket for herself. But Mrs. von Preussach didn't like the jacket either, and Agathe thus seldom appeared in it before her mistress.

Agathe was asked whether there were any leftover scraps of the fabric, and she thought about this. "Yes, indeed, I have a knitting bag full. It's here, in my quarters." The bag had to be brought in and presented during the same session. A sample of the fabric was shown to all the witnesses of the occurrences of that August day. Only the younger Countesses von Koss remembered the "Scottish dress" now; it was the same one Preussach tried in vain to trace during his private investigation at Langnitz.

Therewith, the day's proceedings closed; they had lasted until 5:00 p.m. The presiding judge announced: "During the next session, which will not take place until the third day because of the church holiday now beginning, the prosecutor will make his closing remarks and the defense its closing appeal, and then, if possible, the verdict should be reached."

At this last, decisive session, due to his late arrival this narrator found a seat in the gallery only with difficulty, just as the defender began his speech. Unfortunately, the weak voice of that elderly man let many a word die away in the wide hall. However, we can communicate the closing appeal completely from the copy before us. The reader must merely permit us to pass over the introduction for the sake of brevity and lead him directly to the matter at hand.

From the beginning, the defender disputed the accusation at its main premise, namely the apodictic supposition that

> The dead man of St. Anne's Chapel is Hermann von Preussach, and his wife is the accused.

"This supposition," he said, "the basis of the entire accusation, has not been demonstrated in the evidence as the prosecutor has presented it. Who has proven to us that the two persons are identical, as alleged? Baron Ferdinand von Preussach. He alone. All the other witnesses speak only of a Mr. von Breisach from K***, who disappeared. And this single witness is the party most closely affected by the death of his brother; it is he who attains the paternal estate and title in the event of his brother's death, he is the private plaintiff in this proceeding. What merit can such testimony have? Subjectively regarded, it is invalid. But even from an objective point of view, upon what is it based? Upon an identification of the body? No! Ferdinand von Preussach never saw it! Only upon an ostensible conformity among the descriptions of the person, and the recognition of a ring that bears the Preussach coat of arms, found upon the body.

"And yet how daring is the conclusion: *the dead man wore Hermann's ring, therefore he is Hermann!* And how questionable the identification according to the sketchy description—a corpse, taken up by strangers who never knew the dead man living!

"You will allow me to remind you of several historically proven examples in which a charge was brought, indeed a sentence was pronounced, for taking the life of an individual whose death was, however, legally uncertain, and who later appeared *living* as the devastating witness of legal precipitousness. The annals of law preserve as a warning the case of a similar accusation of spousal murder, which took place not too long ago in a neighboring land whose institutions we otherwise honor as exemplary. A man had been missing for years, his wife had fruitlessly searched for him, and had married a second time. In the home of the missing man a skeleton is found, the neighbors begin to whisper doubtful things to one another, the matter becomes notorious and the wife falls under suspicion; deceptive, fictitious charges lead the unfortunate woman before the court, all the way to the place of execution. There a loud cry rings out through the crowd, the ostensibly dead husband steps forward. The prick of conscience drove the man, hidden nearby up to now, to rescue the innocent woman, and he stayed the sword of judgment—thank God there was still time!—even as it was raised to strike.

"And now, gentlemen of the jury! What if the dead man from the chapel is *not* Hermann, if Hermann is *alive, returns to us living* and demands satisfaction for the accusations against his wife, who was so precious to him and remained so even after their separation? What if the calamitous judgment had been passed? Who would like to share the judges' state of mind, the horrifying feeling of having sacrificed by means of a carelessly pronounced 'guilty' the freedom, honor and life of the defendant? Property that no earthly power can replace!"

The defender continued: "With the invalidation of its foundation, the entire charge is actually nullified. For who would dare, in the matter of the death of the unknown adventurer 'Breisach,' to cast the first stone against my client? We have only been shown proofs which are supposed to demonstrate an association between my client and the dead man from the chapel, an association of such a kind that, were the evidence indisputable, it would indeed appear justified to draw the inference that the dead man could only be Hermann. For this reason it is necessary to examine this evidence more closely, to examine that which the prosecutor has called the subjective facts of the case.

"First we have several pieces of writing. Here is a sheet of paper that was delivered by the schoolmaster in Blumenrode. It's true, it's the handwriting of my client, but the meaning given by the prosecutor to this writing, or rather, to this little flysheet, *sine die et consule*—this meaning is an extremely far-fetched one. This 'A'—who is this supposed to be?

"'A is supposed to be Armand (Hermann).' What an unnatural explanation! Why, in a German letter, the Frenchification of the beautiful German name? And who is this cautioner supposed to be?—for we cannot even tell the sex of the person. An accessory after all to a relationship that is, on the other hand, described as so secret, so intolerant of any uninitiated third party?

"And now this scrap of parchment with the grotesque and awkward characters! The experts themselves publicly admitted: a *certain* judgment could not be made about this product of a disguised or completely clumsy hand. I believe this! But an *uncertain* judgment is no judgment at all! And so let this scrap slip back into the darkness from which it was drawn forth with so much pretension.

"As for the third piece of writing, the strange letter in French, the experts claim to be able to establish an unmistakable similarity to the handwriting of the defendant. That sounds very dictatorial, but we must not merely consider the judgment, we must examine primarily the foundations for it. We are shown the strokes of the letters that are supposed to resemble each other so 'unmistakably.' I call upon every impartial eye to make this comparison for itself. Now, indeed certain features of the writing do resemble those of my client—but: they are those the entire world creates in the same way. The instructing judge claims to see a great deal in another similarity, also orthographic, that he discovered in the word 'coursbondance.' Good heavens! It is true that my client has committed the same sin against good spelling in an authentic piece of writing. But let ten people put the word in question on paper, people who write French more according to hearing and practice than lexical study of it, and surely nine of them will spoil the word in a similar fashion and the tenth perhaps in exactly the same way.

"The handwriting sample is in and of itself a very deceptive means of proof, a never completely convincing means, to be applied with the greatest of care. In spite of this, it has a kind of customary validity in criminal proceedings, and I do not blame the court if it does not want to dispense with it. The handwriting of a person is part of his intellectual, almost his physiognomic, property, and it is not the judge's fault if the means to proof has not reached its goal.

"But—what are we to say to the peculiar condescension with which the court has stooped to a comparison of—*gloves*? To the notion that one can infer from silk scraps and similar plunder the presence of a woman at the site of the murder, during the murder itself, yea, even to maintain that this woman is my client?

"I may pass over the silk scraps; as has been proved they are completely unfamiliar to the defendant. But we must regard the story of these gloves with a more critical eye. It has already occupied us to the point of weariness, but— there is nothing for it; the prosecution still sees, in the innocent right-hand glove, material proof that my client, and specifically my client, was at the ruins on the Raubstein.

"The justice of the peace found the glove during the crime scene examination, in the vicinity of the Raubstein—that is undeniable; he picked it up, because the eyes of a fanciful physician claimed to recognize blood in some dark spots. We cannot find fault with this. Then, female curiosity and sleuthing fever are mixed into the investigation—a name stamp is discovered! A second glove with the same stamp is discovered in the possession of a harmless girl, this one the left, the first one the right! They must be a pair! And—the left is from my client. Everything is clear—*she* lost the right glove at the murder site!

"This from the prosecution. But why do both gloves have to be a pair? Because they are alike in material, size, and workmanship. Fine!, but they are from one and the same works, from Madame Tieffe's business. For the purpose of this punctilious comparison the complete supply of my client's available gloves was confiscated; this similarity was found in all the stamped products of Mrs. Tieffe. What follows from this? That Madame Tieffe finishes all her wares in a similar manner, presumably so typical and beloved in elegant circles.

"But does she work exclusively for my client? No one maintains this. Doubtless she has hundreds of customers, and does not only supply the capital. Gloves are products, like stockings and shoes, that are only produced for inventory according to approximate and graded measurements, according to sizes. If two ladies each have a pair of the same size and quickly exchange their four examples, who claims to recognize which right or left glove belongs to which pair?

"So, the glove that was found is supposed to prove that a woman was at the Raubstein and lost it there—yet from this it does not follow that it was my client, but rather at most that it was one of Madame Tieffe's customers.

"Someone will object that the Raubstein is a notorious spot, avoided, difficult to reach, otherwise never visited by persons of the upper classes while taking walks. Admittedly, as a rule this is so; but I point to the documented exception on the day the body was discovered. The painstaking justice of the peace wrote in his notes:

> We suspected that the corpse was that of a guest who strayed from one of the nearby spas, and since there were many spa guests among the onlookers, they were allowed to come and go freely; but still none among them was found who knew the dead man.

"Well, then! Among these crowds of curious spa guests were certainly many women; it is a matter of experience that the majority of the sightseers at strange events always belong to the fair sex. Now, among these guests from the baths there was one who wore gloves from Madame Tieffe's factory; she besmirched herself at the bloody stonework, on the bloody bushes; in disgust and repulsion she cast off the soiled glove, and lost it—and thus it became the fateful piece of evidence.

"The circumstances touched upon here that refer to my client's visit in Hilgenberg lead me to the time of death determined by the chief prosecutor. Death is said to have occurred during the course of August 24th. This is based on the state of the body as the justice of the peace described it; upon the 'traces of advanced decomposition.' The dead man, says the prosecution, was found during the early morning hours of August 26th; to judge from those 'traces of advanced decomposition' he must have been left to the effects of sun and air for some time. On the early morning of the 24th he was alive, still some hours' travel distant from the chapel; beyond doubt he died in the course of this day, and early in the day.

"First I must deplore here the useless expression 'for some time,' and then, more seriously, denounce the arbitrary assumption of *advanced* decomposition, since the report of the officials at the scene of the crime speaks only of 'traces of beginning decomposition.' To bring this about requires only the August sun of one single day, not counting the time that elapsed from the first discovery of the body to the arrival of the doctors and the justice. It seems extremely probable to me that the dead man found his end only during the night *following* the Saturday of August 24th, if not later; for during the course of the Saturday, even during the evening hours, the path going by the chapel was surely used; after all, it was a holiday, the name day of Her Highness, the Princess ***. If the corpse had already lain in its place it would surely have been discovered. If the deed that took the unfortunate man's life was a work of malevolence, then it most certainly was shrouded in the veil of night, which usually hides such outrages.

"Unlike the prosecutor, I offer all this not as certainty, but only as a hypothesis, but I repeat here as well: what my opponent alleges is also only hypothesis. But if my hypothesis is better founded and preferable for this reason, then my client even has the protection—should she need such aids—of alibi, because by nightfall she was in the circle of those who accompanied her that day to Hilgenberg and with whom she traveled back to Blumenrode; and she did not leave that residence during the following days.

"Should I waste words upon the pitiful servant's gossip about the spotted dress? I can only wish for every woman of delicacy, who shares with many of her sex that so natural distaste of blood—even if it is blood from her own innocent nose; I can only wish that heaven spare her such servants as come running faithfully with every blood-soiled rag and, to the utterance of the most justifiable annoyance at such disgusting presentations, bestow an interpretation from which one draws back in horror. If the blood flecks—to grant them one last word— were really of such an astonishingly noticeable sort, then how would they have escaped the attention of the countess and her daughters? Certainly then, they do not date from that Saturday that was so fraught with misfortune for my client.

"I want to mention here as well another circumstance that could only gain the appearance of such a weighty clue in the prosecution's slanted and superficial presentation, while admitting of the most innocent explanation when properly regarded. I mean Baron Hermann's watch and wedding ring, which were found in the possession of his estranged wife. *I admit it willingly—listen!—it is Hermann's watch and Hermann's ring that lie before us here.* The prosecution says: according to this, then, the accused was in possession of property that the dead man still had upon his person on the last day of his life but which was not found upon the corpse. The dead man? How? Who demonstrates that the dead man *ever* wore *this* watch, *this* ring, let alone on the last day of his life. Not the witnesses! The innkeeper in the forest, the housekeeper of the disappearing Mr. Breisach, his servant—they all speak of '*a* watch,' '*a* thin gold band.' None of them is able to recognize *this* watch, *this* ring.

"Baron Ferdinand? He saw his brother alive for the last time when Hermann's marriage to my client still existed. The divorce process was begun when Ferdinand was away traveling; by the time he returned Hermann had already taken leave of his family and had left the country. Thus Ferdinand cannot know what Hermann possessed after that time, what he carried with him in the way of jewelry.

"Hermann's watch, lying here before us, was a gift from his bride; this ring was his wedding ring. It is customary that engaged and married couples who separate return to each other in mutual agreement those memorabilia that remind them of their dissolved ties. How naturally, then, the divorced wife's possession of these precious objects can be explained; it dates undeniably from the time immediately following the separation! In this way even my client's maid explained this matter; every impartial person must explain it this way.

"My client does not wear her wedding ring since the divorce, either. Did she send it back to Hermann? I don't know, but it can scarcely be doubted; the exchange must have been a mutual one, a symbol to correspond to the one that tied them in marriage.

"If a short while ago I had to accuse the prosecution of a slanted, superficial explanation, then with all due respect for the honorable character of the prosecutor I must now denounce a reprehensible precipitousness. I ask for your particular attention to this point. It concerns the statement of the maid from Möllheim.

"The girl mentions a young man whom she saw in the Widow Veitel's apartment. The prosecutor said, 'This was Hermann; here the secret meeting had its beginning. Mrs. von Seehausen's invitation was a fiction, the letter a construction intended to deceive. From the widow's house, Hermann and the defendant went to the Raubstein and there the meeting found its bloody end.'

"So: the man was Hermann, or, what is the same thing according to the prosecution, he was the dead man at the chapel! Incomprehensibly hasty assertion! Is it supposed to rest on the personal description given by the girl? Assuredly; on what else? But this description does not correspond to that of the dead man, it contradicts it. The dead man was found clothed with long Nanking trousers which extended over his boots; the innkeeper also saw him in these clothes. The young man in Mrs. Veitel's apartment wore, as the witness put it, 'very tight leather pants and boots pulled over them.' How is that to be reconciled? They have my client changing gloves two and three times on one day—fine! A glove can be quickly drawn off or on. But is the dead man supposed to have changed his trousers just as often, and in the morning at that? Blindly concluded, blindly followed opinions lead to this sort of nonsense!

"I am far from doubting that my client was in Mrs. Veitel's house. No! She responded to the invitation from a friend. But that this invitation was a falsification, that Mrs. von Seehausen was an imaginary person,—this is a vague and unsupported assumption on the part of the prosecution. We are told: 'A Mrs. von Seehausen never lived in the Veitel house, indeed, in the whole of Hilgenberg.' Well, who claims she was a resident of the house or the neighborhood? Can she not have been there only in passing, just like the defendant; cannot the widow's house have been her temporary resting place, even intermediate stopping point? Many who come for the cure at the Hilgenberg springs do not live in Hilgenberg, but rather in the neighboring, less expensive surroundings. Seek and ye shall find, says the Scripture! Fine! But seek with reason, *cum grano salis*!

"I have now illuminated all the facts that the prosecution has presented as proof for the allegation 'that the accused stood in contact with the dead man, that she was not without knowledge of his death, and that she was a witness to it.' I have illuminated them, and I now leave the conclusion about their validity to the judges who have been called. But—even if all these proofs were just as the prosecution claims them to be, if it were proved that Albertine von Preussach had seen and spoken to the dead man—her husband, let us add—shortly before his death, yea, even if she was a witness to this death, who would ascribe the death of her husband to her because of this?

"If the prosecution, in its fanciful exposition here, has woven in a strand well calculated to work upon the spirits of his listeners, if it has quoted words—admittedly according to an unsupported story—that the admirable mother of the accused is supposed to have said at the moment of parting, then we'll let stand as true this cry of a careworn mother's heart, oppressed by foreboding; we'll assume that the worthy matron expressed a suspicion that the prosecution was even able to champion as conviction with the aid of keenness and eloquence. Fine, then, let us delve into this suspicion ourselves: Albertine von Preussach allegedly knew that Hermann had died, knew how and where he died. We still have to ask whether this knowledge would constitute an accusation of an actionable nature and bring the power of law to bear upon the accused.

"But the accusation does not purport to be a charge of suppressing a deed *foreign* to oneself: no, it says decisively: 'Albertine von Preussach not only had knowledge of the death, she was the killer!' What are the proofs of guilt, of culpability? Only the old, long-discarded dream of a secret rendezvous, now even spun out into chimerical plans of violence, abduction, of danger and self-defense. The arbitrary idea of the scene-of-crime officers about a meal held in the ruins, put together from crusts of bread and fruit peels gathered there, must provide the weapon—a knife; and a just-as-problematic drunkenness on the part of the unfortunate dead man must serve to give the last brushstroke to this fantasy painting.

"Then the prosecution shows us one more witness; not a witness to the deed, but a statement about the sensibility and spirit of the defendant that is supposed to demonstrate that she was capable of the deed, that this deed appears plausible as a result of the defendant's turn of mind.

"And what do we hear from the mouth of the witness—a person who represents herself as the confidante of the accused, her childhood playmate as it were? Pitiful, almost laughable gossip of scenes of marital discord—admittedly appearing somewhat drastic from the witness's telling, stories of outbreaks of annoyance about servant clumsiness, and finally a couple of unfortunate slaps on the ear, to which their recipient, pampered and prone to not knowing her place, was sensitive. Oh, I fear that these unhappy blows sowed the seed of revenge in the soul of the servant who now brings such sad fruit to light!

"I have reached my goal. I have only a word to say about the last of the many puzzles which this curious trial has presented us. I mean the persistent silence of the accused. This silence has also been puzzling to me, I confess. It is astonishing—even to me, her protector, whom she trusts—that the accused refuses to call witnesses—it is undeniable that she knows of some—who would destroy the charge against her entirely. I say 'witnesses of whom she knows some' not because I know of them, but because I am firmly convinced that there are some, and that certainly not all of them would be as unavailable as the widow Veitel, who is unfortunately in her grave.

"She has a secret, it is possible, that may not be revealed at any price. She keeps it, even under the weight of a charge that could threaten life and freedom; but she keeps it despite the danger threatening her. Why? Because she sees that her most prized possessions are not threatened, because she sees them safe in the hands of her enlightened, incorruptible judges, because she waits trustfully for the verdict. That is why she keeps silent, why she keeps her secret."

The defender fell silent. The gallant old gentleman had exerted himself to the point of exhaustion in the fervor of his speech. Everyone's glance turned to the defendant. Mute and motionless she sat there, absorbed with her thoughts. She only became aware of the nearness of her protector after he had already been at her side some minutes. She turned to him with a few words, of thanks, perhaps, certainly of recognition of his sincere efforts. Moved, the old gentleman kissed her hand.

Soon the valiant man, who had scarcely collected himself, was called to combat anew. Senkenberg stepped forward with the announcement that his client was deeply wounded by many of the defender's attacks upon him.

The chief prosecutor intervened with the remark that he could find fault with the defender for the same reason, but meanwhile time was precious and he had found reason to request the presentation of additional important evidence. Thus the issue of satisfaction was quickly dealt with and the issues mentioned were presented.

The first concerned Mrs. von Seehausen. The state prosecutor requested a renewed detailed questioning of the ladies von Langnitz, to see whether this person had been made known to them as a resident of Hilgenberg. The young countesses could not assert this with certainty, but their mother said, "I remember very definitely that in the letter from Mrs. von Seehausen there were the words: 'I would have come to you myself, but illness confines me to my room.' It would seem to follow from that that Mrs. von Seehausen lived in the area."

The second point concerned the clothing of the young man in Mrs. Veitel's house. The chief prosecutor had convinced himself of the correctness of the contradiction denounced by the defender. Yet he did not want, merely because of this, to let go of the opinion that it was Hermann who awaited his wife in that house. "The defender," he said, "calls it nonsensical that Hermann von Preussach should have changed his trousers; I cannot agree that this is nonsense. He could have had ample opportunity and just as sufficient reason for changing his clothes in the widow's house; she was devoted to him, perhaps privy to his secret. The clothes in which the girl saw him—the close-fitting leather pants—could have been uncomfortable on a mountain walk, he could have exchanged them for the other, more comfortable ones. But the witness could have made a mistake, too. In any case it is advisable to hear her again."

The girl was called. Again there was a scene bordering on the laughable. The silly thing affected to be ashamed and shy, almost insulted, when the strange man's "tight leather pants" were mentioned again. It was difficult to make her understand the seriousness and importance of the matter. Nonetheless, she was sure of herself. The stranger wore white leather pants, she insisted; she knew the color of Nanking very well, it was pale yellow. She also stated now that the gentleman had worn a vest fastened with silver laces, like the ones students like to wear.

The state prosecutor explained that he saw no reason to limit the charge substantively; he reviewed briefly the most important pieces of evidence and repeated his conclusion. Senkenberg likewise held to the civil accusation, speaking for his client. Now the defender got another chance to speak. Following the remarks of the plaintiff, he summarized the main points of his concluding speech just as succinctly: the uncertainty of the identity of the dead man, the paucity of proof supporting the assertion of a connection between him and the accused, and the complete invalidity of the evidence for the actual act of killing.

The presiding judge closed the debate and unfolded the legal summary of the proceedings. It was an example of clarity and precision. He called upon the jury to discharge their office and had distributed to them, in written form, the questions on which they should pass judgment, edited for comprehensible brevity and accuracy. At the same time, the documents were collected that the jury would need to consult.

The defendant rose to leave the hall. Most of the audience got ready to leave as well. Again it was late afternoon, and it was quite clear that everyone would have to wait some time for the jury's decision. In the middle of this pause, full of restless motion, an uproar arose in the gallery; a well-dressed man hastily pushed his way through the crowd. In only a moment he reached the railing and called down, in a thundering voice,

"By God, who is just! I demand to be heard! The accused is innocent!"

Everyone turned to look up at the speaker. Members of the jury, already underway to their chamber, stopped in their tracks; from the corridors and stairways the public streamed back toward the seats it had just vacated. The presiding judge ordered the speaker to be brought to the bench. The suspense about what would happen next was indescribable. An elderly lady who sat behind this narrator went white and broke into words: "Ah, it's Hermann, the one they believed was dead; the defender prophesied it!"

The unknown man appeared in the hall. It was—not Hermann. Proudly and without recognition Preussach looked at him; the stranger walked past without acknowledgement. His gaze sought only the defendant. And she? *She* knew him. With a pale and distressed face she watched him draw near; but, pulling herself together quickly, in an instant she had whispered to him a few words in English.

The presiding judge ordered the immediate removal of the defendant and the clearing of the gallery. It was announced that the verdict had been delayed. Grudgingly the public complied with the instruction to leave. Like wildfire the report of the appearance of the unknown witness for the defense spread through the city. The most contradictory suspicions were aired: first the strange man was Hermann's rival, Hermann having fallen in a duel between them. Next, the man was Hermann himself, scandalously disowned by his own brother but already acknowledged by credible persons. In the end, he was a favored admirer of the defendant; the rendezvous at the widow's house was for his sake and was entirely without connection to the events on the Raubstein.

But none of these rumors was founded on truth. Soon everyone learned that the stranger was a Mr. von Nordeck, now a mining superintendent in the service of ***, formerly an officer, and then and in that capacity known from the past by respectable residents of Hainburg. He had arrived in Hainburg barely an hour before his appearance in the hall, had rushed, never resting, to the courthouse, whose location he hurriedly discovered and, as now became known, had made the most startling disclosures to the presiding judge in a secret meeting lasting for hours.

We cannot keep these disclosures from our readers any longer.

Maximilian von Nordeck—this was the witness's full name—candidly voiced, in answer to the president's first question, the words the defendant had quietly murmured to him. "Think of the oath!" she had said. "An oath," explained Nordeck, "binds the tongue of the unfortunate woman; in an exaggeration of blindness she holds herself to it. And yet I hope to be able to release it. Am I permitted to say a single word to the prisoner? You could be witness!" The presiding judge permitted it. Albertine and Nordeck were brought face to face.

"Dear lady," said Nordeck with a voice full of emotion. "Let go of your unhappy silence! Death has freed the man to whom you held yourself bound."

"God in heaven!" cried Albertine. "My father!"

"Your father is no more. His blessed spirit is already in a world where every earthly disappointment fades; he looks down upon a daughter who was never unworthy of his love, who was driven to the one false step of her life only by the most sacred emotion—a mother's love. But," he broke off his own words, "have I myself been released from my promise?"

Through tears Albertine looked up at her rescuer. "Oh, God!" she cried out. "Why the justification? I am, after all, a murderer, a murderer of the noblest, tenderest father!"

"Your father, dear lady, never received certain knowledge of the danger that threatened you. He died benevolently deceived. His last word was a word of blessing for his daughter. Now, again—am I released from *my* oath?"

"You have kept it so faithfully; I am forever in your debt. Do as you think best."

"Thank God!" said Nordeck. "Your honor, I am ready to answer your questions."

Although he had every confidence in the situation, in sensible acknowledgment of legal prudence the president ordered a separate questioning of Nordeck. The latter began:

"In the summer of 1816, when our troops came home from France, I was with the second squadron of the *** Regiment of Hussars, encamped in this region, which I commanded in the absence of the colonel. Our regiment was supposed to wait here for further orders; but they were delayed from month to month. The leisure afforded by our permanent encampment—mine was in a little village in the country, Winznach—led to excursions in the beautiful area surrounding it. We officers were welcomed hospitably by the neighboring nobility, and in the numerous watering places, as well as in K***, which had an excellent theater at that time, we found the desired amusement.

"It was in the theater in K*** that I met, by chance, a fellow soldier from earlier days, Baron Hermann von Preussach. We were in the same corps in 1809, and I was under many an obligation to him from that time, for reasons that have no place here. The pleasure of reunion was great, but not without a certain pain on my part. I found Preussach to be much altered. The once so handsome, chivalrous young man stood before me, aged early, dulled and slack in body and mind; even his dress was careless, almost shabby. I knew that Preussach was very wealthy; I had heard that after leaving he had made a brilliant marriage; and I could not reconcile all that with his present appearance. He appeared to read my thoughts, but there was no opportunity for a more drawn-out conversation. Nevertheless, we then saw each other frequently. I often came to K***, and later Preussach also visited me occasionally in my final quarters—that was in Möllheim.

"Upon longer acquaintance I became aware of a certain inner strife in him; he lived in unsuitable company that disgusted him himself in his better moments. I was happy that he liked to be with me and that his association with our well-bred corp of officers visibly pleased him.

"In time he became more open; he told me, even if only in bits and pieces, the story of his marriage; that he was the father of two children, that the daughter was still living but that his wife had separated from him and taken the child with her. Ruefully he blamed himself. Moreover, he described how he had become estranged from his family and had left home some time ago, had been traveling for a long time, and had been living now, for several months, in K***, without plan or purpose. A love affair he could not break off held him there, although the relationship had long been repellent to him. The object of this affair was a person from the *corps de ballet* of the theater there.

"Weeks had already gone by since our first reunion, when chance opened Preussach's heart even more to me. Some comrades and I had become acquainted with the well respected and cultured house of Baron von Kettler in Blumenrode. In this house a young lady was staying for a visit; she was called Mrs. von Siegsfeld.

"This young woman, as beautiful as she was gifted, was a far too attractive sight to guests in that home for her not to be mentioned often in our conversations. Preussach was present once, during such a conversation, and even then I noticed his tense attentiveness. The next time we were alone he questioned me in great detail about Mrs. von Siegsfeld. I told him what I knew, and after he had pried everything out, so to speak, he was noticeably quiet and thoughtful. By then I thought I was entitled to a question, and after some beating around the bush he broke his silence. To my utter astonishment I learned that Albertine von Siegsfeld was—his divorced wife. He spoke of her with such love, with such glowing admiration that it moved me deeply. He admitted that he had sunk since the divorce into a state of moral destruction at which he himself shuddered; he still felt the power to pull himself together, but there was only one road to that: a reunion with Albertine. To my sympathetic question whether all hope was lost, whether no intermediary could be found, he was not entirely despairing, but still faint-hearted with dejection.

"From this moment on Preussach sought my company even more assiduously, and whenever possible excluding any third party. Albertine was nearly the only subject of our conversations. Finally he came out with the request: *I* should become the mediator between them. I was horrified; I described for him the chimerical and impossible nature of his expectation. I still remember quoting Schiller while mentioning the difficulties of such an approach to Albertine:

> *Yet a dignity, a loftiness,*
> *Kept intimacy at a distance.*

These words made Preussach completely enthusiastic. He threw his arms around my neck, crying, and called out: 'Yes, that's my Albertine, and I have lost this angel!' He was beside himself to such a degree that, just to calm him down, I unthinkingly gave him the comfort of saying I would consider his suggestion.

"I admit it, I began to avoid Preussach. But I did not avoid Blumenrode, and—how strange—it appeared to me as though Albertine regarded me with a certain attentiveness. Not vain enough to ascribe this to my personality, I formed the suspicion that Hermann had found an opportunity to come to a written understanding without my collaboration and had named me as a confidant. It later became clear to me that in general my suspicions were correct; but I never discovered how Hermann actually found a way to make the connection.

"In short, things finally came to disclosures between Albertine and me. The first took place on an evening, upon the return of an outing on foot during which chance had made me Albertine's escort. I don't remember the turn of the conversation any more; music was the reason for my mentioning a friend I had recently rediscovered, who had a beautiful voice. Hermann really had given us a great deal of pleasure on a few social occasions with his extremely agreeable singing. Albertine asked, apparently dispassionately, for the name of this friend, and I mentioned Baron Preussach. And so the connection was established. Albertine mentioned in the course of the conversation, which gradually came closer to the heart of the matter, that she knew that I was informed of her situation and what expectations Hermann had of me; my character had been estimably described and she would give me proof of her trust, proof that a man of honor would know how to esteem. That proof was the request to tell Hermann that she could not agree to his wishes. She had forgiven him, but her father's wish had set an insuperable barrier to their reunion, and she would never oppose it: 'I swore faithfully never to agree to a plan, much less to encourage one, that would not be blessed by his approval.' Thus ended this first discussion with Albertine. I told Hermann everything unsparingly. The matter appeared to rest. But then I discovered, to my horror, that Hermann had continued his correspondence with Blumenrode, and that he had even received answers. I made serious reproaches. He threw his arms around me tempestuously and cried, 'Max, don't disturb my plans! I'm counting on you, my only friend. Albertine trusts me—and you! Soon everything will become clear to you!'

"My astonishment was indescribable; I still doubted; I believed that Hermann was deceiving me or himself. But it was as he said. Albertine had given her agreement, not to a reunion, but to a meeting at a third place. The motives for this change of heart only became clear to me later: Hermann had known how to attack the loving mother at her most vulnerable point. He had let it slip that his family wanted to reclaim Albertine's daughter, and that he could find himself inclined to support this familial intention if she denied him his ardent wish. It is still a mystery to me how Albertine, with her common sense, could have let her actions be dictated by this picture of horror. At that time no solution was possible; in the few unobserved moments I had during my visits to the Kettler home, I only discovered that Albertine knew of the plan that Hermann devised, that she agreed to it and that Hermann was supposed to acquaint me with it. The plan was this:

"The nobility of that area held social gatherings on certain predetermined days in Hilgenberg, and Albertine generally participated with the von Kettler family. The gatherings were well attended by ladies and gentlemen of all ages; often people divided into groups, or made calls on people in the area, alone or with others; it was possible to get away unnoticed.

"Hermann had arranged it so that Albertine could remove herself from the gathering under the pretext of an invitation, be led to a pre-arranged place where I would receive her, and then be led to another place, where he awaited her. The first rendezvous was arranged in the home of a respectable woman in Hilgenberg, known to me. I have forgotten the name, but I could find the house even today."

"Was the woman called 'von Seehausen'?" asked the presiding judge.

"No! The name Seehausen plays a role in another way. The letter of invitation was written under this name, the letter that would take Albertine away from her companions. I see you know of it. The second rendezvous, where Hermann himself waited, was a cleverly chosen, isolated ruin—"

"We know it," said the presiding judge. "The Raubstein."

"That's what I heard it called. Hermann had tracked down the ruins from the starting point of Möllheim, during the visits which he now more often paid me. Because the Raubstein is a disreputable place, almost forbidden because of the people's superstitions, it appeared indeed to be very well suited to his purpose.

"August 10th was chosen for the execution of the plan. I need only mention briefly that the weather's unfavorability on this day—oh, it was really more heaven's favor!—hindered the plan. If we only had taken the hint! But no! Hermann merely postponed things for a week.

"During this time new concerns rose within me, actually a suspicion that Hermann had more up his sleeve than he had told me and Albertine. I don't know anymore where this suspicion came from. Still, I warned Albertine in writing. I received no answer. But from Albertine's own mouth I understood, fleetingly, when once it was possible, that she was firmly determined to be at the right place again on the 17th.

"Hermann and I were at our posts. But Albertine—thank God! I said to myself then, in silence—didn't come. The Kettlers had been prevented from going to Hilgenberg. Hermann did not lose heart. On the 24th, Albertine would certainly come, he assured me. The unhappy day neared, the day that will always be held fast in my memory as the most horrible of my life.

"As before, Hermann had arrived the previous evening at my quarters in Möllheim. But he could not bear to wait; he went some hours further on foot, in order to spend the night as close as possible to the desired goal. Early in the morning—it was Saturday—I rode directly to Hilgenberg. My servant, who had ridden over after me, was supposed to turn over his horse to Hermann after the meeting was ended, and wait for us toward evening in a village at the foot of the Raubstein. As I caught sight of the Raubstein while riding through the narrow valley, I saw the pre-arranged signal that Hermann was waiting in the ruin. I hurried to Hilgenberg and my first destination was the meeting hall.

"The families who gather there enter their names in a guest book upon arrival; places at the lunch table are ordered accordingly. With my heart pounding I looked at the list; I was hoping that the group from Blumenrode was not there. They were absent, but *Albertine was not*. She had appeared with a countess's family. So there was no choice, no retreat anymore. Without allowing myself to be seen in the salon I hurried toward the house of our confidante; the letter, long since prepared, was sent off; another fearful hour, and Albertine came.

"I freely admit it; the quiet and truly stately dignity with which this extraordinary woman faced such a questionable undertaking, where my man's heart was pounding anxiously—this calm surprised me, almost shamed me. Time was precious; without hesitation we went through the garden of the house and took, unnoticed, the path toward the woods, which soon caught us up in its impenetrable shadows. From here the path leads, first gradually, then more steeply, up to the ruin.

"A few steps from the ruin, Hermann came toward us. He had expected us from the other side, and had been waiting for us there for hours. Albertine's heart beat in quick, sudden pulses—was it the difficulty of the path or the proximity of the significant event? The moment of reunion was here! but oh, the moment already announced the misfortune that hung over us.

"I have already described how Preussach looked when we met again, how painfully his altered appearance affected my soul. And now he stood there, the decrepit, feeble man, before her, the magnificent, charming woman, who bloomed in almost maidenly beauty. Oh, and that was not all! Gladly would I cloak behind a deep eternal veil what I still have to say, *must* say, because it is the key to the tragic outcome of that fateful meeting. Hermann appeared, I noticed only too soon, in a state of unnatural exaltation; he had brought wine to the ruin, and had applied himself too injudiciously to the strong and fiery drink.

"Preussach's condition could also not long escape Albertine, who had not appeared to suspect anything at the beginning. Hermann's entire manner had something boisterous and importunate about it, and the grace that made him otherwise charming and attractive, when he wanted to be, appeared to be completely gone. I read it in her soul that Albertine regretted the step she had taken; but it was already done. I made an effort, as soon as I had mastered my feelings of distress, to start a conversation.

"From the very beginning both spouses had pressed me with the request, when I made known my intention of leaving them alone, to remain an impartial witness to their meeting. I gave in gladly. An old man, who had served Hermann as a guide, also had to take a seat nearby. Albertine appeared to want it this way. The old man could understand nothing of the conversation; it was held mostly in French.

"What should I say about the content of this discussion? Its one, eternally recurring theme was—Hermann's eager attempts to reunite, Albertine's constant referral to her father's wish. It had become midday; we were all exhausted, especially Albertine. Hermann had the refreshments unpacked that his guide had brought, and we men applied ourselves to them industriously; even Albertine enjoyed a few bites. Hermann, that wretched man, drank ever more of the fiery wine; his pleas became more aggressive and finally slid into threats, whose intensity increased almost to brutality. Albertine had risen; she appeared to want to remove herself. I was ready for any signal from her. Hermann became aware of this, and with a truly hellish expression, with wildly rolling eyes, he cried out:

"'You are in league with one another! Oh, I see through you both!'

"Albertine now threw a reproachful look at him. 'Mr. von Nordeck,' she said, 'I'm leaving!'

"'So you are leaving?' shrieked Hermann with a horrifying voice. He held a large, double-bladed knife in his hand. 'You're leaving? Fine! Go, reject me, cast me back into this life that is a hell for me. Life? No! You cast me into death! Go! But first watch me die!' And he turned the knife against his bared chest.

"What happened next? In vain I have tried to recall the events of the next moments in an ordered sequence. I only know that I uttered the unconsidered words: 'Hermann, aren't you ashamed to offer your noble wife such the-atrics?'

"This enflamed Hermann's rage to the point of madness.

"'Miserable wretch! Do you think I don't know how to die?'

"That cry still rang out—and Hermann was lying on the ground, in blood, the knife in the tightly-closed fist that had struck the blade deep into his heart. Albertine had sunk down upon the ground next to him, herself bleeding, close to fainting.

"Scarcely aware of what I was doing, I pulled her upright first. Her right hand was bleeding; at the moment of the death blow she had gripped the blade, a projecting edge had wounded her, and—the knife found its goal inexorably. The guide, thinking quickly, pulled the iron from the breast of the unfortunate man, but it was too late. A single feeble movement of the head, a dim glance, a weak gasp—that was all that betrayed the last glow of the spark of life in Her-mann's breast.

"I was now concerned for Albertine's safety. The blood from Hermann's death wound flowed in streams; my clothes were already soiled; she had to avoid nearing the dead man if this blood was not to betray her. I stopped the wound with Hermann's handkerchief, the guide tore up the long silk shawl that Her-mann wore around his neck, and wrapped it around the upper torso of the dead man. Then we discussed what to do with the body.

"The old man said, 'Let's leave the body here, where sometimes no human foot strays for years. That way everything will stay hidden; but then of course the dead man will decay unseen by fellow Christian eyes.'

"'For God's sake, no!' cried Albertine. 'The body can't stay here!' Amid bit-ter tears she turned to me. After all, the dead man was her husband, the father of her daughter, and had once been precious to her. The thought that he would molder in a grave without the blessing of the church, without a grave in conse-crated ground—this thought would kill her.

"These words, spoken comprehensibly enough for the guide, brought the old man a clever idea.

"'The poor gentleman cannot win the blessing of the church and a grave in holy ground,' he said, 'although he does not so badly deserve such treatment. They're strict around here, if a man has laid a hand on his own life. How would it be, then, if we arranged it so it looked as if someone else had stabbed him, as if he had been attacked and robbed? The little white lie wouldn't harm anything. The dead people in the graveyard won't revolt because of it, and our dear God above probably has a more kindly understanding of the thing than his preach-ers here below.'

"I was pleased by the old man's sensible suggestion, and Albertine agreed to it. With the guide's help I took the shirt, money bag, watch and briefcase from the body; the clothes and the hunting bag of the dead man we intended to burn, but the smoke that could have betrayed us down in the valley, made us abandon the idea. The guide sank the clothes and the bag in a deep cleft behind the ruin, and threw down heavy stones on top of them.

"I was supposed to take the watch, money-bag, wedding ring and briefcase of the dead man, but I felt an inner resistance against taking possession of these belongings of a friend; I pressed them upon Albertine, since she could, if necessary, hide them. Only the signet ring on Hermann's right hand could not be removed; it was firmly ingrown into the flesh and I did not dare to suggest the mutilation of the body. The old man remarked that it didn't matter; robber bands often left such treasures untouched because they could easily betray them. If a compassionate person found the body, then he would see that the dead man was of good society and that would only help him get a respectable burial.

"I scarcely need mention that we brought the body down from the far-flung place of death to the chapel, where it seemed more accessible to people's comings and goings. Here we left it to its fate. Albertine had, against my wishes, followed us to the chapel; I saw her kneeling in fervent prayer before the saint's image when our sad business had been completed.

"It was high time to think of our return to Hilgenberg. The guide offered to take Albertine to a barber-surgeon who could bind her wound properly. As long as we strode through the desolate, unpeopled wilderness I led the unhappy woman, whose pain broke forth all the more intensely and was truly heart-rending since the motion of activity and accomplishment offered no more counterweight. On the way I learned for the first time what means Hermann had used to make her agree to the meeting. She told me that once, when taking holy communion with her family, she had sworn to her father never to see Hermann again. In spite of all the temptations she had kept her oath up to now; but the thought that the Preussach family could tear her daughter away, the anxiety that even legal experts had caused her—that the Preussachs could push through such a reclamation—this had led her to the breach of her promise that she now atoned for in such a horrible fashion.

"'Never,' she went on, 'can my precious father discover how I have offended against him, against my own word; the news of his only child's disloyalty would send him to the grave. I will be silent about what has happened, and if it is ever revealed, yea, even if I am believed to be a murderer, if the arm of justice pursues me—I would keep silent unto the grave, unto the scaffold.'

"I turned my entire eloquence to dispelling the ghastly thoughts with which Albertine tortured herself. I did not succeed. With a tone that cut through my soul, she said that this was her last request of me: that as long as her father lived I should never confide to any mortal that she had seen Hermann. She would keep steadfastly the silence she had just sworn, and *this* oath, at least, she would never break.

"I promised solemnly what she wanted. Even the old guide, deeply moved and with moist eyes, made her the same oath without hesitation. Now it was time for me to withdraw. The woods were already thinning out—what if people should encounter us! My clothes were reddened with blood; on hers there were only some easily hidden spots, which in the worst case could be attributed to the wounded hand. But another worry came to me. Albertine had lost the glove to her wounded hand. Where? She did not know herself, exactly, but she thought it could not have fallen before she was on the actual path, where its discovery should arouse no suspicion; she was also certain that it was not flecked with blood.

"I could not trust her assurance; I hastened to take leave of her—and what leave! I went up to the ruin once more to look for the glove, but in vain! Albertine went on her way in the company of the old man and I did not see her again till—here! You know the rest, your honor! My report is at an end. Eternal God be praised that it did not come too late!"

"Thank providence!" said the worthy presiding judge. "I believe your report; it bears the stamp of inner truth. But the demands of the law must have satisfaction. You named eye witnesses of specific occurrences; could you identify them so that it would be possible to question them? The old man—"

"I can tell you his name!" responded Nordeck. "I did not forget to note it and have kept it safe. The man is called Florian Krauss and has a house in the *** village of Zellenbach."

"Good! Then he can be found, providing he is still living. But there is one more circumstance that your report leaves unexplained. This paper was found in the alms-box at the St. Anne's Chapel, and with it the money-bag of the dead man, filled with gold and silver coins."

Nordeck studied the objects with consternation.

"Here I am myself uninformed!" he said. "It is Hermann's money-bag, that is undeniable; the paper appears to be a leaf torn from his notebook. The script? Is it supposed to be Albertine's? I almost want to believe, suspect, that she laboriously wrote these distorted lines on the parchment with the left or even the wounded right hand."

"But how would that be compatible with the simulation of a robbery?" asked the president.

"Indeed," Nordeck responded, "this is unexplainable to me, too. Did Albertine, preoccupied with the concern of Christian burial for the dead man, concoct an idea so adverse to the plan and carry it out in a momentary confusion of thought? It would be possible; she stayed in the chapel a long time, unobserved."

It developed that this explanation was the correct one when Albertine was interrogated with the same precision by the presiding judge, describing all the events of that unfortunate day in complete conformity with the report of her rescuer. The old man whom they had sought in vain for so long was also fortunately discovered and found still living. Not his testimony alone, but also another indirect, very credible witness lent support to the truth of Nordeck's story. Once during a serious illness, the old man had developed moral scruples about whether his silence and his assistance in the intentional concealment of a suicide amounted to a sin; he had revealed them to his confessor. The enlightened man of the cloth did not hesitate to reassure him completely. God will judge the dead man, was his sensible position; if well kept, the secret can harm no one, but its revelation could endanger the calm and peace of an already unhappy family. Let it rest under the charitable cloak of silence.

After all the mystery has been enlightened there will be one question remaining for the reader just as it was for the judges: How did it happen that Nordeck, the participant in such a fateful occurrence, was so completely separated from the main character? How was it that the news of her threatening danger reached him *now*, when most was at stake?

Here is the answer. Nordeck was, as we know, the commander of a squadron, as it were the military commander at the barracks, who, as such, was not allowed to be away from his post overnight without the prior knowledge of the regimental commander. On this Saturday, he had only left under the presumption that he would return to his quarters before nightfall. Hermann wanted to spend Saturday night with him and return to K*** on Sunday. After he had climbed the Raubstein again upon parting from Albertine, Nordeck remained hidden there until dark. Then he came down, searching for the path to the village where the hussar waited for him with the horses. After wandering, confused, for hours, he lost his path and his bearings completely, so that he felt compelled to stay in the woods and wait for day. The anxiously longed-for morning finally came, but Nordeck saw, to his horror, that he had put great distance between himself and his goal due to a faulty sense of direction. Now where? The path to the village led through a valley livened by numerous groups of churchgoers. In the dress in which he was clad—short, tight civilian jacket that barely covered the white uniform trousers covered with streams of blood—he could not show himself to people. There was no choice: he had to spend the whole, barely broken day—a long August day!—in the woods and wait for twilight anew; one can imagine with what thoughts! Finally evening came. Nordeck slipped up to the chapel again—in his clueless wandering he had not been far away—for he had an urge to see the body again. It lay untouched as he had bedded it; the quiet Sunday, celebrated in Catholic lands primarily through domesticity, had led no wanderers here.

Nordeck said his last goodbye to the dead friend, no longer repulsed, and struck off toward the village anew, now better oriented. It was ten o'clock when he arrived. The innkeepers were still awake; wisely he stayed out in the dark and heard, to his horror, that the hussar had already ridden home with the horses at midday. "The gentlemen have likely changed their minds," he had said, "they'll be planning to walk; the foreign baron is a passionate walker." Comforting news! Tired to death, the poor officer of hussars had to walk the long way to Möllheim on foot. In the gray of morning he finally reached the open town, happy to be able to strip off the bloody clothing unnoticed in his apartment. Day comes, he visits the squadron's stalls—they are empty, the guards are gone, just like his servant. Just as he starts to hurry to the quarters of a comrade, he encounters a civilian.

"What the deuce! Lieutenant!" cried the man. "You're still here?"

"Where are my horses?" asked Nordeck, "my hussars?"

"Oh, heavens!" said the civilian. "Gone, everything gone since midday yesterday already!"

"Gone? What? Where?"

"Now, how do I know? The general was here, and it was: Blow the trumpets, hussars, let's go!"

"And my servant?"

"Now he came just in time with the horse he was leading, and had to go with them right away."

The situation was critical. Where the squadron had gone, and that the general himself had brought the order to march and had set everything in motion, this Nordeck learned quickly. But how to follow? Finally he managed to acquire an old nag and with reins flying the desperate commander galloped after his squadron. The rest is easily guessed. Scarcely arrived, the latecomer had to lay down his sword and accompany the march of the regiment in the sad role of a prisoner.

Thus it remained for the whole of the campaign up to the peacetime garrison. With that he had done penance for his error of duty, but the man who was freed was also more than ninety miles away from the place where all his thoughts remained.

The regiment was reduced and the wealthy officers took their leave. Nordeck went back to his earlier occupation, mining, soon distinguished himself, won the acclaim of his superiors and finally received the honorable call to accompany a mining expedition that his government was sending to Brazil. Nordeck accepted the offer. Satisfied with the prospects opening to him in the new world, he resolved to try his luck there entirely. He traveled back to Europe to arrange everything for his permanent departure from his homeland.

When that was done, Nordeck took the opportunity to visit all the places where he had once fought for the freedom of his fatherland. His path took him through that region in which he had been witness to such fateful scenes. The newspapers of the district announced the opening of the assizes in Hainburg, and among the more important judicial cases they reported one with particular thoroughness; the names of the parties are only characterized by their initials, but they are clear enough to the initiated. There was no doubt—the accused was Albertine! Her bleak premonition had fulfilled itself so horribly!

Nordeck decided quickly. Blumenrode came to mind; there they will surely know how things stand. He hurries there, is received with goodwill; he hears what everyone knows; it is enough to show him the severe and pressing danger. He is told that a heavy suspicion rests on Albertine; incomprehensibly, she refuses every word in her defense. The verdict will shortly be handed down, and one can scarcely doubt what it will be.

"And her parents?" he asks. "Do they know, are they here?"

The colonel is dead, they tell him; he never knew what danger Albertine is in. The unhappy mother had kept him believing, with admirable cleverness, that Albertine was only being pursued, because of the Preussachs' greed, in a complicated proceeding about the fortune. A trusted friend of the house, a competent lawyer, the only person whom the colonel's wife had taken into her confidence, had hurried from the colonel's deathbed to lead Albertine's defense. But the gallant defender still carries the old man's last words to the defendant in his loyal breast; Albertine is said to be in a state of mind that promises the worst, should she now hear of her father's death.

"For God's sake!" Nordeck flared up. "Albertine hasn't yet heard of her father's death? She *must* hear of it!"

The floor burned underneath his feet. He was deaf to everyone who stormed him with questions. He only took the baron aside. "I want to go to Hainburg, I must, immediately! Every minute is precious!"

Momentarily he was ready to travel and on his way. He arrived, asked hurriedly for the defendant's counsel. He was in the courthouse, people said; today the jury is expected to hand down a verdict. The reader knows the rest.

The prosecution did not hesitate to withdraw the accusation after seeing the new documents. Senkenberg, who received the same information in his capacity as counsel for the private plaintiff, was pleased to be able to tell the court that his client had departed without providing him with orders to press onward with the lawsuit.

Albertine was freed. The most well-regarded families in the area, even the princely houses, were eager to provide her with proof of the most respectful sympathy. But she refused every personal consolation. With anxious haste she prepared for her departure, her journey to her sorely tested mother and her unsuspecting, affectionate daughter.

* * *

When I found myself in Marseille in 1820, in the parlor of an inn I met the young governess of a sweet girl of about seven years, called Konstanze by the governess. I fell into conversation with her, once we recognized each other as fellow Germans, and discovered that the charming child was only waiting for her parents, who would arrive shortly, in order to board ship with them—for Brazil.

I almost started; it is such a unique feeling to see people, even those unknown to oneself, at the moment of their parting from a continent—a parting that is usually a permanent one.

The governess said, as I uttered something of the sort, "Yes indeed, no one could have prophesied this even for Superintendent von Nordeck and his wife— my employers. But they have experienced much sadness. Now that my dear lady's mother is dead, nothing more ties her to her fatherland."

Nordeck—the name was familiar to me. In the course of our conversation I further learned that Konstanze was Mr. von Nordeck's stepdaughter, a Miss von Preussach. Then I realized. So that beautiful child was Albertine's daughter, the daughter of the dead man of St. Anne's chapel.

The governess confirmed what I, suspecting it, did not want to say out loud: she mentioned the birth name of the mother of her charge, von Siegsfeld.

A waiter announced that the family was there and waiting in the carriage. The governess got herself and the little one ready to go and hurried down to the carriage, after a more heartfelt good-bye than usually follows so short an encounter. I stepped to the window. A gentleman and a lady sat in the carriage. My now departing new acquaintances waved to me again, and the gentleman noticed it and tipped his hat courteously. Even the lady looked up—her bow was somewhat cold and elegant, but permitted me an even clearer glance at a familiar, unforgettable, still beautiful face. It was Albertine.

The carriage rolled on toward the harbor, and soon the ocean separated them from the fatherland in which they had endured such harshness.

Adolf Streckfuss (1823–1895)

Adolf Streckfuss (or Carl Adolf Streckfuss, as his name often appears on the title page of his works) was born in Berlin, the son of Adolf Friedrich Carl Streckfuss, a Prussian government official who had also made a name for himself as a translator of Dante. The younger Streckfuss was a child with a strong love of the natural world. Too nearsighted to fulfill his original dream of a military career, he had just passed his exams to become a teacher of agriculture when, in the spring of 1848 in Berlin, he lost his teaching career and any chance for a civil service position through his writings and political activities, which were sympathetic to the revolution's democratic aims and earned him the enmity of the establishment.

Streckfuss then turned to writing history, but his publication on the French Revolution and tyranny resulted in a charge of high treason and his writing career was destroyed by police harassment and censorship. In 1851 he became a tobacco dealer in Berlin, and was so successful that by 1858 he could sell the business and return to the literary and civic activities so dear to him: from 1859 to 1861 he edited a newspaper for German craftsmen, which published his first detective story in 1860; in 1863 he reentered local politics as a city representative; from 1863 to 1865 he published serially his best-known work, a history of Berlin called *Von Fischerdorf zur Weltstadt (From Fishing Village to World City)*; by the 1870s he had become a powerful figure in Berlin's leading press organizations; and from 1872 to 1884 he sat on the Berlin city council—no small feat in a city that numbered several million inhabitants by the close of the nineteenth century.

In 1870, Streckfuss's first and most popular detective novel, *The Star Tavern*, appeared, one of a dozen he completed before his death. It is most notable for documenting the shift of narrative focus from the crime itself to the detection of it: the author devotes all eight chapters to the detective's investigation.

Streckfuss's love of the land makes itself felt in the rural setting of *The Star Tavern* and the botanical and entomological activities of a police officer posing as a naturalist, and the author's tobacco expertise is evident in scenes where local merchants interview the traveling salesman, Cornelius Steinert, about his wares. The novel even has a love interest. Interestingly, *The Star Tavern* anticipates the device later immortalized in E. C. Bentley's 1913 detective story *Trent's Last Case*: the detective's suspicions almost result in the conviction of an innocent man. The discovery of the truth causes the detective to question his assumptions about the roles and methods of society's crime-fighters and, ultimately, to abandon detection.

The Star Tavern
by Adolf Streckfuss

Who could have hit upon the strange idea of putting a railroad station at Weidenhagen? The management must have had reasons for putting it there, and His Majesty's Government certainly did not give its approval without some foundation. However, the average mortal is unable to comprehend why on earth a station was constructed at this desolate and untraveled site, and even less, that someone had been found to lease the Weidenhagen station restaurant.

When soon after the completion of the station building the news of the leasing of the railroad restaurant was brought by a railroad man to the small town of Weidenhagen, about three miles away from the station and connected to it only by a miserable dirt road, it was at first not believed. People thought the trainman, who up until then had been known as a solid, reasonable person, had invented the story. But the very next day an attractive advertisement in the local newspaper instructed the gentry of the area and the highly regarded public of the town of Weidenhagen that Christian Braun, formerly the headwaiter at the large station in M**, had taken over the station restaurant in Weidenhagen and would endeavor, by means of outstanding food and drink—a choice wine cellar was especially emphasized—to attain the favor of the afore-mentioned gentry and highly regarded public. A few guest rooms would also be at the disposal of those travelers who might come with the evening and night trains and would not desire to continue their journey at night over the poor roads to the neighboring towns, roads that moreover had the worst reputation with regard to their safety.

The same day that Mr. Christian Braun's advertisement had appeared in the local newspaper in the morning, in the afternoon the worthy burghers of Weidenhagen hurried to the station. The little town with its round thousand inhabitants seemed deserted. Everyone wanted to see this marvel of a man who had dared to lease the Weidenhagen restaurant.

Mr. Christian Braun did a staggering amount of business on that day—he had to telegraph twice to the large station of M** in order to have more provisions sent with the next trains. The Weidenhageners stayed until an hour before darkness set in, but then they all started on the way home in tight-knit groups, for no one wished to go through those notorious woods in the dark.

Since that fine day, in the memory of which Mr. Christian Braun reveled for years, the waiting room of the station had remained a quite lonely place. Even though the through-travelers seldom failed to have the trainman bring a pint of Mr. Braun's really excellent beer to their cars, they seldom left the train, as it generally stopped there for only two minutes. Only those few travelers whose destination was this station itself, from which they intended to go on to one of the neighboring small towns, became real guests of Mr. Braun, thereby enjoying his special attention. When such a guest came, he was capable of broaching a new keg before the old one was half emptied.

It was a good thing for this ambitious innkeeper—at least so he thought— that the roads to all the neighboring towns were in poor shape, and that moreover several murderous robberies that had occurred there in the last few years had brought them into such discredit that no one who resided in the area could be prevailed upon to travel at night across the desolate heath that stretched across the country for miles. Even the mail coach, which used to travel at night, had changed its schedule since it, too, was attacked three years before. In the so-called Thieves' Heath between the Star Tavern and the town of Beutlingen, three men had pulled the coachman from his seat and beaten him half to death. They had slain the guard, and the only passenger, Senator Heiwald from Beutlingen, had escaped the murderers only through rapid flight. Since then the mail coach no longer traveled at night. It met the morning train coming from M**, and at 8:15 A.M. it left the station with its mail, going first to Weidenhagen, then via the Star Tavern to Beutlingen, and from there to Worsfeld and Bartsch. At two o'clock it drove back again and arrived at the station at seven to meet the train from M**. Mr. Christian Braun considered this arrangement of the mail service to be one of the wisest institutions of his government, for it had the effect that almost all passengers arriving in the afternoon or toward evening took advantage of his guest rooms, where, as a matter of fact, they did pretty well for themselves, at any rate better than they would in the smoke-blackened Golden Elephant Inn in Weidenhagen.

It was in the height of the summer of the year 186* when one day Mr. Christian Braun was standing despondently in the doorway of the waiting room, watching the approach of the train from M**. For several days he had not had a single overnight guest, and that bothered him. Even though he was no longer completely dependent on the gain from the restaurant and lodging, since he had taken over the position of postmaster and had rented a nice piece of land in the vicinity, as a former busy headwaiter he still felt this to be a lifelong profession that he could do without for a short period of time but never give up entirely.

The locomotive came puffing to a halt, and when it stopped, to Mr. Braun's joyous satisfaction a passenger alit from a second-class coach. As he held a traveling bag in his hand, and as at the same time the trainman brought forth from the baggage car two stately traveler's trunks studded with yellow nails, there could be no doubt that another passenger had strayed to Weidenhagen.

Mr. Braun immediately hurried up with exaggerated courtesy. Taking the bag from the stranger's hand, he asked, "May I take your things to your room, sir? The mail coach does not leave again until 8:15 tomorrow."

"That won't be necessary. I intend to go farther tonight—perhaps with a rented coach. Can horses be obtained here?"

"In Weidenhagen, three miles from the station, but the road is poor and unsafe. I wouldn't advise it!"

"Do you yourself have guest rooms?"

"Excellent rooms! You will be treated as if you were in the best inn in Berlin, as far as bed, wine, coffee and service is concerned."

"But the kitchen?"

"It's good! I admit I can't serve you a ten-course meal, but I can guarantee you a decent bowl of soup and a juicy veal roast."

"Fine—for the moment that's all I want. Most important, have dinner made ready for me, because I'm as hungry as a wolf. Along with it, a couple of bottles of really good red wine and two glasses. I hope, my good friend, that you will keep me company. While we drink the wine we can talk some more about my journey. But please: hurry!"

"Give me five minutes!" cried Mr. Braun and sped obediently to the kitchen to urge his wife to hurry, while he fetched two bottles of a really good Bordeaux from the cellar. He liked the guest, and he was still hoping to persuade him to spend the night.

In the meantime the stranger had taken a seat at a table that the pretty waitress was covering with a snow-white tablecloth. Who and what could the stranger be? She observed him with the expert look of a waitress who had served beer for two years in one of the best taverns of M**, but she didn't know quite what to make of him. First of all, how old was he? Even this question was beyond her. To judge by his unwrinkled, sun-tanned, but still pink and fresh face, his gaily sparkling blue eyes, his natty blond mustache, his smooth white forehead and full head of curly blond hair, one would hardly have thought him more than twenty-four to twenty-six years old, but this was contradicted by the fact that his tall figure was starting to fill out a little around the waist, according to which his age certainly would have to be placed at more than thirty.

The question as to what line of work he was engaged in seemed even more difficult. When she looked at the two elegant leather trunks, it struck her that he was one of the traveling salesmen who occasionally made sorties to the small towns of the vicinity to seek new markets for the factories of the large cities. His expensive clothing also spoke in favor of this business, but not the peculiarly military bearing of his tall figure, as well as a certain something in the tone of his speech, which reminded one of an officer's commanding voice, even when the stranger was at his most courteous and easiest.

This little student of human nature was interrupted in her musings by Mr. Braun, who came up from the cellar with two dusty bottles.

"Here, sir," he said amiably, holding the bottles up to the light. "This is a little wine that I think will please you and entice you to spend the night here."

"Please *us*, sir, *us*! If my guest must drink poor wine, my host is at fault!"

"Your guest mustn't complain, nor mine either, if he will be just," cried Mr. Braun in the best of moods. "Look, here comes your soup, and the roast isn't far behind. Was I right when I said that the service would be like that of the best Berlin inn?"

"Better, my friend, for there is often much to be desired. If the food and wine are as good as the service, this is like being in heaven!" At these words he bestowed a friendly glance upon the comely waitress, which seemed quite officer-like to her—she had, you see, a special fondness for officers.

The food was really good, and the wine was excellent. The stranger ate with admirable gusto, and the slices of the roast disappeared without a trace. Only when his plate was empty did he lay down his fork with satisfaction. "Now a glass of wine, my good host," he said gaily. "Here's to your good health! A host, who in this desolate, lonely railroad station treats the traveler to such good food and such red wine, deserves—if the bill is not too high—immortality! Drink a toast with me! Long life to you, Mr. Braun!"

Mr. Braun was extremely surprised to hear his name mentioned. "You know me?" he asked.

The stranger laughed. "I'm no wizard. Here on the plate the name *Braun* is written clearly enough in large, handsome letters, and then, too, the owner of the station restaurant in M** also directed me to you. He thought that out of old friendship with him you might take me under your wing a little, and give me information about this or that gentlemen in this area, as this is the first time I've traveled here."

The pert little waitress, Sophie, was all ears. So he was a traveling salesman— why, he looked like a very handsome officer.

Mr. Braun was perhaps no less surprised—he had thought the gentleman to be a landowner. The fact that he found him to be a simple traveling salesman was not at all displeasing to him, as he now had the hope of serving him again in the future whenever he traveled this way. For this reason, quite apart from the recommendation of his former employer in M**, he determined to give this salesman the best information he could. "At your service, as far as my acquaintance extends. With whom do I have the honor of speaking?"

"Here, Mr. Braun, this business card will give you more information," said

Mr. Cornelius Steinert, handing him a large card. It read: "W. Oldecott & Co., factory and wholesale dealer in cigars, pipe tobacco and snuff, wholesale distributor of the best wines of all countries, wholesale buyer and seller of wool, hides, all kinds of grain, seeds and all varieties of agricultural machines, etc. Represented by Cornelius Steinert." The name *Cornelius Steinert* was beautifully written in pen on the printed card.

"Now you know me, Mr. Braun," Steinert continued. "You can see from the great abundance of the products our firm offers that it must be important to me to contact all the best firms in the neighboring towns and also all the landowners, to whom I can give credit as a matter of course. I am completely ignorant about this area, and a person could really lose a lot if he didn't have good advice. But Mr. Bottrich in M** told me, 'You can count on my old friend Braun, he's as good as gold. He will either say nothing, or give you information as well as he can.'"

"That's right, Mr. Steinert. Of course, I count on your complete discretion."

"Of course. Let's see—first"—he searched through his notebook—"in Beutlingen—we'll come to Weidenhagen later—I'll do this little nest on the way back, and before that I'll talk to you again—so, in Beutlingen there's E. H. Heiwald. A distinguished family, right?"

Mr. Braun's face darkened; he obviously had no real wish to answer this first question.—"Hmm—hmm—hmm—he—Senator Heiwald!—to be sure a distinguished family now, but—"

"But?"

"But—there really isn't any but. If you want to do business with the senator, now he is as safe for you as is his brother, Carl von Heiwald in Gromberg."

"Now? But not in the past? What's the story with Senator Heiwald? You said either too much or too little, Mr. Braun."

"Hmm—well, a person doesn't like to burn his mouth!"

"I promise you complete discretion, Mr. Braun. You have my word on it. Whatever you tell me, no one will ever learn that you were the one who told me. Let's drink to it."

They made the toast, and emptied their glasses. The second bottle was already almost empty. At Steinert's signal the waitress brought a third. The drink had loosened Mr. Braun's tongue and made him more communicative than he otherwise would have been. When Mr. Steinert again encouraged him to speak frankly, he pounded the table with his fist and cried:

"And why not? What's Senator Heiwald to me? I'm not the slightest bit afraid of him any more than I am of his brother, that proud von Heiwald! He can act as high and mighty as he will, everyone knows where he got his little pile of money, even though nobody likes to talk about it!"

"Come on, out with it, Mr. Braun! I promise you complete discretion, I give you my word!"

"Well, so be it, but it's a long story! Anyway, I owe it to you to tell you about it, for I can't with a good conscience let you travel to Beutlingen at night to have your throat cut on the way. Have your luggage brought upstairs—you won't go anywhere tonight after you've heard my story!"

"We'll talk about that later—there's a lot left of the day. But now get started, Mr. Braun—you've made me terribly curious."

Mr. Braun filled his empty glass again, then he leaned back in his chair in the consciousness of the importance of the information he was about to impart, and after he had thought it over for a short time, he began:

"It's just six years ago that I came here from M**. I had no inkling what a worthless, God-forsaken region this is, or I'd have gone some place else, for an honest innkeeper who knows his business and combines good service with good wine, beer and good food at reasonable prices can earn a living anywhere. Even here I'm doing all right, I can't complain, but it's not good when you have to be prepared every day to hear news of murder and robbery from nearby!"

"I've already heard it said that your region here has a somewhat bad reputation. But is it really all that bad?"

"Is it really that bad?—I should say so!—The large heath that stretches from the Star Tavern to Beutlingen isn't called the Thieves' Heath for nothing, and might better be called the Murder Heath. Many years ago it was a gathering spot for scoundrels of every description. Scholz the forester, that just a year ago they found dead on the Thieves' Heath, with his head smashed in, is the second forester that this rabble killed since I've been here."

"Does Senator Heiwald have anything to do with this rabble?"

"Who knows? But I'll get back to him in a minute. Just at the time that I started the railroad restaurant six years ago, the whole area was in an uproar over a murder that aroused a general sense of horror. A rich Polish cattle dealer by the name of Saworski, a Jew, who had received a draft for a large sum of money from Senator Heiwald in Beutlingen, suddenly disappeared. He had sent his carriage on ahead from Beutlingen to the Star Tavern in order to go on foot to the Gromberg estate, a little way off the road, because he had some cattle business he had to finish off with Carl von Heiwald. You get to the place by a road that is barely passable in good weather. Since then no one ever saw him."

"And you think he was murdered?" asked Steinert, who had been listening to Mr. Braun's story with the greatest interest.

"There's some certain evidence for this. The Pole's money purse and wallet were found, both empty and smeared with blood, buried under leaves and dirt under a hazel tree not far from Gromberg. When Saworski left Beutlingen they were well filled. The owner of the White Horse Inn, where the Pole had stayed, thinks there must have been bank notes amounting to 10,000 talers in the wallet, and about 2,000 talers in coin in the purse. It's certain that Saworski collected large sums in Beutlingen—5,000 talers from Senator Heiwald alone."

"You said the purse and wallet were found in the vicinity of Gromberg, and this estate belongs to Carl von Heiwald. How does it happen that one of the brothers has a noble name, with *von*, and the other doesn't?"

"Different rumors are circulating about that. According to one, the senator lost his title because of some youthful exploit, and then became a merchant. According to another, he renounced the nobility to become a merchant. At any rate, he called himself simply Heiwald when he came here about twenty years ago and founded the big wool-spinning mill there. Two years later his brother also came to the area and bought Gromberg. But the brothers didn't have much money, and had creditors after them all the time. As soon as they stopped up one hole another broke open—at least, that's what their neighbors told me. I've only known them for six years, but six years ago they were in better shape, even if not as prosperous as they are today. Ever since the Pole disappeared, people noticed that both brothers made their payments most punctually. Once in a while they suffered a financial embarrassment, but they helped each other out—that caused a sensation and a lot of gossip in Beutlingen."

"Didn't the law take any steps to investigate the unfortunate Pole's fate?"

"Of course. They investigated for a long time, filled up a lot of pages with writing, but found nothing. Mr. Carl von Heiwald knew nothing about the whole affair. He hadn't been home that day, but out hunting, so that he hadn't even caught sight of the Pole, who had asked in vain to see him. After Gromberg every trace of Saworski was lost. The law found nothing and the case was closed; but the rumors persisted and they were intensified when that disgraceful mail robbery occurred a few years later."

"I heard about that, but no details. Please, tell me about it."

"I'll be glad to. I know all about this affair, because the poor devil of a coachman lay ill here for a quarter of a year, and my wife took good care of him. He's a distant relative—that's why we took him in. It was three years ago, about this time, that Senator Heiwald was sitting in the very spot where you are now sitting. He had ordered a bottle of wine, and filled a glass for the guard of the coach too. He had just returned from a business trip to M** and wanted to travel to Beutlingen with the mail coach. The guard was waiting only for the train from P**, which was just coming in. The senator talked with the guard in a friendly manner. As I waited on them I heard the guard say: 'Today, senator, we're carrying valuable freight. Ten thousand talers cash in hard coin! Twenty heavy five-hundred-taler bags—the poor horses will have quite a time to pull them through the sand.' 'We can get out and walk a while in the woods—with the bright moonlight we have tonight it will be a pleasure,' the senator answered. I didn't hear any more of their conversation. Right after that the coach left. The next day I heard about the crime, and had Gottlieb brought here from Beutlingen, where they'd brought him, so that he could have better care. The thieves had bashed his head in, so that he was unconscious for many weeks. I'll let you hear what he told about the affair later, and what else I heard about it.

"The mail coach got to the Star Tavern without incident. Because the road was very sandy and poor, the guard gave orders to let the horses catch their breath and drink a little water. He went into the taproom with the senator, where they met Carl von Heiwald, who was conversing with Grawald—that's the name of my friend, the owner of the Star Tavern. The senator and the guard joined them, they chatted with them for a while over a glass of beer, and then von Heiwald stood up and called out the window that the stable boy should bring him his horse. The senator joined him at the window. They whispered a few words to each other. Grawald heard only that von Heiwald asked, 'Is it quite certain?' 'Quite certain!' the senator answered—that was all he understood.

"Mr. von Heiwald hurriedly drank up his beer and before the mail coach left, he galloped away on the road to Gromberg."

"The owner of the Star Tavern told you all that?" asked Steinert, who had been following the narrative with the greatest interest.

"I got it partly from Grawald, partly from Mayor Wurmser of Beutlingen when he was here to interrogate poor Gottlieb.—After Gottlieb had watered the horses the coach left. The moon shone brightly—it was almost full. As the sand was so awfully deep, the guard and the senator got out and followed the very slowly moving coach on foot. But Gottlieb, the coachman, remained on the driver's seat, because he was a little lame, the black horse having kicked him the day before. When you travel slowly through grinding sand you easily get tired, and that's what happened to Gottlieb—he fell asleep. He knows almost nothing about what further transpired. For a second he woke up to feel a violent pain in his head. He thinks he saw three men, but right after that he lost consciousness. A few hours later, the good citizens of Beutlingen, that the senator had gone after, had pulled him out of the ditch next to the road, thinking him dead, his head being all bashed in. The guard lay a little way behind the mail coach, dead for sure. The murderers had battered his head so badly, probably with a stone, that his skull was smashed to bits. They had robbed the mail coach—that is, they had taken only the ten thousand talers of government money, but had not even touched the mailbag, even though they say there were a couple of letters in it that contained money. They even found that the dead guard's purse and watch were still on his person."

"And the senator? How did he escape the slaughter?" asked Steinert.

"Hmm! That's just it! Naturally, he was interrogated, and testified that he hat gotten out of the coach together with the guard, and had chatted with him for some time, but then the guard had fallen behind to cut himself a walking stick from a hazel tree at the side of the road. As the senator went slowly forward, he suddenly heard a piercing cry, and when he turned around he saw that three men had fallen upon the guard and were beating him, he couldn't see with what in the pale moonlight. At first he wanted to run to help him, but when he saw the guard collapse, and realized that he could no longer help him, fear of the murderers overwhelmed him and he ran away, right through the woods, in which he, as a hunter, knew every bush, to Beutlingen, to get help. He arrived there pale as death toward eleven o'clock, with his clothes torn from thorns, and bleeding from a number of wounds also caused by the thorns. He then hurried to Mayor Wurmser's house, and found him still awake. The mayor and the two policemen, along with several private citizens, rode hurriedly into the woods, the senator following in a carriage. But out there things were beyond hope."

Did they find any trace of the murderers and the stolen money?"

"Not a trace! The affair caused a sensation, even more than the murder of poor Saworski. The royal mail coach had been robbed, and robbed of government money, and a royal postal official killed! There was then an endless investigation. A famous police official, I think his name was Dankert, was brought here from the capital for this very purpose, and stayed in Beutlingen for weeks. He interrogated every one in the town and the country around. Half of the Thieves' Heath was dug up in search of the money, but nothing was found. Neither the senator nor Gottlieb could identify any of the murderers."

"Didn't they suspect anyone?"

"Suspect? Well now, my good friend, thoughts are free. It's easy to suspect, whether you're right or wrong."

"Come on, out with it, Mr. Braun! You know that you don't have to be afraid of any indiscretion on my part. Another bottle of the red, dear, a person has to at least keep his throat moist when he's telling such murder stories!"

The waitress rapidly brought the desired bottle. Steinert filled his host's emptied glass again—that was the best way to get him to continue his tale. Mr. Braun continued: "Of course, there was a suspect—at least, a lot of people had one. It was said that only a short time ago the senator was financially embarrassed again, and that his brother had had to help him out with a considerable sum. Now right after the mail robbery or a few weeks later a draft of 3,000 talers had been paid out by the senator in cold cash."

"What did Police Commissioner Dankert say about this? Wasn't the senator arrested? Didn't they search his house? The gentlemen of the police are not exactly stupid!"

"That's true where poor people are concerned. But when they're dealing with a gentleman from a noble, aristocratic family, and on top of that a good Conservative, who for his patriotic services got a ribbon to wear in his lapel, then they put on kid gloves! The commissioner interrogated the two brothers, as they did everybody else, but as witnesses. In the end he got to be good pals with them. He dined several times with Mr. von Heiwald, and finally he left without having accomplished anything. But people will believe what they want to. Nobody in Beutlingen will have anything to do with the senator, and noble Mr. von Heiwald sits all alone in his beautiful estate—all of the gentry avoid him, and his daughter will be an old maid, pretty as she is. The latest affair was the limit. You'd have to be completely blind, if you didn't see this! Whether or not the high and mighty police will see it is another matter!"

"The latest affair! Did something else happen?"

"Don't you know? All the papers are full of the latest murder!"

"I have too much to do to read the papers, but I remember that in M** people were talking about the disappearance of a young landholder, a Mr. von Scharnau. Was he murdered? Did they find out anything about his fate?"

"Nothing definite, and still it's clear as day that he was murdered. And again, anyone who will open his eyes can easily guess who was behind it."

"Tell me about it, Mr. Braun! This gets more and more interesting. In this confounded section of the country you go from one murder to another!"

"You're right, a confounded section! If it goes on like this, pretty soon no respectable man will dare to stay here. I want to tell you, it really does a person good to be able to speak frankly and express his feelings. Well, Mr. von Scharnau arrived here about six weeks ago and the next day traveled on to Beutlingen. There he took a room in the White Horse Tavern and took daily trips into the countryside to look for properties for sale. He wanted to buy himself some property here. For this purpose he had a large sum of cash in his wallet. Nobody knows how much, but there's talk of thirty thousand talers, and some think it was even more. Von Scharnau soon became intimately acquainted with Mr. von Heiwald. He rode over to Gromberg almost every day. They say he wanted to buy the property, except that they couldn't agree on a price. They also say he liked pretty Miss von Heiwald almost more than the property. He went for walks for hours on end with the girl in the garden, or they went rowing on the lake. They made a handsome pair! He a tall, powerfully built man of twenty-six years and she a delicate fairy-like figure with a face such as you see only once in this world. She possesses such a pair of dark eyes that to look into them is like looking into a bottomless sea!"

"You are getting really poetic, Mr. Braun," said Steinert with a laugh.

"And why not? The wine is good." And that was for sure, as exhibited by the joy with which the little man emptied glass after glass: at Steinert's beckoning the sixth bottle was already on the table. The traveling salesman had joined in readily enough, but it didn't affect him. Maybe through his business as a wine purveyor he had become accustomed to drinking a lot of wine, while Mr. Braun, who usually stuck to his good beer, glowed like a peony. "Never mind poetry!" continued Mr. Braun. "The girl is really as beautiful as an angel and nobody has anything to say against her. You'd have to adore her even if her father was the devil himself. Well, Mr. von Scharnau was infatuated with her, but she didn't think much of him. Philipp, the old servant in Gromberg, says that she often returned really sharp answers to his infatuated remarks, and in the end definitely refused to go walking or rowing alone with him any more. So, soon a break came about in his relationship with Mr. von Heiwald as well: both the engagement and the sale of the property came to naught. It was just two weeks ago today that Mr. von Scharnau came to Gromberg again. Old man Philipp says that there was a violent argument between the two gentlemen. Mr. von Scharnau's face was dark red when he left the little sitting room where he had held a long conversation with Mr. von Heiwald. On the threshold he had turned around again and cried, 'Tomorrow I'm leaving Beutlingen forever! I'll go by way of Gromberg. At eleven o'clock on the dot I'll be here to get your final answer.' 'You can spare yourself and me the painful visit,' von Heiwald answered. 'You have heard my final word!' 'I don't believe that! At any rate, I'll come tomorrow.' With these words, they say, the young man left the room, asked for his horse, and then galloped away on his way to the Star Tavern.

"The next morning Grawald, the owner of the Star Tavern, picked him up in Beutlingen himself in his carriage—Mr. von Scharnau had ordered it. All of his trunks were already packed. After Mr. von Scharnau had paid a short visit to the senator, where he had deposited his money, he got back into the carriage and requested Grawald to take him to the train by way of Gromberg. That, however, was impossible. It had rained so hard during the night that the carriage would have gotten bogged down in the poor road. So, Grawald offered to drive him to a small foot path, which goes from the road between Beutlingen and the Star Tavern through the woods to Gromberg, and wait for him there. It's about fifteen minutes' walk from there to Gromberg. Mr. von Scharnau agreed to this. He left the carriage, and Grawald waited for him in vain for four hours. Finally, he got tired of waiting. He thought maybe Scharnau had gone directly to the Star Tavern, but he didn't find him there, either. He then drove back with his hired man. He left his man in the carriage and he himself went to Gromberg by the foot path. Here he heard that Mr. von Scharnau had been on the property more than four hours before, but had immediately returned by the foot path, as Mr. von Heiwald had not been home and Miss Ida had not wanted to receive him. Since that day Mr. von Scharnau and all of his money have been missing. In spite of all the inquiries that were made no trace of him has been found."

Mr. Steinert looked at the floor very thoughtfully. He had rested his chin in his hand, and it was some time after Mr. Braun had ended his narrative before he suddenly asked, "Didn't they ever suspect the owner of the Star Tavern?"

"What are you thinking of?" cried Mr. Braun, as astonished as he was outraged. "Grawald is the most honest and hard-working man in the whole region. He inherited the Star Tavern from his father and with hard work, good and honest service, made what had been just a disreputable drivers' den into the best tavern in the whole region. Today no traveler ever passes by the Star Tavern without tasting Father Grawald's excellent beer. He is known as a smart country innkeeper. People come to him from near and far to ask his advice. Whenever an honest man is in trouble, he turns to Father Grawald, and he will be sure to help him. By hard work, Grawald gradually got to be a rich man. He bought up several farms and part of the heath, so that for him even his flourishing tavern business is almost only a hobby. Suspect him? Only an outsider could ask that."

"That's right! I am an outsider," said Mr. Steinert placatingly. Only I still don't see why, especially in this case, Mr. von Heiwald or the senator has been suspected again."

"Who suspects them? I didn't say anything. I don't suspect them—it just seems strange to me that Mr. von Heiwald, who very well knew that Mr. von

Scharnau was going to visit him at eleven o'clock, went into the woods at a quarter to eleven. He had his rifle on his back, and also, they say, took his big hunting knife along. He didn't return to Gromberg until three o'clock. It's also strange
that the senator, after he paid out the money to Mr. von Scharnau, had his horse
saddled and rode away. He was seen riding into the woods on the way to
Gromberg, but he never got to Gromberg, and he didn't return to Beutlingen
until four o'clock. That's all strange, but I don't suspect anything. I don't have
any desire to burn my tongue!"

"You don't have to worry about that with me—I promised you the utmost
discretion. Anyhow, from your interesting story I can see that I can do business
with either the senator or Mr. von Heiwald without any worry. They are now
beyond reproach as far as anyone can see. W. Oldecott & Co. won't lose anything from dealing with them, and what do I care where their money came from?"

This mercantile philosophy seemed a little frivolous to Mr. Braun, but he
didn't dare to say anything against it, and was only satisfied when Mr. Steinert
declared that he would be his guest for the night, not because he was afraid to
travel at night—he would do that, because he didn't have time to travel by day—
but because he had changed his plans. The next day he would first take care of
his business in Weidenhagen and at some of the estates in the vicinity, then return
toward evening, take care of any letters he might have received, and travel on to
Beutlingen at six o'clock.

II

The next morning Mr. Cornelius Steinert traveled with one of his sample
cases to Weidenhagen after he had procured information from Mr. Braun about
the merchants in this little town. At the Elephant Inn he ordered a carriage so
that he could pay visits to the landholders in the vicinity, then had the inn's servant carry his sample case into the carriage, and embarked upon his business voy-
age in that miserable nest.

His first visit was to Councilman Hildebrand, the richest man and foremost
merchant of Weidenhagen. Steinert found the worthy councillor in his stockroom, engaged in what is certainly the highly honorable task of grinding coffee
with his own hands, but his sharp eyes immediately recognized him as the owner
of the business. Although a store clerk, who was as elegantly attired as he was
able to be, asked him what he wished with affected courtesy, he turned directly
to, the coffee-grinding owner, asking whether he had the honor of speaking with
Councilman Hildebrand.

"You have!" was the short answer. At the same time the councilman straightened up a little, stopped turning the grinding wheel and leaned on the iron fun-
nel, measuring the salesman with a gaze that was anything but friendly.

The young salesman, whose attire was tastefully elegant, even if not exaggeratedly modern, obviously displeased the plebeian old councilman with his somewhat aristocratic appearance. He felt somewhat insulted that he, the owner of an important business, received the elegant traveling man in an old, patched working jacket.

The short "You have," to be sure, sounded anything but encouraging, but Cornelius Steinert did not give up easily. He continued:

"I wanted to take the liberty of paying you my respects in the name of the firm of W. Oldecott & Co. of Berlin."

"Don't need anything. I'm completely stocked up. Anyhow, I never buy anything from firms I don't know anything about."

The councilman rasped this out with his harsh voice. Then, so as not to appear all too rude, he tipped the little black cap that he had placed askew on his gray locks and had begun to turn the wheel again when Steinert continued:

"Perhaps you will permit me to show you my samples anyway. We carry a wide selection of all the most important articles needed by farm owners, the very best wares. I can especially recommend to you our exquisite wines and our cigars, both of our own manufacture and imported."

"I told you I don't need anything!"

"I only ask you just to take a look at my samples."

"I've got no time. Leave me alone."

"Well, then, so be it!" Steinert answered very calmly. "It's my loss, but yours, too."

"My loss? How so, I'd like to know?"

"There's no merchant so smart that he can't learn something every time he looks at the samples of a new firm."

Something like a smile flashed across the features of the cantankerous old gentleman.

"You're not wrong there," he said a little less harshly. "But you're wasting you're time. I've already told you, I'm not going to buy anything. So how can it hurt you if I don't look at your samples?"

"If you look at them you'll buy something."

"Oh? You think so? You think you can catch this old country bumpkin by praising your wares?"

"That would really get me something! You really look as if you could be taken in by fine talk!"

The old man smirked. "Don't be so impudent right away! I just don't want to waste your time on you. I really don't have any desire to buy anything. I'm well stocked with everything."

"A salesman must always have time for business—that's why he's there. Take a look at my cigars—here they are. I'll tell you the price and the quality, and nothing else. You're old and smart enough to know whether you should buy or not."

The councilman's face took on a friendlier look every minute. "If you're always so impudent," he said almost laughing, "you'll never make any big sales.

Now show me your cigars. I'd like to take a few thousand on a trial basis, if the price is right. Have you got anything good in the way of Santo Domingos, with Cuban and Brazilian filler?"

Steinert willingly opened his case and drew forth an elegant little box with the requested sample. "Light one up!" he said, offering the councilman a cigar.

"The cigar is good," the old man said after he had taken a few puffs with the look of a connoisseur. "The price?"

"Twelve and a quarter talers."

"Can you be bargained with?"

"Yes. There are some people who won't buy anything without bargaining. You seem more sensible, and so I'm quoting you the lowest prices."

"You're a resolute fellow, all right!" cried the old man with a laugh. "But you know, I like you. We can do business together. Come into my little office— there we'll get to know each other better over a bottle of wine, and we'll take a closer look at your samples. Here in the stockroom we'd be disturbed too much."

He himself took hold of one of the handles on the sample case, Steinert grasped the other and so they strode toward the office on the most cordial of terms. Soon they were sitting over a glass of wine, testing cigars and chatting. Steinert had to tell all about Berlin and the business of Mr. Oldecott & Co., in the process informing the councilman that his employers had commissioned him to inquire about the property prices in the area, as W. Oldecott & Co. included the buying and selling of real estate in their business. He added that he had heard the day before that among other properties in the area the Gromberg estate was for sale. The owner, Mr. von Heiwald, was said to have been seriously negotiating its sale with Mr. von Scharnau.

The councilman confirmed this, but he warned Steinert at the same time not to get too deeply involved with Mr. von Heiwald. If he was not as unreservedly frank as Mr. Braun in his tipsy state had been the day before, who had accused the senator and his brother of murder, he nonetheless expressed his view clearly enough that there were extraordinarily severe suspicions against the two gentlemen, and that therefore it would be prudent to keep away from them.

Steinert, who exhibited an extraordinary interest in these remarkable horror stories, listened to a precise narration of all the details from the disappearance of Saworski, the Pole, up to the latest events. He found that old Hildebrand's narration was in complete agreement with Mr. Braun's, except that the latter, with a partisanship he perhaps was not aware of, had especially emphasized every detail that could substantiate suspicion of the Heiwald brothers, while Hildebrand remained completely objective. Indeed, he sometimes declared that it was really criminal to completely destroy the reputation of two previously respected men on such flimsy grounds as they had done in Beutlingen, for now no one would have anything to do with the Heiwald brothers except when business made it absolutely necessary.

The actual facts that Hildebrand brought out about the two brothers contained little that was new for Steinert. Only one thing interested him: the fact that Mr. von Heiwald had come to Weidenhagen two days ago to notify old Hildebrand that he was ready to pay up a mortgage of 10,000 talers on Gromberg that the latter held. He had even offered to produce the money before the legal due date if his creditor wished; indeed, to pay it upon demand, given a week's notice. To be sure, Hildebrand admitted, this seems like a further cause for suspicion, but to be just one must take into account that Mr. von Heiwald had had excellent harvests in the last few years, and that by expert management he had brought Gromberg to a high degree of productivity. Precisely because in the first decade of his ownership Mr. von Heiwald had—perhaps with too great an agricultural fervor—sunk every available taler into improvements for the farm, he had at first, naturally, incurred debts, but now this approach was paying off. The estate was yielding extraordinarily high returns which alone probably would have been enough to gradually pay off the mortgages this frugally living man had been forced to secure.

During their conversation Councilman Hildebrand had become very excited and confidential. He found the salesman's open, frank nature especially attractive, gave him many pieces of advice as to how to comport himself in Beutlingen and the other neighboring towns, told him which firms he could safely do business with, and how much credit he could extend.

"Above all," he said, "try to get old Grawald in the Star Tavern for a customer. He is an excellent fellow! As reliable and honest as gold! It may not be easy for you to gain his confidence, but if you once have it, he will remain your customer as long as Oldecott & Co. treat him honestly and well! And the man buys a lot of things! To some extent the Star Tavern is the center of our region. The roads connecting the various towns cross there—seven roads go out from the large open square in front of the tavern, forming a star—that's how the tavern got its name. The inn is so famous in the whole region, Father Grawald is so generally respected and so popular that his tavern at every opportunity is the meeting place for the landholders and also the townspeople from the surrounding towns. No traveler can simply drive on by without first drinking a glass of beer in the Star Tavern and exchanging a few words with Father Grawald. If there's a large political meeting at election time, it's held at the Star Tavern. All the parties agree to this, as Father Grawald does not concern himself with politics. The landholders hold their great balls, two each winter, in the Star Tavern's ballroom. These are great times! Father Grawald has a good wine cellar—he carries the best of wines, such as you wouldn't expect in an inn on a lonely country road. Father Grawald also carries on a profitable trade with grain, wool, wood, and so on. He buys and sells, but he's no extortionist. For instance, he would never force a landholder who is short on cash to sell at a cheap price. Rather, he'd give him an advance for moderate interest. Try to get Father Grawald as a customer—I advise you that again! He's worth more than a dozen landholders and merchants from this region, me, Councilman Hildebrand, included."

The second bottle had been emptied and a considerable amount of business regarding various articles contracted when Steinert took leave of the councilman, who dismissed him with a friendly handshake, pressing upon him the invitation to come again soon.

The salesman called upon three other merchants of the little town who had been recommended to him by Mr. Braun and Councilman Hildebrand. He had varying degrees of success in establishing business relations with each one of them. People trusted him wherever he went—he was very adept at acquiring people's confidence. At first glance he understood the peculiarities of the simple people with whom he had to deal, and he adapted his sales talk to every individual.

With all of these customers, when the business transaction had been concluded, Steinert steered the conversation to the Heiwald brothers. All agreed that there were great grounds for suspicion against the brothers. Mr. Beuster couldn't even comprehend how they could let such dangerous people run loose—after all, they were all but convicted of murder. Mr. Schmidt opined that nobody would touch a hair on the head of such aristocratic gentlemen from a noble family unless Mr. von Scharnau's murder could also be proved against them. Mr. Wolfgang Müller and his partner, Mr. Sorau, were somewhat milder in their judgment. They had every reason for considering Mr. von Heiwald a very respectable man. Whatever might be said against the senator—and much could be said, as the evidence against him was weighty—Mr. Carl von Heiwald certainly had had nothing to do with any crime. For many years he had been a respected customer of Messrs. Wolfgang Müller & Co., from whom he had bought the best agricultural machinery, and even if he hadn't always paid cash, he had met his payments regularly. Just the day before yesterday he had come to Weidenhagen on horseback and paid 523 talers, the last installment he owed.

"Five crisp hundred-taler notes! Here they are yet," said Mr. Wolfgang Müller, tapping the cash box.

"Then you could do me a big favor!" said Mr. Steinert. "For purchases of wool I brought along a few too many big notes, but I'm short of hundred-taler ones. Could you maybe give me the five hundred-taler notes for this five-hundred-taler one?"

"Gladly! With the greatest pleasure!" answered Mr. Wolfgang Müller. The only thing is, I must ask you to write your name on the back of the note—it's a principle of mine never to take big notes without taking this precaution. You can see, Mr. von Heiwald did this to the hundred-taler notes, and for your greater security I'll add my name to them."

He did so, while Steinert added his signature to the larger note.

Very satisfied with the deals he had made in Weidenhagen, Steinert left the little town. He called on two other estates in the vicinity, the owners of which also extended a friendly welcome to him. On these estates he also heard much about the Heiwald brothers, about the mail robbery and the disappearance of Mr. von Scharnau. One of the landholders, Mr. von Willbrand in Sartenthin, had accidentally run into Mr. von Scharnau in the Star Tavern on the day before he disappeared, just when von Scharnau had returned from Gromberg to consult with Father Grawald about his trip the next day.

"Are you going to leave us, then? Did your proposed purchase of Gromberg fall through?" Mr. von Willbrand had asked.

"The devil take Gromberg and everybody that lives there!" had been the young man's angry answer, his whole face glowing red from suppressed emotion. "Grawald, give me another large glass of grog, but put your strongest cognac in it!" he had called out, and then gulped down this terribly strong drink as if it were water. After a second glass had suffered the same fate, Scharnau had galloped away. However, he had come back again, and from the saddle had called into the taproom: "Grawald, I'm counting on you to be in Beutlingen at nine-thirty on the dot. That no-good senator promised me to give me my money at nine o'clock. Then I'm going to get out of this damned place as fast as I can. I feel sorry for you, Mr. von Willbrand, that you have to live in Outer Mongolia here! Adieu, we'll never meet again." With these words he had galloped away.

"I certainly won't see him again," Mr. von Willbrand added. "If the occasion wasn't so terrible, I wouldn't be sorry to get rid of Mr. von Scharnau, for he was a very rude, flippant and crazy fellow. I certainly do not blame the charming little Heiwald girl for showing him the gate, even though it is said to have been unpleasant enough for her father."

"Did Mr. von Heiwald desire an alliance between his daughter and Mr. von Scharnau?" asked Steinert.

"They say so. They say he hoped to get out of a threatening financial embarrassment through his rich son-in-law. Old Hildebrand in Weidenhagen is holding a mortgage of ten thousand talers over the unfortunate man's head and continually threatens to let this sword of Damocles fall. They say that for years it has been old Heiwald's dearest wish to pay off this mortgage, and that he hoped to do so with the help of his rich son-in-law. That's what they say, but what all don't people say? If we were to believe all the rumors that are floating around about the Heiwald brothers, they could be executed on the spot."

Steinert listened to all these remarks with increasing interest. All Heiwald's neighbors spoke much more freely to him, a stranger, who couldn't have any connection with the Heiwalds, than they would to an acquaintance of Heiwald's. Therefore it was all the easier for Steinert to steer the conversation to the disappearance of Mr. von Scharnau at every stop he made. The salesman had devoted almost as much time to the discussion of this remarkable criminal case as he had to the business he transacted.

His curiosity was now appeased and his business finished. Toward four o'clock in the afternoon he pulled into the Elephant Inn again. He asked the owner if he could keep the coach to ride to the railroad station and from there to Beutlingen, but the owner of the Elephant Inn would have none of it.

"The horses are too tired out already," he said, "and besides, my man wouldn't take you. In all of Weidenhagen you won't find any coachman who will take you through the Thieves' Heath to Beutlingen at night."

"I'll give him a good tip."

"That won't do any good! About two weeks ago you might have been able to hire a coach for a night trip, although perhaps it wouldn't have been easy, but now you couldn't do it for any amount of money. No Weidenhagener will let you have his team, and no coachman will take you!"

"Then I'll take a special post-chaise."

"Try it! The postmaster will sooner pay a fine than take you. Don't get the man in trouble—he can't help you, even if he wanted to, because he couldn't find a coachman."

"Is all of Weidenhagen under a spell?" cried Steinert in vexation. "How can people be so damned cowardly? Just because one crime took place in Thieves' Heath, that doesn't mean that every traveler is going to be murdered there."

"If you've got so much courage, my dear Mr. Steinert, then maybe I can help you to procure a night trip to Beutlingen," the innkeeper answered in a somewhat mocking tone.

"Do that—that's all I ask of you."

"Well, we'll see if you still want to go when you hear who it's with."

"It probably won't be Old Nick, and even if it were, he wouldn't get ahold of me right away!"

"It's not quite as bad as all that. Mr. von Heiwald's coachman is in Weidenhagen with his caleche. For a good tip he would take you along and drive to Beutlingen, too—it's not very far out of his way. But I've got to tell you: Friedrich Grunzig is a weird character—I wouldn't ride alone with him through the Thieves' Heath for a hundred talers."

"Go get the man. I think I can make a deal with him."

"Don't do this, Mr. Steinert. You don't know the people around here the way I do. I wouldn't trust old Friedrich out of my sight. I'd reproach myself all the rest of my life if some misfortune should happen to you."

"Don't worry about me. I can watch out for my own hide. Go get the man or tell me where I can find him."

"You can't help someone who won't take any advice!" grumbled the innkeeper in vexation.

Old Friedrich Grunzig, Mr. von Heiwald's personal coachman and trusted factotum, as Steinert later learned, was by no means distinguished by beauty. His bushy red hair, abundantly mixed with gray, protruded around his fat, coarse-featured face. The indefinite color of his skin, with traces of brown, blue and red, led one to conclude both that he got a lot of outdoor exercise and addressed himself frequently to the consumption of that noble beverage, brandy. His bulbous red nose was an almost unmistakable sign of this. The man's unsteady eyes were what gave one the most unpleasant impression. Although he wasn't really cross-eyed, he had the so-called shifty look—his eyes kept moving from right to left, then left to right—they never looked straight ahead.

Moreover, old Friedrich was still a powerful fellow. His small but muscular body, which the close-fitting, somewhat shabby livery coat well accentuated, betrayed significant physical strength that had by no means suffered from age, even though the man was at least sixty years old.

Steinert looked the coachman over with that peculiar penetrating gaze of his.

"Can you take me first to the railroad station, where I have my things, and from there to Beutlingen?" he asked curtly.

"Yes, if you are willing to give me two talers tip and stand for a few glasses of beer from Braun in the Star Tavern!" was the answer that came from the hoarse schnapps voice.

"Do you have your master's permission to do this?"

"I didn't ask him. Besides, that's none of your business. If I take you it shouldn't matter to you whether my master permits it or not."

"It does matter to me. I certainly don't want to run the risk of having Mr. von Heiwald reproach me later on."

"You don't have to worry about growing gray hairs on account of that. Just ask the innkeeper—he knows that my master won't have anything against me earning a good tip by driving a little out of my way to Beutlingen."

"I accept your conditions, Friedrich! But listen to mine. I'll pay you the two talers you ask and pay you an extra one if I'm satisfied with you."

A pleased grin appeared fleetingly on the old man's ugly face. "You'll be satisfied, all right," he said.

"I hope so. But take note: you won't get a pfennig above the agreed-upon two talers if you dare to be discourteous or not obey my commands right away. I'm renting your coach, and I determine how long we stay at the station and at the Star Tavern. You start to drive as soon as I order you to. If you agree to this, fine; if not, I'd sooner go tomorrow with the mail coach."

"Say, for three talers and a few glasses of beer a man like me can be courteous all right!" the old man answered, and demonstrated that he could be by executing an awkward, foot-scraping bow.

"Then harness up right away, so that we can get going as soon as possible!"

"Yes, sir!" With this military answer the old man, who had once been a soldier, turned on his heel. Five minutes later he was already out in the road cracking his whip as a sign that he was ready to start.

Steinert paid his bill, then went to his room and locked the door behind him. From his traveling bag he extracted an artfully contrived six-barreled revolver. He loaded this with great care and stuck it in his breast pocket ready to fire and within easy reach. He also concealed a large double-edged dagger in an inner pocket of his vest. Then he relocked his bag and had the house servant carry it to the coach.

A few minutes later Steinert traveled to the railroad station in Mr. von Heiwald's caleche, drawn by two spirited sorrels. The old councilman, Mr.

Hildebrand, past whose emporium the coach rolled, shook his head as his eyes followed the courteously waving traveler.

III

Mr. Braun's face expressed bewilderment when he saw the traveling salesman of the house of W. Oldecott & Co. drive into the station yard in Mr. von Heiwald's caleche. But he was even more surprised when Steinert told him that he was going to return to Beutlingen in this coach, and on this very same evening. The good proprietor regarded such behavior as being almost tantamount to suicide. In vain he exhausted all his store of eloquence to prevent such a risk, but Steinert only laughed at the timorous man's concern. He was handed a missive that had come for him from the capital, one that didn't look like a business letter. He directed that all of his future correspondence be sent on to Beutlingen to the address of Mayor Wurmser, with whom he was distantly related.

After he had paid the moderate amount of his bill, he took leave of the friendly proprietor, who urged him once more, even though he was already sitting in the caleche, to wait for the following morning, and ride in the mail coach.

When Mr. Braun finally realized that all his efforts had been in vain, he spoke in a purposely loud voice directed at old Friedrich Grunzig: "Well, if you positively cannot be persuaded not to go, Mr. Steinert, then God speed you on your way. Probably nothing will happen to you. I know that you are leaving with Friedrich in Mr. von Heiwald's coach, and tomorrow I'll make inquiries to see that you arrived safely in Beutlingen."

The coachman's purple face took on an even deeper hue than usual when he heard these words. "The old fool!" he said in a rage. "What does the man think? Does he believe that I want to kill you on the way? He can make inquiries of the devil and his grandmother if he wants to for all I care. I'll get you safely to Beutlingen!" With these words he cracked his whip over the horses, but he swung it back so far that the lash struck Mr. Braun a painful blow. They started up at a smart trot, but the speed of the horses soon had to be slackened, for in the deep sand of the roadway even the powerful sorrels could only draw the light caleche slowly along.

Steinert lay back on the soft cushions of the coach. He had had the top turned down to obtain a clear view of the countryside, but this afforded him no pleasure. It was a monotonous road through desolate land. Barren fields, which hardly seemed worth cultivating, alternated with paltry clumps of pine trees, then there was a deep peat bog that extended for five or six miles, crossed only by a single causeway, on both sides of which the morass was unfathomable. Old Friedrich, who up until then had been rather taciturn and had rejected with short, surly answers all of Steinert's attempts to start a conversation, now answered the traveler's question by relating that Father Grawald in the Star Tavern owed his wealth to this bog. Because only the one causeway crossed the bog, all travelers who wanted to go to Weidenhagen or the railroad, whether they came from the right from Papkau and Worsfeld, straight ahead from Gromberg and Beutlingen, or from the left from Samnau and Bartsch, had to go this long, roundabout way past the Star Tavern. Thus the seven roads converged at the famous star, the large square in front of the tavern.

The sun had just set when Steinert arrived at the star, the conversion-point of the various roads. Great, massively built barns, stables and other agricultural buildings, which encircled the courtyard behind the tavern, attested to the wealth of the owner.

Steinert sprang out of the coach. "You can unhitch and feed the horses," he called out to the coachman. "I'll be staying here about an hour."

"Sir!" was the curt military response.

Father Grawald, the proprietor of the tavern, received our traveler at the threshold of his building. "Welcome to the Star Tavern!" he said with a deep voice that yet had a pleasantly friendly tone to it. He opened a door on he left side of the entry, which bore the inscription "Parlor." On the opposite, right side there was a door with the inscription "Taproom."

Steinert stepped into a spacious four-windowed room that faced the star. The blindingly white curtains on the windows, the floor, strewn with fine white sand, the shining polished tables, together gave the pleasing impression of the most excruciating cleanliness. In this parlor guests could not help but feel good, especially when served by such a friendly proprietor.

Father Grawald completely fit the picture that Steinert had formed of him after having listened to the descriptions given him by Mr. Braun, the councilman, and all the other gentlemen in Weidenhagen, who had been unanimous in their praise of him. He was a man of at least sixty years of age, but still blessed with the strength and freshness of youth. His face, framed by snow-white locks, bore the healthy color of a man who spends a lot of time outdoors. Father Grawald was still a stately, one could almost say a handsome man. His lively, intelligent blue eyes had such a merry and frank look about them, the smile that played around the well-shaped mouth was so benevolent and good-natured that one involuntarily trusted this man, upon whom popular opinion quite fittingly had bestowed the generally accepted appellation "Father Grawald." Indeed, Grawald, as Steinert had heard that day from all sides, was truly the father of all those in his vicinity who were in any kind of need.

"Welcome again to the Star Tavern!" Father Grawald said pleasantly. "Please have a seat, sir. How can I serve you?"

"I'd like to have some supper and a good glass of beer. Your beer is famous far and wide, Mr. Grawald."

"I should think so," said the innkeeper with a self-satisfied smile. "What you get in the Star Tavern is good and reasonably priced. You can't expect great delicacies in this out-of-the-way tavern, but today I can serve you a haunch of venison as good as any you've ever tasted."

"Bring me that, and a sizable portion, as I'm extremely hungry. But first a glass of beer so that I can wash down the dust."

While Father Grawald was gone to fetch the beer, Steinert looked around in the parlor. A more detailed study confirmed the first pleasant impression. The large room was furnished in a simple but quite respectable fashion. In one corner there was a glass cabinet with panes so clean you could see your reflection in them, containing several strikingly handsome firearms. The walls were covered with inexpensive but tasteful wallpaper, and were adorned with several good prints in black frames. There was not a speck of dust on the frames, nor on any of the articles of furniture: the most excruciating cleanliness was the primary decoration of this parlor.

Father Grawald soon returned. He brought his guest the beer himself, and sat down with him to chat. This was extremely agreeable to Mr. Steinert, who didn't like to waste time on formalities.

"Your beer is excellent, Mr. Grawald," he said, "and if, as I assume it will be, the meal is just as good, one of the goals of my visit is fulfilled, but I have a second one as well: I'd like to do business with you. I represent the firm of W. Oldecott & Co. in Berlin." Saying this, he gave the innkeeper his card.

Grawald gave it a fleeting glance. "I'm sorry, Mr. Steinert," he said somewhat less amiably, no longer completely the friendly innkeeper, but the wary merchant. "I'm well stocked with everything that I need. You have no idea how many salesmen call on me. They all have to go past the Star Tavern, and they all want to do business with Father Grawald!"

"I believe that, all right. And no wonder! A good payer, who needs to order a lot, will naturally be overrun with callers. Councilman Hildebrand in Weidenhagen already told me it would be hard for me to get anywhere with you, but that I shouldn't let myself be scared off by the first refusal, for if I gave you honest and good service you would certainly end up being my best customer."

"Did old Hildebrand buy anything from you?"

"Yes, he gave me a considerable trial order, and I don't ask any more than that. Later the goods must speak for themselves, and they do. Anyone who buys from W. Oldecott & Co. stays on as one of our customers."

"Hildebrand is a good man, but a really odd bird. A salesman generally doesn't get anywhere with him. I'm surprised that you were successful."

"Not me, but my samples. He found them of good quality, and the prices right, so he gave me a trial order. Won't you at least look at my samples?"

"It doesn't cost anything to look," Grawald answered. "Have them bring in your sample cases, as far as I'm concerned. While you're eating supper I'll try a few cigars."

Grawald gradually fell into an excellent humor, having been warmed by Steinert's witty remarks. He laughed and smoked while a pale, shy girl, Grawald's daughter, served the guest his evening meal. Grawald was pleased with the test, and gave Steinert a not inconsiderable order for cigars, also permitting Steinert to add a number of fairly large wine samples for a projected wine shop.

Suddenly, however, Grawald's gaiety gave way to a gloomy reserve when a new guest entered the parlor. It was a tall, handsome man of about fifty years of age. To judge by his bearing and clothing he belonged to the upper classes—it was easy to recognize him as a landholder. His greeting was rather perfunctory as he seated himself at a distant table. Grawald returned his greeting with a deep bow, then hurried off himself to procure the beer that the distinguished gentleman had ordered, but he did not do so with the same joy that he had displayed when he had waited on Steinert, but moved instead with a certain reluctant, grumbling subservience.

Steinert had time to survey the stranger minutely, for the latter was looking out the window. He was sitting in such a way that the full light of the large lamp hanging in the center of the room fell directly on his face, which was only half turned toward Steinert. Seldom had Steinert beheld such handsome, expressive, but at the same time such unattractive features. His fiery black eyes had an almost savage look, its sharpness appearing all the more sinister because of the dark bushy eyebrows that grew almost together above his nose. His compressed but well-formed lips, not hidden by his thin black mustache, gave his face an expression of defiant pride. The stranger's entire person exuded a repellent arrogance that deterred any friendly approach.

Father Grawald returned with a pint of beer. "Would you like anything else, Mr. von Heiwald?" he asked.

"Not for now," answered Mr. von Heiwald curtly.

So that was the notorious von Heiwald. Steinert observed him with even closer interest than before. After all, in the last twenty-four hours he had heard the most disparate verdicts about this man. The unfavorable opinion people had of him, was now that he could see him, understandable. Although he had the intention of calling on Mr. von Heiwald at his estate the next day, for good reasons he wished to avoid becoming acquainted with him here on another's property. He therefore decided to continue his journey. He called Father Grawald and requested his bill. Grawald wrote it out.

Steinert gave it a fleeting glance, then took a thick wallet out of his breast pocket, which he opened and laid down on the table in front of him so that the light of the lamp fell directly upon its contents. Probably to show Father Grawald that the house of W. Oldecott & Co. had seen to it that he was provided with ample funds for making purchases, Steinert riffled through a sizable pile of bank notes of high denomination, from which he drew a draft for a thousand talers and handed it to Grawald, with the request that he change it for him. As he folded the notes up again, his glance flitted over to Mr. von Heiwald, and he noticed that the latter was contemplating Steinert's wallet with great attention, but looked away when he caught Steinert's eyes upon him.

"If you could possibly give me a few one-hundred-taler notes, Mr. Grawald, I'd be especially grateful, as I'm all out of them!" said Steinert. "I'd also like to request pen and ink so that I can write my name on the back of the bank note for your protection. There's so much counterfeit money going around these days, and it's the large notes that are so frequently counterfeited that a person should never omit this precaution. You have to know who the former owner was so you can go back to him, if once you get a counterfeit note."

Grawald agreed with this. He did the same thing, he said, and, as he counted out the money and handed it to Steinert—eight hundred and some talers—he also wrote his name on the reverse of eight hundred-taler notes.

"Would you be so kind, Mr. Grawald, as to ask my coachman to hitch up?" Steinert asked when the transaction was over.

Mr. von Heiwald intervened: "Not yet, if you please!" he said. He walked over to the table at which Steinert was sitting, and nodding slightly to him, he continued: "Perhaps you are not aware that the caleche that you have used for your trip here is mine?"

"So I have the honor of speaking with Mr. von Heiwald of Gromberg?" asked Steinert, standing up and bowing courteously.

"That's who I am! I cannot deny that I was unpleasantly surprised when I saw my caleche standing outside and heard from my coachman that he had promised to drive you to Beutlingen in return for a good tip. I don't like the idea of his using my coach, to some extent, as a hired vehicle."

"I regret this, Mr. von Heiwald, and beg your pardon. But at the same time I'd like you to note that I expressly asked your coachman if he were permitted to accept such a passenger, and only when he assured me that was the case, and the proprietor of the Elephant Inn in Weidenhagen confirmed his word, did I accept his offer. I would have been all the more unwilling to insult you or to cause you unpleasantness because I had—and still have—the intention of calling upon you in Gromberg tomorrow."

"You haven't insulted me and will be welcome to call upon me. I know that my coachman by virtue of his years of service to me allows himself some liberties. I put up with a lot from him because of that, and in this case I will do the same. So, you may travel to Beutlingen in my caleche without concern. All I ask is that you let the horses rest another half hour at least. In the last few days they have made long and strenuous trips into the woods, and I wouldn't like them to get overtired. They are valuable and noble beasts."

"Just as you wish, Mr. von Heiwald! Will you be so kind as to set the time yourself when I may leave?"

Mr. von Heiwald looked at the clock. "It's now a quarter after eight," he said. "If you leave at nine you will still have bright moonlight for the whole trip and you will get to Beutlingen early enough. Goodbye. Till we meet again tomorrow in Gromberg." He made a stiff, scarcely perceptible bow, then left the parlor, followed by Father Grawald.

Steinert stepped to the window. He surveyed the open star-shaped area from which the various roads departed. A servant from the inn was leading a noble steed, Mr. von Heiwald's, around upon it. The unhitched caleche was standing a short distance away from the window. Old Friedrich was sitting on the shaft, calmly eating his supper as if he didn't have a care in the world. Mr. von Heiwald stepped over to the carriage and spoke to the coachman, but so quietly that Steinert could understand only the occasional word: "Money ... hatchet ... on foot through the sand..." Friedrich listened attentively. He nodded his assent without answering his master in words, and once looked toward the parlor window with his characteristic grin. When his master left he didn't even stand up, but continued calmly to devour a tremendous slice of buttered bread. Mr. von Heiwald sprang into the saddle with youthful agility and rode off at a full gallop.

Steinert watched him ride away thoughtfully until a tap on his shoulder woke him from his reverie. "You've pulled something damned stupid, Mr. Steinert, if you don't mind my saying so," said Father Grawald, who had been standing behind the salesman for some time without being observed by him.

"Something stupid, Mr. Grawald? How so?"

"Well, I think it is always very careless to open a cage that contains the kind of birds that your wallet does, in any public room in a tavern, but especially in our damned unsafe region. But whatever possessed you to do this in the presence of Mr. von Heiwald, of all people, is completely beyond my comprehension. It's like saying, 'Look, here are thousands of talers that a single unarmed traveler will carry through the Thieves' Heath tonight.' Are you a complete stranger to this area? Don't you know what's been happening here?"

"This is the first time I've been here, and I have no idea what you mean. According to what I heard in Berlin, Mr. von Heiwald is a respected and wealthy landholder in this area, one with whom I hope to do business tomorrow."

"Tomorrow? Maybe sooner than you wish, maybe as soon as tonight! You did talk to old Hildebrand in Weidenhagen—didn't he tell you anything?"

"No, we didn't have time to chat very much. As I had several other business calls to make, and wanted to go on tonight, we could only talk about business matters."

"Well, then I'm no longer surprised that you wanted to make the trip to Beutlingen at night, and even in Heiwald's caleche. Nobody who knows this area would do that with such golden birds in his pocket. But it would be a sin to leave you in ignorance. Sit down, enjoy another glass of beer, and then I'll tell you what you have to know. You still have more than half an hour's time before you can travel on, if indeed you'll still want to."

Steinert accepted Grawald's invitation, and the innkeeper now told Steinert in great detail the story of Saworski the Pole, of the mail robbery, and the disappearance of Mr. von Scharnau. When Father Grawald was done with his narrative, he said, "If you will follow some well-intentioned advice, then stay with me in the Star Tavern tonight. I'll see to it that you have a good room and bed. Then tomorrow morning I'll drive you to Beutlingen myself. You'll get there on time, even before you can make your business calls."

"It's very kind of you, Mr. Grawald," replied Steinert firmly, "but I cannot accept your offer. I would think myself a miserable coward if I crept into bed in the Star Tavern out of fear of robbers. I'm going!"

"As you wish. I just hope that you get through all right. Apropos, it occurs to me that a little while ago you spoke of needing a few more hundred-taler notes, or do you have enough now?"

"No, it would be a great convenience to me if I could change a few more big notes. Most landholders, especially the peasants, don't like to take large bank drafts. Could you perhaps change some for me?"

"No, I can't. All the hundred-taler notes I had you already have, but Mr. von Heiwald and his brother, the senator in Beutlingen, can help you out. The notes that you got from me I got from the senator. He still possesses, as I saw on that occasion, a good supply of them in his cash box, and the same is true of Mr. von Heiwald, who wanted to know yesterday if I could change some hundred-taler notes into smaller notes for him."

"Thank you. I'll prevail upon the gentleman's kindness tomorrow."

"Yes, tomorrow! Well, I wish you luck! Listen—old Friedrich is already cracking his whip. He's hitched up the horses. The old boy is punctual, you have to give him credit for that. It's exactly nine o'clock."

So Steinert had his luggage loaded. He took his leave of Father Grawald, then took his seat in the caleche, and away they went at a smart trot as long as the sandy road permitted it.

This time Steinert didn't lean back in the cushions as carefree as he was on the way to the Star Tavern. Before climbing into the coach he had ascertained by a rapid check that the revolver and the dagger were ready for instant use. As they drove, he drew his revolver half out of his pocket again to be quite certain.

Involuntarily he was forced to think of Grawald's warning and then of the few words he had overheard of Mr. von Heiwald's conversation with his coachman. What could this grim-faced gentleman have ordered the old man to do? What connection was there between his present ride and the words *money* and *hatchet*? He would have given a lot to know the answer to this without having to ask. He reached for his revolver again but, almost involuntarily, withdrew his hand: it was just too foolish to worry like this. He was almost ashamed of himself because of this, but nevertheless he decided to observe every precaution.

The pale moonlight favored him, as with his sharp eyes he could survey the road for some distance. He was sure that he could not be taken by surprise.

For about a half hour Friedrich had driven first at a brisk trot, then at a slow one. But now the road was so sandy that the pace became slower and slower, until finally the horses were reduced to a walk. The old man got down from the driver's seat and walked slowly alongside the coach.

After a quarter of an hour or so he stepped up to the door of the coach and said, "The sand is so deep here—wouldn't you like to get out for a while and stretch your legs, sir? Just for the sake of the poor animals."

Steinert was just about to accept the invitation, had in fact already opened the door, when, taking a quick survey of the forest, about two hundred paces ahead of the coach he perceived someone who seemed to be hiding behind a tree.

At the same moment he thought of the mail robbery, and considered that he would be far safer in the coach if there were a sudden attack. Therefore he settled back in his seat again and declared curtly that he was tired and would stay in the coach.

"It's only a short distance that the sand is so deep. It's only about five minutes, and then you can take your seat again, sir."

"I'm staying in my seat. The horses probably won't perish if they pull me along, too."

"Right! It wouldn't matter to me," grumbled Friedrich, "but my master specifically ordered it."

"What did he order?"

"That you should get out when we came to the deep sand, sir."

"Mr. von Heiwald didn't say anything to me about that."

"But he said it to me. So don't make any more fuss. It won't take long—in five minutes you can get in again."

The old man's tone at these words was half imploring, half impatiently threatening, so that Steinert was all the more convinced that he should be on guard. He cast another glance ahead, and more clearly than before he thought he perccived someone concealed behind a big pine tree close to the road. This reinforced his decision not to get out of the caleche by any means.

"I'm going to stay in the carriage!" he said shortly and decisively.

"We'll see about that," cried the old man angrily. "Whoa, whoa!" He stopped the horses, pulled open the door to the caleche and said threateningly, "Will you get out now or won't you?"

"What do you think you're doing, my man?"

"I'm not your man! I'm asking you if you'll get out peacefully or not?"

"And if I won't?"

"Then, so help me God, you can spend the night here in the woods. I won't drive a step farther until you're out of the carriage."

Steinert reached for his revolver, but he withdrew his hand again. It was still not necessary to take extreme measures. Although he was convinced that friendly words to the old man would be of no avail, he nevertheless decided to employ them.

"Did you forget that in Weidenhagen you promised me to be polite?" he asked calmly.

"Am I not being polite? I can't help it that my master ordered me to have you get out of the carriage."

"I'll take the responsibility before Mr. Heiwald. I'm going to call on him tomorrow. Drive on!"

The old man laughed scornfully. "You're going to call on him tomorrow?

Maybe and maybe not. I'm telling you, if you don't get out, you can spend the night here or I'll pull you out myself!"

"Are you going to drive on or not?"

"I will like hell. Get out of the carriage, or I'll pull you out!"

"Then I'll drive myself..." He reached for the reins.

The old man grabbed the reins himself. With a leap he was on the driver's seat and from underneath it he pulled forth a small hatchet, which he raised above his head.

"If you touch these reins you're going to get hurt!" he cried in a voice that trembled with rage.

Did he think he was going to intimidate this city gentleman? He was wrong. The very next moment he felt a gigantic hand constricting his throat. With his left hand Steinert, who had jumped from the carriage, grasped the raised hatchet, with his right hand he shook the sturdy old man, who collapsed under this force. With a mighty shove he cast him into the bushes at the side of the carriage, then he picked up the hatchet, which had fallen to the ground. He pulled himself up onto the driver's seat, grasped reins and whip, and with a mighty stroke urged the horses on. The noble beasts pulled the harness with all their might. They started up, slowly at first, but when Steinert didn't spare the whip, they went faster and faster.

Had old Friedrich purposely exaggerated the depth of the sand, or had the road improved? Steinert didn't concern himself with the answer to this question, but with renewed strokes of the whip urged the horses on, so that soon the light caleche was traveling at a hard gallop along the sandy road, past the tall pine tree. Because of the speed of the vehicle as it went past, Steinert was unable to see if anyone was really concealed behind the tree.

A shot rang out among the trees behind him. Steinert looked around, but could not see who had fired the shot, nor did he take the time for a long investigation. With mighty strokes of the whip he drove the tiring horses to exert their strength to the utmost, and they attained a wild gallop. After a quarter of an hour or so he had reached the edge of the forest, and not too far in the distance he saw the gleam of the lights of the town of Beutlingen.

Only now did he reduce the speed of the horses, first to a trot, then to a walk. After about a quarter of an hour—the tower clock was just striking 10:30—Steinert drove slowly through the old gate of the town. In the third house on the street he recognized the White Horse Inn he sought by its big sign, and stopped before it.

There was still light in the taproom, as the dignitaries of Beutlingen were accustomed to frequent the White Horse, the foremost inn of the town, and generally left in the neighborhood of ten o'clock. Therefore Steinert found the inn's servants still active, and the porter took charge of his vehicle. In surprise he said, "Why, that's Mr. von Heiwald's team!"

"Quite right," answered Steinert calmly. "Perhaps tonight yet, or early tomorrow old Friedrich will pick them up. Just take the horses into the stable and give them a good rub-down, as I had to drive rather rapidly. I'll make it worth your while. Bring my baggage to my room—I'm going to stay in the inn a few days."

The porter and the waiter each took a trunk and Steinert himself carried his valise and the captured hatchet, which he concealed from the eyes of the servants by carrying it under his overcoat.

Our traveler found his room to be spacious and attractive. Steinert ordered a bottle of wine and some cold cuts for supper, and arranged to have them brought to his room. He requested that Mr. von Heiwald's coachman be brought to him as soon as he appeared.

After the waiter had left the room, Steinert bolted the door, and then surveyed more closely the weapon he had captured in battle, and which up to now he had carried hidden under his overcoat. It was an ordinary small, old kitchen hatchet. The numerous nicks showed that it had already been used a lot. Every household has hatchets like this, and still Steinert regarded it with extraordinary, tense interest. His attention was drawn to several dark spots, which the wooden handle displayed near the metal. His trained eye recognized them to be blood spots.

With a care that the nicked and rusty old hatchet certainly did not deserve, Steinert wrapped it in a white linen cloth and locked it up in the trunk that contained his linen and other pieces of clothing, and only then unbolted the door.

The waiter brought the supper. Steinert ate it with relish. Anyone watching him would have a hard time believing that he had performed admirably at table scarcely two hours ago in the Star Tavern. At any rate, the adventure in the woods hadn't deprived him of his appetite.

He was still sitting with his glass of wine, smoking his cigar, when the waiter announced that Mr. von Heiwald's coachman was there. Old Friedrich stepped into the room, but stopped at the door, twisting his hat, obviously in great embarrassment. Steinert couldn't help laughing when he beheld the old sinner's face.

"Well, Friedrich," he said, "here already? You must have come at a good pace, or else taken a shortcut."

"I came through the woods," the old man answered grumpily.

"I hope you didn't hurt yourself when you fell?" asked Steinert derisively.

"My bones aren't that tender, but damn it all, you've got a strong arm!" This exclamation bore testimony to the respect that Steinert's really remarkable physical strength had elicited from this man he had defeated in battle.

Steinert laughed. "If you had known beforehand how strong I am, maybe you would have been a little more polite. Right? You made that mistake to your detriment, so I will forget and forgive the whole affair, for you've had your punishment. Here are the three talers I promised you. Now drive home without worrying. Give my best regards to Mr. von Heiwald, and tell him that I will come to Gromberg tomorrow myself."

Friedrich put the money away quite calmly, as if he had taken this business for granted. However, he obviously had something else on his mind, for instead of leaving, as Steinert had expected, he kept his position by the door and twisted his hat in embarrassment.

"What else do you want, Friedrich?"

"My hatchet," was the dejected answer.

"You'll have to look for that in the woods!"

"It's not there. I looked all along the road where you pulled it away from me."

"Then it must be in the brush. I seem to remember that I threw it there."

"Oh? I thought you might have taken it with you."

"What would I do with that old hatchet?"

"Right. The old no-good thing is of no value. I'd just like to have it, because the master told me to take a moment on the way back to cut down the little ash tree that's growing out over the Gromberg driveway. Well, that can wait until tomorrow. But now I've got one other thing on my mind. If you're not altogether too mad at me, I'd like to request something."

"Out with it, old man. What do you want?"

"That you don't tell the master anything about the whole business. Sometimes he gets downright furious at me, and so I think that what he doesn't know won't hurt him."

"Hmm. So you're not going to say anything at home yourself?"

"I won't be that dumb. In this case there would really be hell to pay, first because I was so fresh, and second, because I let the horses be taken from me. Galloping in the sand! They'll be all worn out. It's a good thing the master doesn't know about it. You won't say anything, will you?"

"It's all right with me. Another time be more polite to your guests, old man, and now good night."

Friedrich Grunzig thanked him with a clumsy bow, then turned on his heel and left. Steinert watched him derisively. When he had closed the door behind him he said, "A good act, old man, but not good enough. I see your purpose, and it annoys me."

IV

About nine o'clock the next morning Steinert stepped into Senator Heiwald's office. "Enter without knocking" was written in large letters on the outer office door, and Steinert had followed these instructions. He stood before a tall, elderly gentleman who was smoking a cigar while he paced to and fro in his office. He interrupted his pacing when the stranger entered. Steinert recognized the senator through his similarity to Mr. von Heiwald, especially by the characteristic gray bushy eyebrows that almost met above his nose.

"Do I have the honor of addressing Senator Heiwald?" he asked courteously.

"I'm he. What can I do for you?"

"My name is Cornelius Steinert from the firm of W. Oldecott & Co. in Berlin. I wish to take the liberty of presenting to you a draft for 2,000 talers from the firm of Carl Jachner's Sons, payable on demand after three days."

"That is perfectly agreeable, and I have already been informed of it. I was expecting you yesterday. Perhaps you would like to receive the money immediately? It is at your disposal."

"That would be very nice. Then I could report back to Berlin today."

"Quite right. Kindly present the draft at the cashier's office, and give us a receipt. I hope to see you again after the business has been transacted."

Steinert bowed, and betook himself to the cashier's desk in the adjoining room. The cashier asked him obligingly what kind of notes Steinert would prefer to receive.

"You're very kind," Steinert returned. "I'd prefer hundred-taler bank notes."

"I regret that by chance we haven't got a single one in the cash drawer. But it's possible that the senator still has some in his private cash drawer, and I'm sure that if you asked him he would gladly change them for you if he has them. If it's all right with you, for the time being I'll make the payment with one bank draft for 1,000 talers, and a thousand additional talers in twenty-five-taler notes."

It was all right with Steinert. He received the money, made out a receipt and returned to Senator Heiwald in his office.

"Is everything all right?" the latter asked.

"Perfectly. I just have one small request."

"Let me hear it. I'm at your service."

"For the business transactions I hope to make here among the landholders, hundred-taler notes are the money of choice. I don't have any, and I hoped to get some from your cashier, as Mr. Grawald incidentally informed me yesterday that I could get a number of them from you. But your cashier directed me to your private supply, as he himself didn't have a single one in stock."

"It's the same way with me," the senator answered. "And I don't understand why Father Grawald should think that I had these notes in particular."

"He himself gave me a few hundred-taler notes, which he, as he said, had received from you. On this occasion he said he thought he had seen that you had a number of them in stock."

"That is extremely odd and incomprehensible to me. It's true that a few days ago Father Grawald received a payment of a thousand talers from me for worsted wool, but if I am not mistaken there wasn't a single hundred-taler note in the lot."

Steinert had become very thoughtful. He was struck by the contradiction in the statements made by Grawald and the senator, and especially by the latter's obvious effort to prove that he hadn't paid Grawald in hundred-taler notes, although a single word of denial should have been enough to give to an unknown traveling salesman. At any rate, the senator had his good reasons, for he repeated several times more his expression of amazement at Grawald's claims after Steinert had dismissed the matter, which was too insignificant to deserve attention, from his mind.

After the exchange of a few courteous expressions, Steinert left the senator, from whom he had obtained permission to call on him again and at that time to present his samples. He returned to the inn, where the one-horse carriage he had ordered for the trip to Gromberg already stood hitched and waiting for him. He got in immediately and ordered the coachman not to drive straight to Gromberg, but rather first to drive along the road to the Star Tavern as far as the spot where the footpath led off across the woods to Gromberg.

Steinert now traveled in broad daylight the same road he had traveled after nightfall the day before. In the great speed with which he had raced along he had had little opportunity to observe the terrain beside the road, and now he took a better look when the carriage slowed down to drive through the sand.

The Thieves' Heath was a lovely pine forest interspersed with an occasional birch or oak; thick undergrowth lent many spots a particularly inviting appearance. It was especially suitable as a hiding place for wood thieves and poachers, and perhaps for even worse rabble.

After a drive of about three quarters of an hour the coachman stopped. "To the left here," he said, "the footpath goes off to Gromberg. You can scarcely get lost if you don't turn off to the left or right. You can easily be in Gromberg in a quarter of an hour."

Steinert paid the coachman and ordered him to return to Beutlingen. He would return from Gromberg on foot. Then he went a little way into the forest on the footpath.

Under a shady oak he sat down upon the moss. Before he continued on his way he desired to inform himself thoroughly about the area by means of a detailed map in his possession. On this he easily found the footpath leading to Gromberg. The map showed that another footpath branched off from this one and led straight to Beutlingen, bypassing a considerable bend in the road. It was probably the path that old Friedrich had taken after the fight the evening before.

The map showed a little farther on a second footpath branching off to the right, leading to a lone house in the woods, probably a hut for a game warden or for workers.

Steinert impressed the entire situation upon his mind in detail, then he turned back to the footpath nearby. He searched the area with great attention. His gaze was attracted by a tall pine tree. He recognized it as the tree behind which he thought he had seen a person concealed the night before. It was only a few paces away from the spot where the footpath led off to Gromberg.

Tensely Steinert riveted his attention upon the ground around the pine tree. Not a broken stem of grass, not a bent-over blossom escaped his practiced eye. The examination, however, did not present the result that he had expected. The grass around the pine tree stood up so straight and strong that no one could possibly have stood in ambush there the night before for any length of time.

Steinert realized that either the moonlight had deceived him the night before, or that he had not found the right tree. To make certain of this he walked along the road toward the Star Tavern for a short distance.

He soon found the spot where he had tussled with old Friedrich. No other coach had come that way since, so that all the indentations were still present in the deep sand.

He clearly saw the footprints that extended along next to the traces of the wheels. They came from old Friedrich, who had walked next to the carriage. Here they were pressed in more deeply.

Here Friedrich had stood, demanding that he leave the carriage. Close by the footprints overlapped, and were all mixed up: it was the spot where he had fought with the old man. The underbrush at the side of the road displayed some broken branches—this was where he had thrown his antagonist.

Had Friedrich had an accomplice last night? Did the shot that had been discharged in the woods perhaps come from him? If that was the case, there must be other footprints. There was no doubt that Friedrich, if he had acted with an accomplice according to a prearranged plan, certainly must have met with him again after the fight to discuss further steps to take, as the attack upon the traveler had failed.

Steinert examined the road for a long distance with the greatest care, but found no other prints except his own and the unmistakable ones of the old man, who obviously, after he had picked himself up out of the undergrowth, had walked in the sand to the Gromberg footpath, but then had taken the path through the woods.

There was no room for doubt, for the footprints in the sand were still so sharp and clear that even an eye with much less training than Steinert's could have followed them without trouble.

Friedrich had been alone, he had had no accomplice who had awaited him, the figure of the person concealed behind the pine tree had been a figment of Steinert's imagination produced by the deceptive light of the moon. But this theory was contradicted by the few words that Steinert had caught from the conversation between Mr. von Heiwald and his coachman, for they clearly pointed toward a premeditated attack.

"Money ... hatchet ... on foot through the sand!" What else could these words mean except: "The traveler has a lot of money on his person, take your hatchet and strike him dead with it when he is on foot in the sand." In order to execute this plan Friedrich had forcefully urged his passenger to leave the coach and go on foot. Steinert could not free himself of this opinion.

Once more Steinert turned back a little way along the roadway. He selected those footprints of the old man that were clearest and most sharply impressed in the sand, then took a piece of paper out of his wallet, and with a small scissors very neatly and skillfully cut out the forms of the prints, both of the left and right foot. Some of them were so clear that one could even see the impression of the nails with which the old man's shoes or boots were studded. Steinert completed the precise picture of the footprints by drawing the traces of the nails upon his cut-outs.

Only when his work had been carefully completed did Steinert start out on the path to Gromberg. He obviously was in no hurry, for he went forward slowly only a pace at a time and often stopped to look around. His sharp eye searched every tree, every bush, every little depression or swell on the pathway.

He might have been following this path for about five minutes and had already passed the path on the left that led to Beutlingen, when suddenly a small swell in the pathway, imperceptible for any one else's eye, caught his attention. The pine needles with which the ground was covered lay here in a somewhat thicker layer than elsewhere, so that the soil was not visible among them.

Steinert knelt down and again examined the suspicious spot with great intensity, then carefully he took his knife and removed a portion of the needles from the ground until he came to the soil. He found what he had been looking for, a black spot, the color of which sharply contrasted with that of the surrounding soil.

"So here is where it happened," he said quietly. "Here are the traces of the blood that these needles were supposed to conceal!" He took a sample of the blackened sand, which he wrapped up in a small piece of paper, then again covered the scratched-up surface with needles so artfully that no one would have been able to distinguish it from the surrounding untouched surface.

Now he rose to his feet. A little to the left of the path his attention was drawn to a bright spot on the ground at the foot of a large pine. Here the sand was devoid of needles. They had been removed from this spot in order to cover the bloody spot on the path. Whoever had grabbed them had gone to work with a bloody hand. Steinert found the proof of this on some darkly stained pine needles that were lying at the edge of the sandy surface.

Mr. von Scharnau had been slain on the way back from Gromberg to Grawald's coach, which had been waiting for him. This conviction forced itself upon Steinert with irrefutable certainty. The murderer had picked up the pine needles with a bloody hand and borne them to the footpath to cover the blood stains on it. Who was the murderer and what had happened to the corpse?

Steinert's penetrating gaze swept over the area until he noticed that some twigs had been pressed down in the underbrush that grew densely in the woods to the right of the path. He carefully pulled the bushes apart, his sharp eyes searching for footprints on the ground, which was covered with grass here and there among the bushes. And—lo and behold! he found them, but they were so faint that they were revealed as human footprints only to the most highly trained eye. Steinert followed them, pushing through the dense brush. With every step he took he first very carefully examined the ground and the bushes nearby before he moved forward. He saw nothing suspicious, except that, hanging from a black-berry bush he perceived a fragment of woolen thread, caught on a thorn. Stein-ert examined it with close attention, this insignificant gray-and-black-striped thread appearing to him to be of extreme importance. With a delicate ivory ruler he measured the height of the thorn from the ground, about three feet, then removed the thread from the thorn and placed it in his pocket, carefully wrapped in paper. He continued on his way, and the footprints disappeared, for the ground became more solid as the underbrush became less dense.

Steinert could only follow the direction that the prints had last taken, and they led him to a dense growth of alders, where he had the satisfaction of finding them again, and this time more clearly imprinted, even though still faint, in the swampy soil.

They were, as he now determined, the prints of two men who had walked, not next to each other, but one behind the other. The footprints, which now sank deep into the soft soil of the moor, often overlapped. Steinert could no longer see them clearly delineated, but he noted that, to judge by the size of the prints, the two men must have worn coarse, thick, clumsy footgear.

Suddenly he stopped again and bent down toward a blackberry branch which hung about a half a foot above one of the footprints. Only a hawk's eye could perceive the fine blue hair that was caught on a thorn, but Steinert saw it, removed it and wrapped it in paper as he had the woolen thread.

Onward. The ground got swampier and swampier, and the deep footprints, now partly filled with water, appeared more and more clearly. Now it was pos-sible to measure them.

Steinert took out the patterns he had made of old Friedrich's feet, and real-ized immediately that Friedrich could not have been either of these two men, for his foot was shorter and wider than either of these two footprints.

Again Steinert cut out a paper copy of each of them the best he could, and then continued on his way.

The water of the marsh became deeper. The footprints, although still visi-ble, were no longer recognizable, as the water had washed them away. They finally led to a deep pool of swamp water, situated in the midst of a growth of alders. Here they were all in confusion, as the soil at the edge of the pool, filled with black stagnant water, was well trampled. To the right of the brook the terrain again rose to sandy heath. Here there were several large field stones, among which three empty spots were visible where formerly other stones had lain which were now missing. Among the stones stood wild rose bushes, on one of which Stein-ert again noted a fragment of gray-and-black-flecked wool, which he removed and wrapped up as carefully as before.

Close before the rise to the heath the bank was overgrown with thick grass. At one point the stalks had been pressed flat. Partly they were still flat, partly they had sprung up again. Around this spot the grass was completely trampled down, and the footprints were visible here, deeply imprinted in the marshy soil up to the edge of the water. On the other side they led through the high grass toward the forest, now side by side.

Steinert again examined the entire area around the pool with the closest attention, but could not discover anything else of interest. He sat down on one of the large stones, and remained there for some time. In deep thought he reviewed the whole distance he had traversed. So that his memory would not fail him, he wrote down short but precise notes in his notebook about everything he had perceived and then finally resumed his walk, following the footprints.

In the high grass they were clearly visible, and for a short way through the alder growth they were also unmistakable. They went side by side, but as the soil became firmer they became fainter and fainter and finally disappeared. Steinert could only continue in the same direction in the hope of encountering them again. A third piece of black-and-gray yarn that he plucked from a blackberry bush about three feet from the ground showed him that he was on the right path. He found nothing further of interest, and soon he reentered the more open woods. To his astonishment he emerged from them almost at the exact spot where the path to Gromberg led into the road from Beutlingen to the Star Tavern.

He did not tarry here to make further investigations. After he had straightened out his somewhat disarranged clothing, he turned into the footpath to Gromberg. Now he walked somewhat more rapidly than he had done before. Although his gaze continued to sweep the terrain searchingly, he nevertheless no longer applied the same diligent attention, for he believed that he had found what he had been looking for.

Steinert now walked past the place in the path which had busied him so long before, and soon reached the little footpath that led off to the right. Here, however, his glance was riveted by a peculiar sight.

At the side of the path a poorly but quite neatly dressed woman was sitting in the moss, a lad of about three at her side. The woman's head was bent down, resting on a large farm basket filled with mushrooms standing on the ground before her. When she heard a man's footsteps approaching, she raised her head a little, and Steinert gazed into a beautiful but deadly pale countenance. The woman was obviously very ill, the expression of the most profound physical suffering stamped unmistakably upon her features.

Steinert stopped. The piteous appearance of the poor woman aroused his compassion. "What's wrong, madam?" he asked her sympathetically. "You seem to be ill."

"I can't go any farther! I was picking mushrooms in the woods, but now my strength has left me, and I can't carry the basket any farther," answered the woman in a weak, trembling voice.

"Are you ill?"

"I had typhus. I only got out of bed for the first time a week ago."

"How could you be so rash as to try to do work like this so soon? You must have been picking for several hours to fill that big basket with mushrooms."

"Since six o'clock this morning! And now the whole work is in vain, for Friedrich leaves for Weidenhagen at twelve o'clock. He was going to pick up the mushrooms, but I'm too weak to carry them home."

"Where do you live?"

"Not far—I could be home in about ten minutes. This path leads directly to our house, but I can't go any farther. I can't get the basket up on my back again."

"And it's important to you to be home at twelve o'clock?"

"Oh, yes. Friedrich can sell the basket of mushrooms in Weidenhagen for half a taler, but if I'm not home at twelve o'clock they're not worth anything, as Mr. von Heiwald doesn't like mushrooms and in Beutlingen they have so many that the people won't pay anything for them."

Steinert reached into his pocket to recompense the poor woman for her loss, but then he thought better of it. He was afraid he would offend the woman, who did not look like a beggar, so he said kindly, "If you wish to get home by twelve o'clock, it's high time we got started. Let me take the basket—I'll carry it that short distance. You probably have enough strength to walk next to me."

He picked up the heavy basket with such ease that it seemed to be a toy. Laughing, he fastened the straps around his shoulders, and when he had the burden placed properly on his back, he offered his hand to the woman, who had watched him in great confusion, without knowing what to say. "Now, madam," he said with comforting and boundless good nature in his voice, "do get up and allow me to help you, then things will be easier for you. How about this little rascal here? Can he walk that distance?"

"No, I'll carry him. He's too fat and has weak legs."

"You're going to drag that heavy boy along, and you can hardly move yourself? That would be something! If you're going to do something, do it right, my old teacher used to say. I'll carry the boy, too. Now, my little man, you're not afraid of me, and you'll let me carry you, won't you?"

The boy needed no coaxing. Steinert took him up on his arm, and now they started forward on the footpath to the right. After a short march of hardly a quarter of an hour, Steinert stepped out of the forest onto an open area that surrounded a tiny house that was situated right on the road leading from Gromberg to the Star Tavern. Mr. von Heiwald's coach was standing in front of the house, and next to it stood a simply but elegantly clad young woman in spirited conversation with a laborer.

"It's Miss von Heiwald," cried the woman joyfully.

So this was the fairy princess of Gromberg, the charming Ida von Heiwald, about whom Steinert had already heard so much. The gossip hadn't exaggerated. Ida von Heiwald was wonderfully sweet and wonderfully beautiful. Her delicate and at the same time strong, extraordinarily graceful form really had something fairy-like about it. With her large, dark, eloquent eyes, which were overshadowed by black eyebrows that were joined together and perhaps too sharply drawn, she observed the world dreamily and with such marvelous earnestness that it seemed that she didn't belong on this earth. Ida hurried toward the woman.

"That was wrong of you, Mrs. Schurre," she said with a sweetly good-natured but scolding tone, "Didn't you promise me that you would spare yourself completely for at least another week? And here you are again already, in the woods since six o'clock picking mushrooms, exerting yourself far too much, maybe catching cold and getting a relapse. I'm quite angry with you and have already scolded your husband for letting you do it."

"But, milady, I had to earn some money again after being in bed sick for so long."

"You didn't have to earn anything, you are supposed to get well! But what's all this?" she interrupted herself suddenly.

She had caught sight of Steinert for the first time, who had gently let the boy slide down to the ground and was undoing the straps of the basket.

"I couldn't go any farther," Mrs. Schurre answered with tears in her eyes, "and then this good gentleman came along. He carried the basket and the boy so that I could get here in time to give Friedrich the basket to take to Weiden-hagen."

If Steinert had really had great distress and pain from this—for him—small load, the look that he received from Ida's large, serious eyes would have been a sufficient reward. It was admiring, grateful and sweet.

"That was noble, that was wonderful," she said, and unaffectedly offering him her hand, she added, "You may well have saved Mrs. Schurre's life, for any overexertion could cause the sick woman to have a deadly relapse. I thank you with all my heart!"

As she spoke these words she squeezed his hand, as if he were an old acquaintance, but then, without waiting for an answer she turned to Mrs. Schurre.

"Now you go into the house, madam, go straight to bed and stay there for at least an hour if you don't want to make me really angry."

"But the basket with the mushrooms, milady."

"Don't worry about that any more. Friedrich will take it to Weidenhagen all right and sell it there at the best price he can get. Won't you, Friedrich?"

The laborer, Mrs. Schurre's husband, lifted the basket up to the coach. Friedrich tied it fast and then asked again, "Anything else to take care of in Weidenhagen, milady?"

"Nothing else. Don't forget the medicine for the shepherd."

"I won't forget."

He waved to the young lady with such a friendly, kind and still respectful grin on his face that Steinert, to whom he had nodded almost confidentially, was almost reconciled with him. Then the old man drove away at a slow trot on the road to the Star Tavern.

Ida, who had picked up the small boy, accompanied Mrs. Schurre into the house to assure herself that her patient was really obeying her commands. The man followed her, and Steinert remained alone. He sat down on the bench next to the front door of the house and allowed himself to sink into a contemplation that was anything but pleasant.

How much he had experienced that day! He had come closer to the fulfillment of a difficult obligation that he had undertaken. He owed it not to chance but to his own acuity that the secret of the wicked deed that had been committed in this woods a few days before was beginning to become clear for him, and still he couldn't feel any joy about the success he had achieved.

How often he had laughed at the fairy tale of heart-rending love at first sight! Just a few days ago he had expressed himself in this way with complete conviction to a group of friends, and already today he felt only too clearly that he himself had fallen victim to the spell of the very love that he had damned and ridiculed, love at first sight!

Yes, he loved Ida von Heiwald, the daughter of the man whom he considered a murderer and whom he was resolved to deliver into the hands of the law. He loved her, he told himself with pain, yea, almost bitterness, but he was resolved not to be deterred even by this love from the fulfillment of a difficult duty.

V

Steinert was so deeply immersed in the raging sea of his agitated gloomy thoughts that he had completely forgotten the external world. He didn't notice that Ida von Heiwald had come out of the house, that she was standing next to him, and that she was observing him with sympathetic attention. He was aroused from his reverie only when she addressed him in a friendly way.

"Mrs. Schurre has gone to bed, and I hope that the exertion won't do her any harm. I thank you again for looking after my poor patient with such humane kindness."

He gave a start, almost disconcerted, but he quickly recovered. The young girl must not suspect what strange thoughts had occupied his mind. Towards her and her father he had to be the frivolous, shallow and carefree traveling salesman Cornelius Steinert of the house of W. Oldecott & Co. in Berlin. With the powerful self-control that was characteristic of him he forced himself to give a gay laugh, and to answer in a light tone that was not easy for him at this particular moment.

"Is the poor woman feeling better? Well, I'm glad to hear that, for then at least I didn't haul that dirty basket and that rather unappetizing fat boy in vain! It was a foolish notion of mine, but when I saw the woman sitting in the grass I couldn't resist that amusing idea. Cornelius Steinert with a farm basket on his back and a fat Bacchus in his arms! I just wished that my Berlin friends could have seen me. I must have cut a really ridiculous figure, didn't I, miss? That is to say, I have the honor of introducing myself as Cornelius Steinert from Berlin.

I am a salesman for the firm of W. Oldecott & Co. and am about to pay my respects to your father, with whom I hope to establish business connections."

He had spoken these words with the unmistakable glibness of tongue and that complacent self-satisfaction that tends to characterize traveling salesmen from Berlin, but to his astonishment he noticed that his words had by no means produced the impression that he had desired and expected. For a moment Ida stared at him, half in wonder and half in alarm, but then, as he babbled on, a very lovely, half roguish smile played around her beautiful lips. She shook her curly locks and said calmly:

"You're wasting your efforts, Mr. Steinert! You will not make me believe that you helped my poor Mrs. Schurre only because of a silly whim! I know you better than you think!"

"You know me, miss?"

"Yes! Mrs. Schurre faithfully reported every word to me that you spoke to her and little Fritz! She also told me that at first you reached for your purse to give her some money, but that you got a better idea and carried the basket and the boy for her. I thank you for that. You would have deeply offended the poor woman with a gift of money, whereas now she reveres you like a god."

She spoke so simply and naturally, so candidly and honestly, that Steinert was almost ashamed of his attempt to deceive her. Toward her he could not preserve the frivolous tone that he had adopted—it was quite impossible. So he simply broke off the conversation about this subject and asked if he might have the honor of accompanying her on her way to Gromberg. He also expressed his amazement that the young lady dared to walk alone through the infamous and much feared Thieves' Heath.

At these words of Steinert's a dark shadow passed across Ida's lovely countenance.

"Did you too hear the terrible stories that are circulating about our poor part of the country?"

When he confirmed this she continued, "I'm glad, Mr. Steinert, that you turned the conversation to this subject yourself. I believe I can now risk a request that I ordinarily wouldn't make to a stranger, but I can make to you because I know that you have a deep feeling for misfortune."

"My dear Miss von Heiwald, you are judging me too hastily, too favorably," Steinert answered earnestly. "Believe me, appearances are often deceiving. You must not entrust your confidence to a strange man whom you consider to be noble and full of human kindness. Such—don't take offense at the expression— such a frivolously bestowed confidence is always met with disappointment."

She walked next to him for a while in silence, then she looked up at him.

"I don't know," she said, "what the reason is you want to appear to me to be less good and kind than you really are. Toward Mrs. Schurre you had no reason to dissemble, and you showed her your real nature. Why are you trying to hurt me by dimming my joy at your goodness of heart? Whatever reason you may have, I still must speak to you about my father. You have heard the rumors about him that have been spread abroad by miserable slanderers and repeated by thoughtless people?"

"Yes."

"I'll not ask you if you believe a word of these insane stories. I know that is not possible. Otherwise, as my father told me, you would not have traveled alone through the Thieves' Heath to Beutlingen last night in my father's carriage, and you wouldn't be going on foot and unarmed through the woods to Gromberg today. You are contemptuous of the disgraceful gossip, but my father is not contemptuous of it. He is wounded in the depths of his heart by this everlasting slander. In the last two weeks, since Mr. von Scharnau left, my father's unhappy state of mind has gotten worse—he's gruffer and more misanthropic than ever. I had to tell you this, Mr. Steinert, so that you will be prepared for some sharp words. My father doesn't mean to be insulting, he's just very, very unhappy. Don't be angry with him and, I beg you with all my heart, spare him. Avoid turning the conversation to those abominable rumors."

Steinert was painfully embarrassed at Ida's request. With every moment that passed he found himself more attracted to this dear girl, and still her words again strengthened the suspicion that he harbored toward Mr. von Heiwald. It went against Steinert's natural feelings to interrogate Ida, and still his duty to unveil the crime commanded him to do this. He didn't dare overlook a favorable opportunity that would not recur. After short intense meditation he said:

"You show me great confidence, Miss von Heiwald, and I thank you for this. As far as I am able, I shall strive to spare Mr. von Heiwald's feelings, but if I am to do so, then I must learn more details, especially about the relationship between Mr. von Scharnau and your father, and also with you, than rumor and the distorted tales of gossipy innkeepers have imparted. I am not asking you for your confidence, Miss von Heiwald,—on the contrary, let me warn you again, don't let yourself be misled by your too favorable opinion of a stranger to confide more in him than any stranger should know. Imagine that I am a policeman who has come here to shed light on the disappearance of Mr. von Scharnau. You should tell me what you would tell such a policeman, and nothing more!"

Ida smiled. "You take a strange pleasure in depriving me of the trust that I would so much like to have in you. You a policeman!"

"I don't say that I am one, but I beg you to confide in me only as much as you would confide in any policeman."

"Then you would certainly hear very little from me, for I abhor the police, and even more those people who lower themselves to be police spies."

"Now you have spoken hard and unjust words, Miss von Heiwald!" returned Steinert earnestly, almost severely. "A young girl should judge more gently and justly. Do you think a man worthy of abhorrence who devotes all his life's energy to the service of the law, who feels the lofty calling of delivering criminals into the arms of the law, of avenging crimes, of purging society from the scum that disgraces law and morality? The policeman who carries out his duties with love and fidelity, who struggles just as hard to free the innocent of a false charge as he does to deliver the guilty to their well-deserved punishment, who often must risk his life when he follows criminals into their most remote hiding places, deserves the thanks and the respect, not the contempt, of his fellow citizens."

"You are an ardent defender of the police; but can you approve of it when spies in disguise sneak into the midst of a family, when they deceptively obtain trust by hypocritical protestations of friendship, only later to use a careless or jesting word or a confidential communication to ruin these unsuspecting unfortunate people? I read about a very famous policeman who, in the guise of an artist, received a friendly welcome in the house of a Silesian landowner and rewarded the trust shown him by sending his host to the penitentiary because of an alleged conspiracy."

"I know the case to which you are alluding," answered Steinert with a little less self-assurance. "I cannot approve of it at all. It was a crude, disgraceful breach of trust, and moreover it was not committed to bring a murderer to a just punishment, but rather to entangle a man in a long, tedious investigation, a man who had perhaps been led astray politically but was honest and respectable. At any rate, you can't condemn policemen if they don't always identify themselves as such. Then they would never reach their goals, and the crime in most cases would remain unpunished and would triumph over the law."

"Any deception, any ruse or lie, even if committed for what may be a good purpose, seems to me to be reprehensible, and a man of honor should never sully himself that way. But why does my repugnance toward the police trouble you? You are, as I've heard, a merchant, who has nothing to do with that odious profession. We are no longer far from Gromberg. If I am to tell you about father's connections with Mr. von Scharnau before you talk to him, it's high time I did so."

She told her story. Steinert found that what Mr. Braun and Mr. Hildebrand had told him was confirmed. Mr. Scharnau, who had entered into negotiations with Mr. von Heiwald with regard to the purchase of Gromberg, had been in and out of the house almost daily and had been received in the friendliest way by Mr. von Heiwald. Ida was the only one who had acquired a strong repulsion toward this coarse person who often indulged in unseemly jests. This strong repulsion increased when Scharnau pestered her with proposals of marriage. She turned him down harshly, but even this failed to protect her, as Scharnau demanded that her father force her into this detested union.

It is true that Mr. von Heiwald would have liked to see an engagement, but the happiness of his only daughter, whom he loved above all else, was more precious to him than this wish. He gave the importunate Scharnau a negative answer.

Ida did not know exactly what else had transpired between her father and Mr. von Scharnau. Her father had told her only that Scharnau had threatened him with terrible revenge, and had left him with the choice between complete forgiveness and deadly enmity, between a family connection based on Ida's hand and a duel that would end with the death of one of the participants. Mr. von Heiwald, who was opposed to duels on principle, had rejected the choice, because according to his principles he could neither duel nor, after what had taken place, grant his daughter's hand to a man who felt degraded by it. Then Mr. von Scharnau had sworn on his honor that he would not rest until he had brought his enemy to the scaffold. He would give Mr. von Heiwald one more day to think it over; on the next day he would return to receive his final answer. Then he had hurried off, and although her father had told him that his decision was irrevocable, and that Scharnau might spare himself another visit, the latter had come back the next day anyway, but found that her father, who was determined to avoid another confrontation, was not at home.

"He's been missing since then!" Thus Ida ended her tale. "I am convinced that he secretly left our region. He knows the disgraceful rumors that malicious enemies have been spreading about my uncle and my father for a long time; he knows that his disappearance would heap fuel upon the fire. Maybe he even hopes by so doing to evoke so much suspicion against my father that it will provoke a dishonoring criminal investigation of him. I don't know what else he may have attempted, or will attempt, but I do know that we are suffering from the terrible blows that his hatred has aimed at us."

Steinert had garnered only a few new facts from Ida's narrative, and these were likewise not of a character to lessen his suspicion of Mr. von Heiwald, but rather even to increase it. Not greed alone, but also revenge and the fear of persecution by his furious enemy could have driven the murderer to his dark deed. It lay in his interest to make such a dangerous enemy harmless.

Steinert would have liked to direct a few more questions to the young girl but did not have the heart to entice her to make statements that would be injurious to her father. He walked silently and pensively alongside the lovely girl, who now led him on a narrower path through fairly well-maintained grounds to the manor house of Gromberg.

They had reached their goal. Ida opened a garden gate, and Steinert stepped through the gateway into a small flower garden which adjoined the house. On the wide gravel path that traversed the garden Mr. von Heiwald was sauntering, smoking a cigar and surveying his beloved flowers in the beds to right and left. The click of the closing garden gate drew his attention, and he immediately recognized in Steinert the stranger whom he had encountered in the Star Tavern the evening before. With a slight nod he went toward the newcomers.

Mr. von Heiwald was wearing an old wool, black-and-gray colored shooting jacket with a green collar. At about the level of his thigh *one of the coat-tails was a little damaged.* This old-fashioned and somewhat shabby coat was matched by the dark trousers of coarse cloth, the clumsy shoes almost fit for a peasant, and the stockings of thick *blue wool.*

"You have given me permission to call on you, Mr. von Heiwald," he said ingratiatingly. "You see, I have hastened to take advantage of this kind permission. Permit me to hand you this letter of recommendation from Colonel von Soltau."

Mr. von Heiwald, who had neither been especially friendly toward the traveling salesman, nor greeted him effusively, took the letter and scanned it hastily. It read:

"My dear Heiwald,

"Mr. Cornelius Steinert, a traveling salesman for the large firm of W. Oldecott & Co., is warmly recommended to me by an intimate friend as a highly educated, kind man of excellent character. In order to establish business connections for his firm, he will spend some time in your part of the country. As I have heard, he is also to examine various estates, as W. Oldecott & Co. is considering acquiring large amounts of property there. Incidentally, they are talking here of constructing a branch railroad line from M** to W** which will pass right through the Thieves' Heath. Perhaps, if you want to sell, you can strike a good bargain with Mr. Steinert; at any rate, I would be very much obliged if you receive him kindly and assist him with word and deed.

"In friendship,

Your

H. von Soltau."

"You are acquainted with my old friend Soltau, Mr. Steinert?" asked Mr. von Heiwald, who after perusal of the letter of recommendation had become quite friendly.

"Not personally, but I was recommended to him by a dear friend."

"Well, at any rate, you have brought me his recommendation, and that's enough for me. Soltau is my oldest friend, and anyone whom he recommends certainly deserves it. You are welcome here, Mr. Steinert. You will be my guest today and, let us hope, frequently in the days to come. Ida, see to it that lunch is soon served, and that a good bottle of wine is put on the table. My daughter Ida—Mr. Cornelius Steinert from Berlin, whom my friend Soltau has warmly recommended," he said, by way of introducing them to each other.

"I have already had the honor of introducing myself: I had the pleasure of chancing to meet the young lady on my walk through the woods."

"Then all the better, then you have already made each other's acquaintance. At the table and after lunch you can continue it, for I won't be deprived of my midday nap. Anyone who sleeps as little at night as I do, really needs it. If it's all right with you, Mr. Steinert, we'll stroll up and down in the garden here while Ida sees to it that we get something to eat. We can use the little stroll right away, to talk a little about your business."

It suited Mr. Steinert. They promenaded to and fro in the garden. Steinert gave an account of the business that W. Oldecott & Co. engaged in, while Mr. von Heiwald, who was a great lover of flowers, stopped here and there to fix something in the beds: here he tied a flower more firmly to its stick, there he cut off a withered bloom or a branch that was growing longer than it should. On such an occasion he once stepped out of the gravel path onto the soft soil of the flower bed, on which his foot left an extraordinarily clear imprint. Steinert likewise bent far over the bed to admire a magnificent dahlia that Mr. von Heiwald was tying to a stick.

They strode on and turned into a side path of the garden. Here there were a few flower beds that were less well-tended than those near the main gate. Mr. von Heiwald again busied himself, this time to free a lovely white-blooming dahlia bush of many withered flowers, when Steinert suddenly exclaimed, "I've dropped my little pocket-knife somewhere! Pardon me a moment, Mr. von Heiwald, I'll be right back. It must be lying among those magnificent red dahlias. When I bent over the bed it must have fallen out of my pocket."

He hurried back along the path while Mr. von Heiwald unsuspectingly continued his work.

When Steinert reached the spot where Mr. von Heiwald's footprint was clearly visible, his heart pounded almost audibly from his tense expectation. He looked around cautiously. He couldn't be seen from any side. Then he bent down close to the footprint and compared it with the two cut-outs he had made in the marshy ground of the Thieves' Heath, and really, it coincided exactly with one of the two forms. Even if it was a little shorter, by about the thickness of a pencil, still the whole shape of the foot was exactly the same.

The comparison was the work of a moment. Steinert straightened up. "I found what I was looking for," he called out to Mr. von Heiwald, and soon after he was again at his side, chatting as unconcernedly as before as they continued their stroll through the garden. He inquired about the value of the estates in the area and mentioned openly that the house of Oldecott & Co. was thinking of making large purchases of land here in order to be able to exert pressure toward the construction of the branch railroad line. His firm was also considering Gromberg, declared Steinert—he hoped to be able to agree on a price with Mr. von Heiwald in the event that the latter was still inclined to sell.

"More than ever!" cried Mr. von Heiwald with all his heart. "I wish nothing more eagerly than to be able to leave this area, in which I have spent the unhappiest years of my life, as soon as possible. It is only the possession of Gromberg that holds me here. Pay me any halfway reasonable price and you will find me ready to make any reasonable concession."

"Then we will certainly come to terms, as W. Oldecott & Co. never demand anything that's unfair. My firm delivers payment promptly and with regard to price and delivery will make you offers with which you will certainly be satisfied. To be sure, I myself am not entitled to close a property purchase definitely, but I am commissioned to report all the conditions of sale, to examine carefully all the properties for sale and to give my opinion about their value. I therefore beg you to put your conditions of sale in writing and to permit me to come to Gromberg a few times to examine the property thoroughly at my leisure."

"You will always be welcome here, Mr. Steinert! The more closely I observe you the more certain I am that your firm will buy Gromberg! The estate is in such an excellent condition that it hardly has its equal in the whole region. It was like a wilderness when I took it over, but in eighteen years of continuous work I have made it into a little paradise. I would never sell it for any price, but would rather enjoy the fruits of my labor here to the end of my days if staying here in this region hadn't become intolerable to me. So come as often as you want, the more frequently the better."

The two gentlemen's conversation was interrupted by Philipp, the old servant, who announced that the meal would be ready in a quarter of an hour. Mr. von Heiwald begged Steinert to excuse him for this period of time so that he could devote himself somewhat to his appearance. In the meantime Philipp conducted the guest to a guest room of the palatial manor house, where Steinert could likewise put his apparel in order, it being somewhat in disarray from his walk through the woods.

After a spare quarter of an hour Philipp announced that the meal was being served and that Mr. von Heiwald was awaiting him in the dining hall.

Steinert was conducted to a spacious, simply but elegantly furnished room, in which the table was set. Apart from Mr. von Heiwald and Ida he found that two young men were present, who were introduced to him as agricultural inspectors.

They took their seats at the table. Steinert was seated between Mr. von Heiwald and Ida, thus obtaining the opportunity to chat frequently with the lovely girl, as Mr. von Heiwald used the time at table in the fashion of landholders to discuss agricultural affairs with his inspectors, to hear their reports and to give orders for work to be undertaken. Only when the discussion of agricultural affairs had been concluded did the conversation become general.

Mr. von Heiwald was in the best of moods. The prospect that he might soon sell Gromberg made him feel good-natured, and he therefore joined in with Steinert's cheerful conversation more than he normally would have, as he was usually melancholy and taciturn. Steinert proved to be excellent company. He knew how to talk in such a lively and interesting manner that pretty Ida listened to him spellbound.

The young girl, who had grown up in the quiet solitude of the remote farm, where only seldom did a neighbor stray in, for the first time in her life took part in a clever and witty conversation that went far beyond the sphere in which the monosyllabic discussions, generally devoted only to the interests of agriculture, usually took their course in Gromberg. Ida felt greatly attracted by Steinert's clever and spirited remarks. When he chanced to mention that he had been in America, she didn't tire of asking him questions about it, and he was pleased to answer her, for the conversation with the charming girl exerted such a magical effect upon him that for a short time he completely forgot the purposes that had led him to Gromberg.

At Ida's request he gave an outline of his adventurous life. He had been an officer, but had had to resign his commission after he had worn the epaulettes for only a year because at a drinking party he had been grievously insulted by an intoxicated friend and could not bring himself to challenge him to a duel, as he was his sister's fiancé. He had been active in agriculture for a few years, but as he did not possess the necessary capital to buy himself a sizable farm, and did not wish to remain forever in a subservient position, he had become a merchant. After he had traveled for the house of W. Oldecott & Co. for several years, he had been seized with the desire to see the New World. He had gone to America, and here he had devoted himself completely to an adventurous life. At times he had traveled through forest and plains as a hunter, at times he had gone into service as a laborer for one farmer or another. Only the wish of his aged mother, whom he dearly loved, had finally called him back to Europe. Since then he had been in his present position, which, he said, ending his narrative with a sigh, often afforded him joy and granted him great satisfaction, but also imposed on him at times duties that were hard to fulfill.

The meal was ended, old Philipp brought the black coffee, and the two inspectors took their leave. They would have liked to stay a while, for the witty guest had bewitched them, too, but the local custom demanded that they should leave as soon as the coffee was served.

Mr. von Heiwald offered his guest a cigar, a sign of special favor which the somewhat snobbish landholder usually only extended to members of his own class. "You won't be offended, I hope, Mr. Steinert," he said, "if I now surrender to an old habit, albeit it not one to be praised, but indispensable to me, namely, my afternoon nap. If you should be tired too, you will find a comfortable sofa in the room assigned to you. If not, Ida will have to entertain you, maybe show you our pretty little lake in the park. The shady lanes along the shore afford a cool, refreshing stroll."

Steinert was not at all tired. The stroll along the lake with Ida seemed to him much more pleasant and enticing than a rest on the soft sofa of the guest room.

"Well, if it's all right with you, I'll pick you up by the lake in my carriage in an hour or so," continued Mr. von Heiwald. "We can then take a drive around the boundaries of Gromberg so that you can get yourself oriented. But I have another proposal for you, too. You intend to examine Gromberg carefully in order to give your firm detailed information, so it would be very inconvenient for you to have to come over here from Beutlingen all the time. How would it be if you stayed here with us for a few days? As you've seen, the guest room is ready for you, and your staying here would give us pleasure, wouldn't it, Ida?"

"Certainly, papa," was the answer. Steinert could see that it came from her heart when he looked into the large, expressive eyes that regarded him expectantly, almost imploringly.

He fought hard with himself. His inclination impelled him to accept the invitation. How nice he imagined it would be to be able to spend some days in close contact with Ida! And a sojourn in Gromberg could also be very helpful for carrying out his plans. But still, it was impossible: he could not stay here as the guest of the man whom he was resolved to hand over to a vengeful justice.

He turned down the invitation. He had to visit other farms and the neighboring towns, and Beutlingen was the proper central point, he said, and would not let himself be moved either by Heiwald's insistent persuasion or by Ida's very friendly supplication. He would promise only that he would come to Gromberg as often as at all possible.

He almost regretted that he had been so decisive when he took the charming stroll along the shore of the little lake in Ida's company. What a rapturous hour of undisturbed, intimate togetherness! Ida was so naturally trusting, so simply benevolent. This darling country child had completely enchanted the strong man, tried and tested in the battle of life! If only she were not the daughter of this Mr. von Heiwald! This was Steinert's only thought, ever recurring and inconsolable.

The hour flew by so fast that Steinert could hardly believe his eyes when Mr. von Heiwald came with his carriage to pick up his guest and drive him around the estate. Ida accompanied the men, sitting next to Steinert in the little two-seater while Mr. von Heiwald occupied the driver's seat, as he took the reins himself.

Did Steinert, whose sharp, inquisitive eye never rested, who saw everything with one glance, gather a clear picture of the boundaries of Gromberg as they drove around them? Hardly! This drive seemed to him like a beautiful dream. He sat so close to the dear girl in the narrow carriage, his arm touched Ida's, her little white hand lay there so temptingly that he just had to grasp it, and she did not withdraw it. Thus they drove quietly hand in hand through the fields and the woods. Steinert was happy that Mr. von Heiwald was now carrying on the conversation, and that, when he drew attention to this or that parcel of field or forest, he required no answer. Otherwise our friend probably would have made the wrong reply more than once, for he thought of nothing but the small, soft hand that he held in his, and saw only the large, dark fairy-princess eyes that enchanted him with their dreamily loving gaze.

They returned to Gromberg. He thought they had just started out. But now he had to be firm! He took his leave. He was going to walk back to Beutlingen, but Mr. von Heiwald wouldn't hear of it. Old Philipp had to drive the guest into town in the two-seater.

VI

It was not yet dark when Steinert returned to Beutlingen. He changed his clothes rapidly in the inn, then inquired as to the whereabouts of Mayor Wurmser's residence. The waiter directed him to the house nearby.

The mayor couldn't be disturbed, he had company, said the pretty maid-servant who opened the door to Steinert's knock. It was only with difficulty that the girl could be persuaded to bring Steinert's card in to her stern master, as she was not allowed to interrupt his card games. If the stranger had not had such an aristocratic appearance she would not have risked interrupting the mayoral card game, but finally she yielded to Steinert's earnest and decisive entreaties, and brought his card in to her master. After only a few moments she returned with the message, which she had received to her great surprise, that the mayor was very pleased with the gentleman's visit and would see him in his study.

Steinert was conducted into a rather remote room, which revealed itself by the presence of a massive desk covered with documents as the mayor's study. He was alone only a few seconds when Mayor Wurmser, a small, very lively man, entered and greeted his late guest with obvious pleasure.

"I bid you welcome with all my heart, inspector," he said, shaking Steinert's hand warmly. "The day before yesterday I received the news from the police superintendent in M** that you would take over the investigation into this dreadful business, and I'm exceedingly pleased about it. The acuity of the famous Inspector Werder will finally succeed in freeing our poor region of the band of murderers that makes it unsafe. I greet you with truly heartfelt pleasure, my dear inspector!"

Steinert, or rather Police Inspector Werder (for now I suppose we must give him his real name and title, as revealed to us by the mayor), bore the little man's exuberant greeting very patiently. He took a seat on the sofa and let the mayor babble away disconnectedly for a while. From the mayor's inconsequential chatter Werder immediately drew the conclusion that this man would be of no use whatsoever to him in his further investigations. He was not surprised by this perception, as he had already heard that the mayor was a good-natured gossip, a very useful official for a small town and an honest man, but completely useless for any task requiring a keen understanding, courage and strength of character.

After the good mayor had calmed down a little, Werder said, "You see me ready, cousin, to assist you to the best of my abilities in your inquiries as to the fate of Mr. von Scharnau, or rather to relieve you of the burden. But for my endeavors not to be in vain I must urgently request that from this moment on you no longer address me as 'inspector,' but rather always as 'cousin' or 'Cousin Steinert.' No one in Beutlingen and the surrounding area must have any inkling of my true name and position. For everyone except you, or rather from this moment on for you too, I must be merely your devoted cousin, Cornelius Steinert, a traveling salesman for the great concern of W. Oldecott & Co. in Berlin, if I am to hope for any success in my inquiries."

"Certainly, inspector …"

"There's that forbidden title again!"

"It won't happen again. Only here in my study …"

"Even the walls have ears! Besides, you'll get used to Cousin Steinert more easily if you don't think of the police inspector. I can assure you that the traveling salesman for W. Oldecott & Co. learned more around here in two days than the most experienced policeman would have learned in a week! As soon as I know something positive you will of course be the first one to hear it. In order to obtain success I must count on your insightful cooperation above all!"

The good mayor felt tremendously flattered. He shook "Cousin Steinert's" hand warmly and assured him that he was entirely at his service. At Werder's request, he outlined everything that he himself knew about the two Heiwald brothers and about Mr. von Scharnau and his appearance in Beutlingen and Gromberg.

The mayor confirmed that he himself up till now had considered the rumors circulating about the two Heiwald brothers to be false and maliciously spread lies, and that he had contradicted them to the best of his ability. But since the disappearance of Mr. von Scharnau he had come to doubt his former belief. He couldn't help admitting that a heavy cloud of suspicion rested upon Mr. von Heiwald, but that it was hardly sufficient to justify opening an inquiry.

For this reason he had not ventured to undertake anything, although Father Grawald of the Star Tavern in a private conversation had, for that reason, accused him of malice, and even of partisanship toward the Heiwald brothers. Old, honest Grawald couldn't comprehend how such leniency could be shown when the whole surrounding area and especially the Star Tavern suffered from the fear that Mr. von Scharnau's disappearance had reawakened.

"Did Father Grawald directly accuse Mr. von Heiwald?" asked Werder.

"Directly? No! But he expressed himself as clearly as possible and even added that he would cut off all business connections with the two Heiwalds, as nothing good could come of them."

"When did he say that?"

"Two or three days after Mr. von Scharnau disappeared."

"Then he didn't keep his word very well, for I know that he has had dealings with the two brothers several times since then. Now, one more request. I'm going to go back to my room in the inn now and write a report on my investigations thus far to the police superintendent in M**. Of course, I will not omit praising your activities in the case. It's important to me for the report to get to the Weidenhagen station tonight so that it can make the night train. Will you be so kind as to transmit it by a messenger on horseback?"

"I'll immediately order one of the policemen to get ready for the ride."

"Excellent, cousin. I thank you and I shall not forget to mention your great cooperation. Tomorrow morning I'm going to the Weidenhagen station myself. There I'm expecting to meet an acquaintance coming from M**, a naturalist, who wishes to examine the plants, vermin, butterflies, bugs, snakes, and so on. He will probably put up at the Star Tavern for some time. I hope I can count on his not being asked for his identification papers by the police from Beutlingen or by the gendarmes. I'll vouch for the man—he's well known to me. But this, too, must be between us, incidentally."

"I understand, cousin. Everything will be well taken care of."

Werder had brought his first official visit in Beutlingen to a successful conclusion. He had accomplished his purpose, so he returned to the inn to write that important report to his superiors about his activities to date.

In this report he first told in simple words what he had seen and heard, without drawing any conclusions: the tales told by Braun, the merchants in Weidenhagen, by Mr. Hildebrand, and Father Grawald. He told of his nocturnal adventure with old Friedrich Grunzig, his visit with the senator, his discovery in the forest, and finally his visits in Gromberg and with Mayor Wurmser. To this short, compressed narrative Werder added in the report an account of the conclusions that, in his view, should be drawn from the facts.

Werder emphasized especially the serial numbers on the hundred-taler notes that undoubtedly came from Mr. von Heiwald; the clothes he wore in the garden: the shoes, blue woolen stockings and the gray-and-black-striped woolen old hunting jacket with patched coattails; and the correspondence of the footprints.

He concluded his report:

"From all this evidence I feel myself compelled to request that an inquiry with respect to the murder and robbery of Mr. von Scharnau, or perhaps for complicity in this crime, be instituted against Mr. von Heiwald, and that his arrest be undertaken.

"In the interest of the public welfare, the arrest of Senator Heiwald might also appear justified, although the evidence we have against him, if not taken in conjunction with the evidence against his brother, in itself would not suffice to permit an action against him.

"In the interest of the inquiry the arrest of the two brothers as well as a most careful search of both their houses seems indicated. Only after this has taken place will it be possible for me to take further steps here, especially to institute the search for Mr. von Schnarnau's body. A search of the quagmire before the arrest of the probable murderers would draw their attention to it and could easily lead to an obfuscation of the facts.

"Finally, I should like to add dutifully the request that the arrest of the two brothers and the search of their houses not be allocated either to me or Police Commissar Ewald or the local authorities, but that a reliable and discreet official be sent here for that purpose. It would impede my further activity, as well as that which I expected Mr. Ewald to undertake, if we were recognized as police officers. The local authorities are all unsuitable for a difficult criminal inquiry."

After Werder had finished his long and detailed official report, he wrote a private letter, which he enclosed with the report. The letter bore the address:

To the Honorable Mr. von Soltau
Police Superintendent in M**   ·
(Private)

It said:

"My dear Julius,

"The enclosed report is for my superior in rank, but these lines are for my friend and brother-in-law.

"Julius, are you my good or my evil angel? All the good and bad luck I've had in this life seems to have come from you! Whenever I've been tossed around badly by Fate, you were the guilty or innocent cause.

"The fact that I didn't want to shoot you, my dearest friend and future brother-in-law, because of an insult you delivered to me in an intoxicated state, compelled me to surrender my uniform and gave an unexpected turn to my life—and yours. Things went well for you, you got to be a distinguished man, the police superintendent of M**, but I had to drift along through the world first as a farm hand, then as a traveling salesman. A careless word from you, the description of the enticing hunts in the American wilderness, which Semrau gave when he returned from there, drove me to the Far West, to the squatters and Indians, to the adventurous life of the wilderness hunter. Then your admonition, the description you gave in your letters of the grief of my dear old mother, called me back home.

"Again it was you who determined my fate—I am almost a puppet subject to your whims. You made me a policeman, through your recommendation I was hired and promoted, under your direction I have made a name for myself—I don't know whether I should say I'm famous or infamous—as the boldest and smartest solver of the most baffling crimes. And that's not enough! Finally, it was you who, in your friendly concern that I have a magnificent career, sent me here. My prudence and acuity—so you kindly wrote in your letter to the minister—would certainly succeed in freeing this region of the band of murderers that is making it unsafe.

"Julius, you wanted to provide for my happiness, and have made me unspeakably unhappy! You will understand when I tell you after you have read my report: 'I love Ida von Heiwald, love her to the point of insanity, and still I must deliver her father, the murderer, to the executioner.'

"Love and duty! This conflict is causing me to despair. But don't worry: even though all my life's happiness will be ruined by the fulfillment of my duty—I shall not waver! The report will prove this to you.

"I shall carry out the task that you allotted to me. I shall unmask the criminals and hand them over to the court for punishment, but with this deed my career as a policeman comes to an end. How proud I was hitherto of the outstanding successes of my intellect and my professional activities, how proud even this morning! A few words from a simple country lass have destroyed my intellectual pride, ruined the proud delusive edifice of my excessive ego and shown me that my much-vaunted cleverness is nothing but vain deception and delusion. 'Every disguise, every ruse and lie seems contemptible to me, and a man of honor should never sully himself that way.' These are her simple maidenly words, but for me they are true and devastating. They judge my past unrelentingly.

"How miserable I felt when I stood before this dear girl in the sad consciousness that with a lie on my tongue, with deception and guile in my heart I was about to enter her father's hospitable house in order to destroy him. And still I could not and cannot retreat. I am bound by my oath of office. Precisely because here for the first time in my life my love and my duty are in conflict, honor demands that I persevere although my heart is bleeding. I shall not rest or desist until I have completed my task here. Tomorrow I shall lie and disguise myself the way I did today, I shall call at Mr. von Heiwald's house as Cornelius Steinert, shall offer a friendly hand to the man whom I wish to deliver to the executioner, I shall entangle him with merry jests and at the same time observe him so sharply that not one of his words, not one of his glances, escapes me. I'll do all of that. But when I've succeeded in murdering the father, and breaking a pure, noble maiden's heart through my infernal intrigues, then cursed be the Judas reward! Cursed every prospect for promotion! Cursed every groschen of blood money that I take as a reward for my disgraceful actions! I'll go insane, Julius, if I think of the future any more. Away to America! Maybe there I can find again the peace of heart I have lost.

"Pity me, friend, but don't be angry with me. As ever,

"Your Carl."

Werder sealed up the letter and the report and brought them to Mayor Wurmser, who sent them that night with a mounted messenger to the railroad station in Weidenhagen.

VII

Werder spent the next week in excited, almost exhausting activity. He was on the go almost continuously. He paid a call on all the neighboring landowners, and likewise all the more important merchants of the little towns round-about. The firm of W. Oldecott & Co. could indeed be satisfied with the restless activity of its salesman. At the end of a week he was as precisely informed about all the business connections of the Heiwald brothers and Grawald with the farms and little towns as if he had already lived in this region for years.

He had to arrange his daily routine so that his way led him to the Star Tavern, where he usually took a walk in the woods with the professor, who had made himself right at home, or he kept the learned gentleman company in his room while he dried his collection of plants and prepared his butterflies and insects.

During these visits the two friends conversed so animatedly and merrily that the little professor's hoarse "hee-hee-hee" and the traveling salesman's booming, merry laugh could often be heard in the taproom below. It would be hard to imagine two friends less alike, said Father Grawald, nor could there be two merrier, more harmless people than the two of them. Grawald held the professor in especially high esteem. There's a man for you, he would say, so good-natured, modest, satisfied with everything, so companionable, and still such a great scholar!

The little professor was on his feet day and night. Already at the crack of dawn he started out on his excursions through forest, field and meadow. He roamed for miles, tireless, but this left him with an insatiable thirst. He stopped in at every village tavern to drink a glass of milk or beer. He would then converse in the most affable manner with the bartenders and farmers about the economy, the harvest, business. He could talk about anything, but he liked best to chat about his host, Father Grawald, for whom he displayed a real reverence. There was no better person, no more attentive host, no more capable businessman in all the world, he would say; too bad that Andres bore so little resemblance to his father.

Generally the professor, loaded down with the treasures he had collected, would return to the Star Tavern about noon. Afternoons he put his naturalia in order, and prepared them for his collection. All the tavern workers would have to help him with this, and they all liked to do so, for the merry, harmless little professor was everyone's favorite—even surly Andres had to laugh at his merry jests. Father Grawald had put his entire house at the professor's disposal. The professor dried the paper that served as a wrapping for his plants in the attic. In the cellar, wrapped in damp moss and paper, resided those plants that the professor wished to bring home alive and plant in his garden. In the shed next to the house stood a chest containing snakes, and in the parlor a glass-covered box full of caterpillars that the naturalist was cultivating.

Even at night this busy little man didn't rest. He went into the woods with a little lantern to catch night moths and other nocturnal creatures. Often he didn't return until close to one o'clock, and then he still had to put his catch in order. In the middle of the night he wandered down into the cellar, to the attic or the shed. Father Grawald had given him a house key, as the tavern workers usually went to bed early. So no one disturbed his coming and going—even the watch dogs no longer barked, as the professor had made friends with them too.

Their tireless activity caused the days to fly by swiftly for the two police officials. After all, both of them had a special secondary interest along with their official duties. Ewald was happy with his collections and worked away merrily at his hobby. Werder, however, paid a daily call to Gromberg. He inspected meadow, field and forest with model precision, but always had a little time left over to call at the manor house.

During the first few days after Ewald's arrival Werder treated Ida much more coldly and taciturnly than when they had first met: he no longer resembled the merry and interesting traveler of that first day. When Ida, in her ingenuous unaffectedness, offered to be his guide to a distant field, he accepted her offer, but he remained so silent, so cold and unlikable the whole way that Ida often wondered how she had offended this welcome guest.

She became all the more joyous when after a few days Werder's mood suddenly altered. He became merry, talkative, confiding. He asked her himself to be his guide on a path through meadow and forest. On the way he offered her his arm and she felt a slight pressure from it. Toward Mr. von Heiwald Werder displayed in these days a respectful amiability and cordiality. While in the first few days he had declined every invitation to be a guest of the family at lunch or dinner, he now willingly accepted them. He stayed in Gromberg until late at night as the most welcome guest for Mr. von Heiwald, who never tired of hearing the much-traveled man describe life in America. "If we can agree on a deal, Mr. Steinert," he would say after he had eagerly listened to a description of the plant life there, "I'm going to cross the ocean with my Ida and seek a home in that beautiful land, an asylum where I can live and work far away from people's slanderous tongues. How happy I'll be, once I can breathe over there in that free land!"

"Then will you take me along too, Mr. von Heiwald?" asked Werder, but even if he directed the question to the father, his eyes sought for an answer in Ida's dark ones. He hardly heard it when Mr. von Heiwald said amiably and cordially, "I can't think of a more esteemed or more welcome traveling companion!" Much more important for him was the beaming smile that transfigured Ida's countenance, the joyous "yes" that her eyes signaled to him.

It was on the morning of the tenth day after the first call that Mr. von Heiwald had received from the traveling salesman, Cornelius Steinert. The proprietor of the estate was sitting at his desk, busy checking some accounts, while Ida was at her usual place by the window, from where she could keep the road to Beutlingen in view. Werder had promised to come in the forenoon and spend the entire day in Gromberg, so that Ida very frequently raised her head from her embroidery to see if the expected guest still could not be seen.

Finally a carriage was to be seen coming from Beutlingen.

"Here comes Mr. Steinert!" Ida called out joyously to her father, but in the next moment she said disappointedly, "No, that's not he. That's not the little caleche from the White Horse, it's the mayor's big open coach. How odd, three strange gentlemen are sitting in it."

The coach drove into the yard. The very next minute, without being announced, a tall gentleman with a military bearing stepped into the room. "Do I have the honor of speaking with Mr. von Heiwald?" he asked with a slight bow.

"That is my name."

"I should like to speak with you alone!" The stranger said this in a curt, almost commanding tone.

"With whom do I have the honor?"

"I am Police Commissar Dunkelword from M**."

Mr. von Heiwald gave an involuntary start when he heard the name and the position of the stranger. The police department in M**, famous throughout the country for its great activity, owed its reputation mainly to the inexhaustible efforts and the acuity of three officials who had succeeded in several almost desperate cases in solving the mystery of crimes that had been perpetrated. The names of Werder, Dunkelword and Ewald were famous and feared. One of this famous trio was now standing before Mr. von Heiwald. What could he want in Gromberg? A sad premonition told the unhappy man, who turned pale as death. His limbs trembled, he clutched the arms of his chair convulsively, so as not to fall down. He could hardly utter the few words, "Leave us, Ida. I must speak with the gentleman alone."

Ida, too, trembled when she heard the feared name, but she didn't collapse. She had expected, even longed for, what was now to happen. She didn't lose her composure for a moment. She rushed to her father, she threw her arms around his neck, and while she kissed him tenderly she said sincerely, "No, father, I shan't go! I'll stay with you, no matter what may happen! Your daughter's place is at your side!"

"I beseech you earnestly, my dear young lady, to leave me alone with your father. What we have to discuss is not fit for the ears of a young lady!" The police commissar said this imploringly, and with emotion, as Ida's beauty had not failed to make its impression on him.

"I am strong enough to hear everything that you might say to my father, sir! I beg you, don't send me away!" When she spoke these words Ida looked so imploringly at the policeman that he couldn't resist. He answered, "If Mr. von Heiwald wishes you to stay, miss, I have no objection. From Inspector Werder I have the strict order to treat you as well as duty allows."

"From Inspector Werder? He's here too?" cried Mr. von Heiwald, deeply shaken.

"He is in Beutlingen. He will be in Gromberg in an hour."

There was no longer any doubt. Dispatching the two famous policemen from M** could have only one purpose—Mr. von Heiwald knew that. Now he knew his fate. The first shock had shaken him, but he soon regained his composure. He no longer trembled when he said, "Tell me, sir, what do you wish of me?"

"Mr. von Heiwald, I have the sad duty of arresting you."

"Do you know the reason, and may you tell me what it is?"

"Yes! There is strong suspicion against you of complicity in the murder and robbery of Mr. von Scharnau."

Mr. von Heiwald had become pale as a ghost. "I knew it," he said in an almost inaudible voice. "That's the final blow that vile slander can deliver against me. Have courage, my child!"

"I shall, father," returned Ida, embracing her father more tightly. "I thank God that finally an open charge has been leveled against you! As long as your disgraceful enemies were agitating against you in secret, as long as they slandered you, your strength was weakened. But now you can look them straight in the eye openly and boldly, and will destroy their worthless plots! Your innocence will finally come to light. Father, I bless this moment, which I have longed for with all my heart!"

"I thank you, my dear, dear child! Your confidence gives me courage and strength, too. Sir, I am ready to follow you. May my daughter accompany me?"

"To my regret I cannot allow that. I have been ordered to send Mr. von Heiwald to Beutlingen alone with one of the officials who accompany me. I myself will remain with the other official until Inspector Werder arrives. I have been commissioned to begin the most minute search of the premises, and therefore, as deeply as I regret this, and as much as I must beg your pardon, I cannot even permit the young lady to leave this room until the house search is over."

"Do your duty, sir," answered Ida earnestly and firmly. "Don't give us any consideration, not the slightest. Goodbye, father dear, we'll meet again soon and happier."

What a marvelous transformation a few minutes had wrought! The childlike, simple country maiden was suddenly elevated to a strong, composed young lady. Her large eyes, previously so dreamy, now saw clearly, firmly and seriously. Mr. von Heiwald regarded his beautiful child with admiration and pride. He also felt strengthened by Ida's strength. "Yes, we'll meet again, my precious child," he cried. "No farewell, just *au revoir* until we soon meet again! I'm following you, sir!" He kissed Ida again, then followed one of the two officials who had been called in. In Mayor Wurmser's coach he started the little journey to Beutlingen. The officer joined him, but modestly took his place in the back seat. On the way to the city not far from Gromberg Mr. von Heiwald encountered Mr. Cornelius Steinert, who was headed for Gromberg in the White Horse's little caleche. He recognized his friend from afar. He would have liked to inform him of his fate in a few words, so he turned to the officer.

"Here comes a friend of mine. May I speak a few words with him?" he asked.

The officer regarded the caleche. "Do you mean the gentleman with the blond mustache sitting in the carriage there?"

"Yes, he is a Mr. Steinert, who wants to buy my estate."

"Hmm. You can speak with that gentleman all right. Although I really shouldn't allow you to consult with anyone, I have nothing against it if you wish to speak to Mr. Steinert and nobody else." The amiable officer himself ordered the driver to stop when the two vehicles came together.

Werder greeted Mr. von Heiwald with his usual savoir faire. "You're driving to Beutlingen early, Mr. von Heiwald. I hoped to see you in Gromberg. May I wait for you there? I'd like to make my last survey of the estate today."

"You will hardly be able to wait for me today, Mr. Steinert. I'm not going to return to Gromberg today. I've been arrested!"

If Mr. von Heiwald had expected that his communication would horrify Steinert, or even cause him extreme astonishment, he was disappointed. His friend remained remarkably calm and composed. "I suspected this morning that something of the sort was in the works," he said. "I wish you luck, Mr. von Heiwald! Now you will finally be in a position to silence certain disgraceful rumors forever."

"Ida said the same thing to comfort me, and she is right! Now I beg you, Mr. Steinert, to drive on to Gromberg. Ida respects you and is fond of you, the way I am. She has complete confidence in you. Maybe they will permit you to speak with her, and then you can bring my dear child a greeting from me. I know that you will be a true friend and comfort to her in her distress."

"You can rely on that, Mr. von Heiwald! Whatever I can do ..."

"I believe you without any assurances! Goodbye! Forward, driver!"

"Goodbye. We'll soon meet again."

With these words the friends parted. Werder continued on to Gromberg.

After her father had left her, Ida had remained alone with Commissar Dunkelword in his study. The second official kept watch over the servants so that they could not disturb the search of the house, while Dunkelword took his seat at the baron's desk in order to begin immediately with an examination of his papers. With respectful courtesy he invited Ida to keep watch over his actions. It was, he said, a painful duty to rummage around in another's papers and money, and he would be very much relieved if the daughter of the house would check what he was doing.

A quarter of an hour might have passed when footsteps resounded in the corridor outside. The door opened and Werder stepped into the room.

"Thank God you're finally here!" cried Ida.

She had waited so eagerly for her friend, from whom she hoped to receive help, advice. She hurried toward him, unconsciously following the impulse of her heart when she grasped his hand and leaned against him.

He gently squeezed her hand. "Pull yourself together, dear, dear Ida! We are not alone!" he said quietly, tenderly. Almost ashamed, she drew back.

Commissar Dunkelword was too well-trained an official to betray even by a glance his amazement at the tender reception the daughter of the murderer had given to his superior.

He greeted Werder with a respectful bow.

"Your orders have been carried out to the letter, inspector," he said. "Mr. von Heiwald was arrested with all possible consideration and is on the way to Beutlingen. The servants are being watched over by Sergeant Letke. I have begun examining the papers in the presence of the young lady."

"Thank you, my dear Dunkelword. Everything is going splendidly. Please be so kind as to leave me alone with the young lady for a few minutes."

The official left obediently.

Ida thought a terrible dream was torturing her when she heard the way Dunkelword addressed Werder. Inspector! Was it possible? Steinert, her father's friend and favorite, the man to whom her trust and heart were drawn so rapidly because she thought she had recognized his noble humanity—he was the feared inspector! He had sneaked into this hospitable house under a false name, he had trickily obtained the father's trust, the daughter's love, in order to engage in base spying! Yes, it was possible, it was only too certain! Under this frightful blow her strength failed. She teetered, she started to swoon, she would have collapsed if Werder had not caught her in his arms. His touch brought her back to life. She tore herself loose; with deep repugnance she pushed him back.

"Get away from me! Don't dare to touch me!" she cried with a cutting voice. Her eyes blazed—Werder had never suspected that they could express so much hatred, so much contempt.

"Ida!"

"You're wasting your efforts, inspector! Now that I know you, you'll no longer be able to play the spy!" Cold and cutting though the tone of her voice was, still her heart was almost broken with the most profound pain. Her eyes filled with tears, and her artificial composure left her. In pain she cried out, "My God, this is too terrible. I can't bear it!" She hid her face in the cushions and wept bitterly.

Werder was deeply shaken. A tear appeared in his eye as well. For a long time he didn't dare to disturb his beloved in her pain, but finally he approached her. "Ida, I beg you, listen to me! Just grant me a few words!" he said, beseeching her quietly, tenderly.

A deep, convulsive sob was her only reply.

"You must hear me, Ida! You mustn't condemn me unheard. After all, I'm no less unhappy than you are. I love you, Ida, my heart belonged to you from the first moment that I beheld you in the forest, and still I was condemned to be your enemy. I didn't dare tell you who I was. A terrible duty, my oath, commanded me to suppress my feelings, no matter how much my heart bled. I had to pursue your father, against whom the weightiest evidence was present, step by step, even though I knew that in so doing I was destroying my own happiness. Ida, I was victorious in the terrible battle of my conscience between duty and love! The official remained true to his oath and his honor, sacrificing himself in the process. You may hate him as an enemy, but you mustn't despise him!"

He grasped her hand. She withdrew it, but not hastily, as she had before. She looked at him with her large dark eyes, in which there appeared the expression of infinite pain. With gentle reproach she asked, "Do you really think my father is a murderer?"

"No, Ida, thank God, no! I considered him the murderer when I first called on you. With a bleeding heart I sought evidence of his guilt, I thought I had found it, and then…but I mustn't tell you all that today, but I may give you this comfort: your father is innocent, and tomorrow he will be with you again. In the last few days you have seen me so merry and gay, so inexpressibly happy! I could be that way, Ida, because in my search for evidence of the guilt of the man whom I would have liked to love as a father, I found evidence of his innocence."

"And still you had him arrested?" asked Ida, but there remained scarcely a note of reproach in her words; indeed, she allowed Werder to retain her hand, which he had grasped again and kissed.

"It had to happen, just to prove his innocence. Upon my request, which I had made when I still considered him guilty, the arrest was ordered. In spite of that, perhaps I would not have allowed this order to be executed if I hadn't believed that Mr. von Heiwald would gladly tolerate a few hours of arrest if in so doing his name would be freed of any blemish. For this reason I am also undertaking the search of the house. Your father's money and letters will produce the complete proof of his innocence. If he had handed them over voluntarily to the court, doubts might have arisen as to their accuracy, but now they must die away. Enough, dear Ida, I won't press you any longer to bestow your pardon on me. I have great hopes for the future."

The luminous gleam in her eye told him better than any words could do that she had pardoned him. With a relieved mind and a light heart he could now devote himself to his important official business. With the assistance of Commissar Dunkelword he carried out the search of the premises with painful thoroughness. He checked all of Mr. von Heiwald's papers, giving special attention to the examination of his estate and account books. These were packed up for conveyance to Beutlingen, along with the proprietor's gray hunting coat and all of his cotton stockings. Several hours passed before the thorough work was finished. It was almost noon when Werder took friendly leave of Ida, in order to return to Beutlingen with the two policemen.

In the meantime Mr. von Heiwald had been received with great courtesy by Mayor Wurmser and placed in a back room, where he, as the mayor said, would remain until it would be possible for Inspector Werder to carry out the interrogation himself.

The hours passed by with leaden slowness for the captive. Finally he was informed that the inspector was awaiting him in the mayor's office. That he was no less astonished than Ida when he recognized that the same Steinert that he had become so fond of had been transformed into the feared police inspector, hardly merits mentioning, but he quickly gained his composure. Bowing to the official with mock courtesy, he said:

"I can scarcely express here my admiration for the skill with which you played the role of a friend of my family, inspector, nor for the way you certainly faithfully put down in writing many an unconsidered and now already forgotten remark made by me or my daughter. At any rate I owe the considerate treatment which up until now I have received to the inspector's kindness, which probably is intended as thanks for the hospitable and cordial reception Mr. Steinert received in my house."

Werder took the reproach lying in these words very calmly.

"You are angry with me, Mr. von Heiwald," he responded amiably, "and you have every right to be. I hope, however, that you will soon be convinced that you are doing me an injustice. I beg you now to forget your annoyance and to answer all of my questions freely and candidly, even those that might seem irrelevant to you. But consider in so doing that the scribe will write down your answers and therefore that every word you speak is of importance for you and perhaps for others."

The interrogation began. Mr. von Heiwald answered calmly and clearly all the questions directed to him about his relationship with Mr. von Scharnau. He narrated the events already sufficiently known to our readers without concealing his own violent behavior, which had impelled him to insult the young man.

"You didn't wish to see Mr. von Scharnau again and therefore went out hunting before his arrival. Do you happen to remember what clothing you wore that day?" asked Werder when Mr. von Heiwald had finished his story.

"Very clearly. I had my light, brown summer coat on."

"Are you sure that you did not wear the old gray hunting coat with the green collar lying there on the chair?"

"Positive. It was a very warm day, and therefore I wore the light coat."

"Did you wear blue wool stockings?"

"Yes. That's what I always wear."

"Did you wear boots or shoes?"

"Boots. When I go hunting, which often takes me into the swamp, I always wear high hunting boots."

"In what direction did you go?"

"I can't tell you exactly any more. I wandered around in every direction in the woods, the meadows and fields. That day I was less intent on good hunting than on not running into Mr. von Scharnau, so I avoided only the short path to Beutlingen and the road from Beutlingen to the Star Tavern."

"Did you meet anyone in the woods?"

"Only one of my laborers by the name of Schurre."

"Now we come to another question, and I beg you to search your memory thoroughly before answering. About two weeks ago you were in Weidenhagen and there you paid Wolfgang Müller & Company a sum of money for various agricultural implements. Do you remember this?"

"Certainly. It was 523 talers."

"What denominations did you use to make the payment?"

"I remember that precisely too. I paid out five one-hundred-taler notes and change. At Mr. Müller's wish I signed my name on them."

"Are these perhaps the notes?"

"I think so; at least the signature looks like mine."

"Do you have any more one-hundred-taler notes in your cash box at home?"

"No."

"Did you perhaps have some and give them to Innkeeper Grawald?"

"No, quite the contrary! Grawald gave me the five notes a short time before for a consignment of rye."

"You are positive about this?"

"Quite positive. In my account book the day of payment must be noted. In the margin, if I'm not wrong, I wrote the numbers of the notes. I always do this with big notes, and I don't think that I would have omitted to do so on this occasion."

The inspector took the account book, thumbed through it, and soon found the notation and the numbers written in the margin. "Correct, Mr. von Heiwald," he said very kindly. "You confirm what I already suspected, or better, knew. Permit me to ask only one more question. You owe Councilman Hildebrand in Weidenhagen a mortgage of 10,000 talers that you have offered to pay with a week's notice. Is this correct?"

"Yes."

"Did you have the cash at hand?"

"No."

"Where did you expect to get it?"

"A friend offered to lend it to me."

"A friend? May I ask his name?"

"He expressed the wish that I shouldn't mention it."

"He couldn't have imagined that serious grounds for suspicions against you would be inferred from this silence on your part. Believe me, it is of great importance that you answer me. I implore you quite earnestly."

"Well, I don't think Father Grawald will hold it against me if I mention his name. Anyhow, I didn't promise him not to."

"So it was Father Grawald! I thought so! Did he already hand the money over to you?"

"No, but he promised me I can collect it any time."

"Are you certain of that?"

"You don't really know Father Grawald, inspector, or you wouldn't ask this question. He is an honorable man, and for him his word is as binding as a legal contract."

"Mr. von Heiwald, I thank you. Your testimony has had precisely the result I expected. I can inform you with a joyous heart that the present charges against you are completely withdrawn in every respect. If you wish, you may freely return to Gromberg immediately. However, you would place me considerably in your debt if you would voluntarily play the role of a prisoner for a few more hours until the real murderers of Mr. von Scharnau are arrested. It's possible that the culprits could get wind of your release and be perhaps warned by this."

"The real murderers? Is Mr. von Scharnau really dead?"

"He was murdered and robbed! In a few hours I will conduct the shameful murderers to the morass in the Thieves' Heath where the unfortunate man's corpse is entombed. The carriage that is to drive me to the Star Tavern is at the door. Father Grawald himself and his son Andres are the murderers!"

Mr. von Heiwald was deeply shocked by the unexpected news. "Impossible!" he cried. "You are mistaken! You have been deceived!"

"I am completely certain about what I say. We have absolutely irrefutable evidence for the guilt of the murderers."

"Evidence? Didn't you think you had that against me? Were you not convinced of my guilt? Don't deny it—now that I know your position, I know what your examination of Gromberg meant!"

"I considered you guilty, Mr. von Heiwald," responded Werder earnestly. "I don't deny it. That's why I came to Gromberg, and I would have turned you over to the law without mercy if my opinion had been confirmed; but I already told you that all reasons for suspecting you have disappeared. You are free. It depends upon your good will whether or not you will remain a prisoner a few more hours in the interest of the impending investigation."

"I'm free and still there is evidence against me that could deceive the sharp-witted, famous Inspector Werder so much that he considered me the murderer! The evidence found against Grawald, although it may seem to be foolproof, may—no, must—also be deceptive. You were unjust toward me, inspector—I implore you don't again be so much against an innocent man, against that fine man, Grawald! He is as little the murderer as I am! I have known him for many, many years. A nobler and better person does not exist. He is incapable of any crime, let alone murder and robbery."

"Your noble confidence increases the respect I feel for you, Mr. von Heiwald, but it doesn't shake my conviction. This worthy Father Grawald for many years played the role of an honest man with wonderful success, and in secret piled up one crime after the other. He is the murderer of Saworski the cattle dealer; with his sons he committed that murderous mail robbery in which your brother the senator was almost a victim. Mr. von Scharnau was also murdered and robbed by him and Andres. While he harvested the fruits of his crimes, with incomparable cunning he shifted the blame onto you and your brother. He is the source of all the shameful rumors spread against you. But enough, Mr. von Heiwald. I know that I will hardly be able to convince you, as I am not able now to show you all the evidence that speaks irrefutably for Grawald's guilt. Time is getting on: I have to go to the Star Tavern to arrest the guilty pair. Will you remain voluntarily in apparent arrest for a few more hours?"

"But Ida—"

"She knows that her father is innocent, and that tomorrow he will return happily to Gromberg."

"Then I'll remain."

VIII

On the afternoon of the same day three vehicles pulled up in front of the Star Tavern. In the first of them, Mayor Wurmser's coach, sat the latter and Inspector Werder. The mayor insisted on being present at Grawald's arrest, for the Star Tavern as a hereditary leased property of the City of Beutlingen belonged to its police district.

In the second carriage Commissar Dunkelword had taken his seat along with the two officials from M**, while in the third, a farm wagon, sat the two policemen from Beutlingen and several workmen equipped with picks, spades and shovels.

Father Grawald's eyes widened when he received the unexpected guests, but he called out his hearty welcome to them as cordially as ever: he had no idea what reason had brought these numerous guests to him. He bowed respectfully to the mayor, he shook the inspector's hand amiably as that of an old friend, and courteously invited the commissar and his two companions to enter the parlor, the door to which he dutifully opened. The policemen from Beutlingen and the workmen were shown to seats in the taproom opposite.

In the parlor at a table pulled close to one of the windows sat Professor Ewald. Today he had chosen this seat against his wont to arrange his plants. He had not bestowed his usual attention upon them, for since noon his glance had been fixed more on the road to Beutlingen than on the copious content of his botanical basket. When finally, later than he had thought, the people he had been expecting finally entered, he greeted Werder and Dunkelword with a look of agreement. With Werder he exchanged a friendly, jesting word, and had himself presented to the mayor.

The gentlemen took their seats and Grawald himself brought them the foaming beer and, in accordance with the custom that prevailed in the Star Tavern, sat down among them. "To what do I owe the honor of seeing you today, mayor, and in such a large company?" he asked curiously.

Instead of the mayor Werder answered. "We have come on a peculiar matter, which closely affects one of your best acquaintances. Don't you know that Mr. von Heiwald was arrested in Gromberg this morning?"

"I heard it from a Gromberg worker, but I don't know anything further about the reason for it. Officials from M** are reported to have been there."

"Quite correct. The gentleman here is Police Commissar Dunkelword from M**. You can easily imagine the reason: you yourself warned me against Mr. von Heiwald when I arrived here. Don't you remember? You told me the story of Mr. von Scharnau's disappearance. Now it's all over for this distinguished gentleman: he's sitting in jail accused of murder."

"But is there evidence against him?"

"Certainly. We have come to search for the body of the murdered man in the Thieves' Heath."

"You've come for that reason? But Mr. Steinert, what do you have to do with all this?"

"Enough, friend Grawald. You will understand if I introduce myself. I just assumed the name Steinert. I am Police Inspector Werder from M**."

Suddenly Father Grawald felt quite uneasy. A deep suspicion welled up within him. He looked across timidly at Professor Ewald, who, busily engaged with his plants, seemed not to pay any attention to the conversation taking place at the large guest table. He would have preferred to leave the uncomfortable company of the police inspector, but when he slowly started to rise to his feet, Werder pulled him amiably down on his chair.

"Stay here, Father Grawald," he said. "We have a lot more to talk about. Where is Andres?"

"Outside in the shed. What do you want with him?"

"I have an order to give him from Mr. von Heiwald. One has to be nice to a prisoner. Professor, would you be so kind as to call Andres in?"

The professor was immediately ready to do this favor, but Grawald wouldn't permit him. "I'll call him myself," he said. He jumped up—his only thought was to get out into the open. Now he suspected the fate that awaited him, but he still did not give himself up for lost. If he just succeeded in getting out into the open, in a few minutes he would be in safety in the peat bog. He knew every square inch of it: he knew where he could hide. Any stranger less familiar with the treacherous swamp than he was who would attempt to ferret him out would have to sink into the mire without hope of succor. Just let him get out into the open! But he was held back by an iron hand. "Remain seated, Father Grawald," said Werder firmly. "The professor will find Andres, and bring him here."

The professor exchanged a significant look with Werder and then left the parlor, the two officials from M** following at a sign from him.

Fate drew closer and closer, Grawald felt. Great drops of perspiration appeared on his forehead, and everything was hazy before his eyes. He decided to make another attempt to escape. The opportunity seemed favorable, for Werder's beer mug was empty. He grabbed it. "I'll bring you a fresh mug, inspector," he said in as close to a businesslike tone as he could muster.

"Not yet. Stay here."

That was a command, no longer a friendly request. All doubts faded; now he had to flee, and soon. Grawald was sitting near the door to his bedroom. If he succeeded in reaching it he was saved. The door could be locked from the inside by a heavy iron bolt, a jump out of the window would land him in the garden, and with a few steps he could reach the heath and soon after the swamp. Now what he needed was caution and self-control. He had to seem as unworried as if he had no inkling of the threatening danger in order to be able to take advantage of the first unguarded moment.

"As you wish, inspector," he responded, sitting down again. "Just tell me when you want a fresh mug."

A few minutes passed in deep silence. Werder no longer thought it was worth the trouble of continuing the conversation. He knew that Grawald was on his guard, that he suspected his fate, so that there was no longer any hope that he would make an unconsidered remark. He merely waited for Ewald's return to make the arrest.

The door opened. Conducted by the two officers from M**, Andres entered, his hands cuffed together. Ewald followed him. All eyes were directed toward the prisoner, who was looking around with dull eyes without really comprehending what had happened to him.

Grawald took advantage of this moment. With a powerful leap he reached his bedroom, slammed the door behind him and locked it with the iron bolt.

Werder ran after him. He slammed his shoulder against the door to burst it open, but this was impossible even for his mighty strength. The thick oak withstood his greatest exertions. He heard the window being opened and Grawald leaping out the window into the garden.

"After him! Come on! To the chase! You, Letke, guard the prisoner. The others follow me." With these words he hurried ahead, through the house to the garden.

Father Grawald was still a sturdy, powerful man, and swift of foot. The realization that he could only save himself by the utmost exertion of all his muscles increased his strength. With furious speed he ran through the garden, reached the dense brush of the Thieves' Heath and disappeared in it. When Werder, followed by Ewald and the two officers from M**—the mayor, who was not fond of great exertions, had remained behind to help the sergeant guard the prisoner— came into the garden, the fugitive was no longer to be seen.

"He's gone!" cried Ewald and Dunkelword angrily. "He's reached the woods. There's not much we can do for the time being. How can we find him in the brush?"

Werder smiled. He thought of his hunts in the Far West, where, with an Indian companion at his side, he had followed the spoor of big game through the dense wilderness. How easy it seemed now to follow the trail of the heavy man's footsteps, clearly pressed into the sand. Following them through the woods offered not the slightest difficulty to his trained eye. "Follow me!" he cried to his companions. He hurried forward with such speed that the other policemen soon fell behind, panting.

He reached the brush area. He followed the trail here with the same speed. He never lost sight of the trail for a moment, and soon he saw the fugitive in front of him, hurrying toward the swamp with the greatest expenditure of all his strength.

He probably would have reached his goal if Werder hadn't been in the forefront of the pursuers, but he was not capable of continuing the race against him. He felt his muscles weakening, his speed diminished, and he heard his pursuer coming closer and closer. He would be overtaken in a few seconds if he could not free himself of his opponent. In the moment of the flight in his bedroom he had torn the double-barreled pistol from the wall, where it always hung loaded above his bed. Now he grasped the weapon, cocked it on the run, then stopped, awaiting the enemy. When Werder was scarcely three paces away from him, he shot with a sure hand.

The hammer fell, but the cap failed to ignite. In the next moment a mighty blow of Werder's fist knocked the criminal down unconscious. Ewald, who soon came up panting, could put the handcuffs on him without the stunned man's being able to defend himself.

A few drops of water, which Ewald fetched in a collapsible cup and sprinkled on his face, soon brought Grawald back to consciousness. Now he had to begin his way back to the Star Tavern. With suppressed rage he was forced to listen to the mockery about his vain attempt to escape. He would have liked to murder the would-be professor when the latter told, giggling hoarsely, that shortly before noon, expecting that Father Grawald would offer resistance, he had replaced the caps in the pistol with others that were already used. His rage increased even more when, during the search of the premises of the Star Tavern, which took place immediately after their return, Ewald was the knowledgeable guide who, in the wine cellar, showed the inspector an iron safe hidden in the wall, in which Grawald had secured his fortune.

The house search was finished in a short time. Grawald's account books and money were sealed up and entrusted to Commissar Dunkelword, who stayed behind in the Star Tavern with one of the officers from M**, and then Werder and the mayor with one of the policemen from M** took their seats in the first carriage, Ewald with Andres and the two policemen in the second. The farm wagon followed them with the laborers.

On the way Werder tried several times to initiate a conversation with Grawald, but the latter remained grim and silent. He didn't even respond to the inspector's remarks.

"You're pursuing the wrong course, Mr. Grawald!" said Werder finally with his usual calm amiability. "You won't get anywhere with defiance and stubbornness. The game is up—you can't save anything any more. You know that the bank notes of the murdered Scharnau, the numbers of which we know, were found in your secret safe, to the extent that they were not already circulated. The proof that you and your son Andres committed the murder and robbery is in our hands. There's only one means for you, not to save yourself, but to win a lenient treatment in prison and perhaps some leniency after the sentence is passed. That one means is an open confession. Now the best opportunity for this is being afforded you. Lead us to the place where you hid the murdered man's body."

"I don't know anything. I'm innocent," was Grawald's only answer.

All of Werder and the mayor's entreaties were in vain. Werder tired of the wasted words.

"So you won't say anything, Mr. Grawald!" he said, bringing to a close his repeated urgent entreaty. "You'll see that it's to your detriment. I'll find the murdered man's body without your help. You smile incredulously, but soon I will produce the proof that I am familiar with all your foul deeds."

The carriage stopped at the place near the pine tree where the Gromberg footpath empties into the highway to Beutlingen.

Conducted by the policemen, Grawald and his son were forced to follow Werder, who strode vigorously ahead into the woods.

Suddenly Werder stopped.

"Here's where you murdered him!" he cried, pointing to the ground with one hand and clapping Father Grawald on the shoulder with the other.

Grawald stood as if struck by lightning. The unexpected accurate accusation devastated him. How did the inspector discover the concealed site of the

crime? Then his glance fell upon Andres, who, staring at the ground in embarrassment, did not dare look at his father. He was the cowardly traitor, he and no
one else.

"You betrayed me, you wretch!" he cried, exploding in wild rage.

The words were spoken! The hardened criminal felt what they meant in the
very moment that, following only the inspiration of the moment, he had unthinkingly brought them forth. They could not be taken back.

"You heard, gentlemen, and will testify to it in court, how the murderer has
just accused himself!" said Werder earnestly. "Are you going to continue to deny
it, Mr. Grawald? Conduct us yourself to the spot where you concealed the body.
I'm asking you for the last time!"

"Go to hell, all of you. I'm innocent! I'm not going to say another word,"
screamed Grawald furiously, and stuck to this. Not another word could be gotten out of him. Andres, too, surlily followed his father's mute example.

Werder had to be the one who led the company to the quagmire; on the
way he had noted every tree, every bush with unerring certainty, and he strode
forward, never deviating from a straight line. They reached the quagmire.

"Here is where the body lies in the water," cried Werder.

Again old Grawald cast a furious glance at his son, whom he considered to
be the informer. This time, however, he held his tongue, and remained a mute
witness to the labors that the inspector ordered for finding the body.

Werder had so closely identified the place where the murderers had sunk
their victim into the water that in a short time the laborers discovered the body
and pulled it out of the quagmire. Putrefaction had already distorted the facial
features so much that the mayor could no longer recognize them as Mr. von
Scharnau's. Unaccustomed to such scenes, the man turned away from the grue-
some spectacle with a shudder.

At Werder's order the body was carefully wrapped in blankets they had
brought with them and carried to the farm wagon. At the moment it was impossible to make any further examination as the sun had already sunk and darkness
was fast approaching. Werder conducted his prisoners to Beutlingen, where he
delivered them to the jail and ordered them to be guarded with especial care by
the two officers from M**.

On the same evening, after he had taken cordial leave of the inspector, Mr.
von Heiwald returned happily to Gromberg.

Our story is at an end. We have only a few words to add.

How Inspector Werder became convinced of the erroneousness of his original hypothesis and of Grawald's guilt can be seen in large part from that which
has been narrated. His deeply entrenched opinion was first shaken by a chance
encounter with a laborer by the name of Schurre on one of his walks across the
heath. He heard from Schurre that the latter had encountered Mr. von Heiwald
in the woods on the day Mr. von Scharnau had been murdered. The laborer
remembered perfectly well that on that day his employer had been wearing a light

brown summer coat and high hunting boots. From another laborer he gathered the news that between 11 and 12 o'clock on that day Grawald's carriage had stood for a long time without an occupant on the road to Beutlingen; the horses had been unhitched and tied to a tree with the reins. The contrast between the innocent testimony of the laborer and Grawald's statement at court that he had waited four hours in vain in his carriage for the first time turned Werder's suspicion, harbored against the son, toward the father as well. Thorough investigations, in which Ewald had been especially active and zealous, furnished new evidence.

Through the testimony of various witnesses it was ascertained that on the day of the murder Andres, in a gray woolen summer coat, and with his gun on his back, had gone hunting in the Thieves' Heath, and that Grawald on that day had been wearing shoes and blue woolen stockings. Werder was able to procure a few threads of the wool from which Mr. von Heiwald's stockings had been knitted and from the landowner's gray hunting coat as well. The blue woolen thread found in the woods was much coarser, the black spots on the wool swatches were farther apart than they were on the sample from von Heiwald's clothes; on the other hand, as was ascertained by Ewald, they agreed perfectly with the wool threads from Andres' coat, just as the blue thread agreed with the dye of the wool in Grawald's blue stockings.

With indefatigable zeal Ewald collected new evidence. He ascertained that Father Grawald in the last few years had lent out far greater amounts than he could have earned in an honest way. It had not been easy to determine this, for the cunning criminal had taken care to keep the amount of his fortune secret. It had been lent out in small amounts, and the debtors had had to promise him not to talk about it. As they had generally been in need when good Father Grawald had helped them out with a loan, they attributed his wish to the noble-minded intention of doing good in secret.

The most telling evidence for Grawald's guilt, finally, had come from the discovery of the secret safe in the wine cellar. Ewald had used a quiet hour of the night, long after all the residents of the house had gone to their beds, to use his picklocks. In the safe he found the greater part of the money stolen from Mr. von Scharnau and also a watch with a heavy gold chain, which he immediately recognized from the description that he carried with him, as the watch that had been stolen from Saworski, the murdered cattle dealer.

Even the most cunning criminal eventually commits a foolish action that finally unmasks him. Thus Father Grawald had not been able to bring himself to bury the valuable golden watch and chain in the woods, but preserved them in the secret strongbox that he thought he had concealed so well that no human eye, least of all that of the ridiculous little naturalist, would ever be able to discover it. After Grawald's arrest the evidence increased daily against him and Andres. The blade of the kitchen hatchet that old Friedrich had taken with him fit perfectly in the deep cut in the skull of the slain man. The ropes with which the stones had been tied into the clothes of the corpse to keep it at the bottom of the quagmire had proved to be sections of a line belonging to Father Grawald that, like the hatchet, he always carried with him in his carriage. This was a sensible precautionary measure because of the poor roads, on which it was easy to damage a wheel. A poorly washed blood stain on Andres' gray coat, the precise correspondence between the father and son's footgear and the footprints measured by Werder in the swamp completed the chain of evidence.

In jail Grawald remained true to his system of defiant denial, and refused to answer the questions directed to him by the investigating magistrate presiding over the court of inquiry. He rejected the evidence that continued to accrue against him as inventions of Inspector Werder, who wanted to destroy him in order to absolve Mr. von Heiwald. He stuck to this assertion. He never became entangled in contradictions because he could never be induced to make any definite statement. Even solitary confinement, generally so feared by criminals, had no effect upon his hard, tough mind. He sat almost motionless all day long in his solitary cell.

In the beginning Andres was just as defiant, but his strength soon collapsed. When the magistrate unrolled the whole chain of evidence collected against him, when he told him that the jurors would pronounce him guilty even if he did not confess, but that a repentant confession would perhaps procure a mitigation of his sentence, and when then in his solitary cell his conscience became active; when exhausted after hours of interrogation by day he tossed restlessly on his bunk at night, he could no longer maintain his old defiance. He made a comprehensive confession not only of the murder of Mr. von Scharnau, but also of the other crimes he had committed in the company of his father and his deceased brother.

Grawald with his two sons had slain and robbed Saworski the cattle dealer, and also committed the mail robbery, the victim of which had been the mail guard; finally, with Andres he had slain Mr. von Scharnau. Once he had started to confess, Andres concealed nothing. He even revealed a fourth murder committed against a traveler who had stayed at the Star Tavern, even though the magistrate didn't ask him about this, as no one knew anything about that unfortunate departed, whose name Andres didn't even know.

Calmed by relieving his conscience, Andres went back to jail.

Grawald was called before the judge immediately after the interrogation of his son. The magistrate had Andres' recorded testimony read to him word for word, but even this did not shake the grizzled criminal. He stuck to his denials. He was brought back to jail. When the next morning the turnkey brought him his breakfast gruel, he found him dead on his bed. He had managed in some inexplicable manner to provide himself with a knife, and this with a sure hand he had plunged into his heart.

Andres stuck to his confession. He was condemned to death, but the monarch commuted his sentence to lifelong imprisonment.

Grawald's arrest and the recovery of the body of the murdered von Scharnau were Police Inspector Werder's last official acts. The very next day he returned to M** without visiting Gromberg again. He immediately submitted his resignation.

In vain his brother-in-law, the police superintendent, urged him to remain in the service in which he had distinguished himself so brilliantly. Werder would not be moved. "Never again," he said decisively, "will I work as a policeman. I have learned a terrible lesson. How firmly I was convinced of innocent Mr. Heiwald's guilt! With tireless zeal I collected the evidence leading to his destruction, and if I had not accidentally run across that laborer, Schurre, if I had not been supported by such a clever and active official as Ewald, then perhaps Mr. von Heiwald would today be standing in front of the jury, and a guilty verdict, a death sentence, would be probable in the face of the generally prevailing belief that people had. Never again will I take such a responsibility upon myself!"

He remained adamant, and his resignation was accepted. Ewald became his successor in office.

Werder's small inheritance from his mother was not sufficient to grant him a pleasant existence in the fatherland, and he could advance no claims for a pension. He therefore decided to go to America for the second time. But before his departure his heart urged him to pay another visit to Gromberg in order to take leave of the two people who were so dear to him, to part, reconciled, from them forever.

Some weeks had passed since Werder had seen Ida for the last time. In all this time no news had come to him from Gromberg. He had not written. How could Mr. von Heiwald have found any reason to turn to him!

The coach that bore Werder through the woods on a beautiful day of late autumn rolled slowly along on the poor road of the heath through the grinding sand. When he came to the estate boundary our friend could no longer keep his impatience in check. He left the cumbersome vehicle, and hurried through the estate's paths toward the manor house. There, making his way on the winding paths, he came around an evergreen bush and suddenly stood facing Ida.

"Ida!"

"Werder!"

With a loud cry of joy she flew into his arms.

He didn't go to America. He lives in Gromberg with his charming spouse. Mr. von Heiwald, who was formerly so misunderstood in the whole area, and now is greatly respected, is happy in the happiness of his children and grandchildren.

Auguste Groner
(1850–1929)

Auguste Groner was born Auguste Kopallik in Vienna in 1850. Her father was a civil servant in Vienna's expanding middle class, and Auguste received extensive schooling: she studied painting and music, and traveled widely in Europe. She trained as an elementary school teacher, and taught in Vienna's public schools from 1876 to 1905, when she retired to devote herself completely to her writing. In 1879 she married the journalist and lexicographer Richard Groner, who also came of a civil, servant background. Together they pursued their journalistic, authorial and editorial interests: Richard edited three family newspapers and co-founded a biographical yearbook, and Auguste collected folklore, wrote juvenile fiction, folktales, and detective fiction, and founded two youth newspapers.

Groner was nearly 40 before she turned to crime fiction, writing more than three dozen detective stories, novellas and novels between the late 1880s and 1927. Her social idealism prevented her from developing a detective whose focus was strictly logical and scientific. Her detective would be methodologically brilliant, of course, but primarily he would have to be interested in people, would have to empathize with their suffering and care about their fates.

In a move that presaged G. K. Chesterton's creation of Father Brown, Groner invented Joseph Müller, a police detective more concerned with justice than with the strict administration of the law. As the reader will see in *The Golden Bullet*, an early Müller novella, this philosophy eventually cost him his police career and he became a private detective, although the bafflement of the "secret police" in difficult cases was still the source of most of his work.

Though Müller was Groner's only series detective (appearing in at least thirteen novellas and novels), he was not her only sleuth; she also wrote works featuring both civilian and police detectives who made single appearances. Groner's social idealism gave all her detective fiction a strongly didactic flavor. Because her focus on crime always included its contributory social factors, she expended great energy exploring the nexus of crime and society's outcasts (ex-convicts, nobility who have fallen from grace, ethnic minorities, etc.), primarily the difficulties they face integrating or re-integrating themselves into the Austro-Hungarian empire's rigid and oppressive social system. Though the detection in her detective fiction is solid, her primary gift is as a storyteller, and her best detective fiction is characterized as much by her dexterity in manipulating several plots as by its detection.

The Golden Bullet
by Auguste Groner

"What does the man want?"

"To make a report."

"Show him in."

The servant left the room. Detective Inspector Horn looked at the door impatiently. It was 11:00—the hour at which he was accustomed to being relieved—and yet not only had his colleague not arrived, but duty now called.

Inspector Horn was very annoyed, and in this spirit he received the man whose presence had been announced. The caller was a young man upon whose forehead nature had forgotten the stamp of intelligence. In an attitude of helplessness and fear his little eyes roamed the large bare room and he twisted his hat in his hands.

"Your name?" the inspector bellowed at him.

"Johann. Johann Dümmel."

"And you are—?"

"What am I? I'm Professor Fellner's manservant." The detective inspector suddenly became friendlier. Fellner was an esteemed fellow diner at the White Swan. Had something happened to him?

"What do you want to report?" the police officer asked quickly.

"I don't know whether I should have come, but at home—"

"Yes, get on with it," Horn urged him.

"In short," Dümmel burst out, "my master won't get up."

Horn sprang up and reached for his coat.

"Is he unconscious?"

"I don't know. The door is locked. That never happened before."

"And you know for certain that he is at home?"

"Yes, because I saw him during the night, and besides the key that locks the door is still in the lock, on the inside."

Horn was ready to leave. Just then the colleague arrived who was to relieve him.

"Goodness, it's cold today," the latter remarked, and Horn replied sarcastically, "Well, then, you'll have no objection to my sparing you an investigation. It's about Fellner, otherwise I wouldn't bother. Adieu. But there is one thing you can do: please send a doctor right away to Professor Fellner's house, that's Feldstrasse, number 7."

Thereupon he opened the door and strode, followed quickly by Johann, through the adjoining room. He was already on the threshold when he turned and looked unkindly at a small man, extremely modestly dressed, who sat in the corner in a visibly downcast mood.

"Well, what about it, Müller. Suppose I took you with me?"

"Oh, inspector!" the little man burst out, and his sad eyes lit up.

"If nothing more comes of it, it's at least a little investigation. I know you can use it."

In response, the man seemed about to burst with combined humility and half-suppressed excitement. A moment later the three were climbing into one of the hired carriages located in front of the police station.

"When did you see your master for the last time?" Horn interrogated the servant.

"Last night about 11:00 P.M."

"Did you speak to him?"

"No—I looked through the keyhole."

"Hm! Is that a habit of yours?"

Dümmel turned red, but he seemed to possess a fair amount of refinement, because he was also genuinely indignant and almost became rude.

"It wasn't like that," he growled. "I only did it this once and because I was nervous about my master. He had been very excited for a couple of days. Yesterday evening I went to the theater, like every Saturday. When I came home after 10:30, I knocked on his bedroom door, as I always did, and when he didn't answer I quietly withdrew. As I went through the dark anteroom to my bedroom, I noticed a ray of light coming from the keyhole to the door of the study. That made me wonder, since usually my master isn't up anymore at that hour. So after a bit I crept up and looked through the keyhole."

"And what did you see?"

"He was sitting at his desk. He looked perfectly calm, so I went to bed and didn't worry anymore."

"And why didn't you go in to him?"

"I didn't dare. My master was hot-tempered and didn't like to be surprised while he worked."

"And this morning?"

"I got up at the usual time and went about my duties, laid the table in the dining room and then went to wake my master. When I got no answer, I thought:

'Ah, it's Sunday—and last night he went to bed quite late,' and so I waited until 10:00. Then suddenly I was frightened and went to his bedroom again; this time I didn't just knock, but tried the handle too, and then I found that the door was locked. I pounded and called out for a long time—and when nothing helped, I came to you, inspector."

That was Johann Dümmel's story.

Horn was visibly distressed. But Müller's cheeks had become flushed, and something like secret joy, like expectation and passionate interest shone in his deepset, dark, clever eyes. He laid his nervous hand on the carriage door.

"Not yet," said the inspector.

"No, but at the third house," responded Müller modestly.

"You know everyone's residence?" Horn smiled.

"More or less," came the soft answer—and then the carriage stopped. They got out in front of an elegant small house, built in the villa style like almost all the houses here on the edge of the city.

But this house had three stories. The windows in the third floor were covered. Ordinarily the owner of the house lived up there, but at the moment he was in Italy with his convalescent wife. So for the time being only Fellner and his servant occupied the charming little villa, which was constructed in the Nuremberg style with a heavy door and windows fitted with bull's-eye panes. With its bays and its gables, its front garden and the wide view to the north and south the house made a very nice impression. There was nothing across the street from the villa, and there were no outbuildings; it was merely flanked, left and right, by similar, quiet, elegant villas.

The three men entered the quickly unlocked house. The inspector and the servant strode ahead, and Müller followed slowly. His eyes glided as sharp and quick as lightning over the colorful tile in the entry, over the white stairs, over the carpeted hallway. Once he bent and picked something up, but then he went on, his face calm.

The men had reached a dim anteroom. Johann turned up the gas flame to add to the weak winter daylight. Horn, who had visited the professor before and thus knew his way around, hurried through Fellner's small dressing room and tried to open the high, deeply recessed, darkly stained door to the study, but it would not give way. The key stuck in the enormous lock with its cast iron ornamentation, but in such a way that the bottom part of the wide keyhole was exposed, as Horn noticed when he held a flaring match to illuminate the lock.

"You're right. It's locked from inside. Let's go into the bedroom first," he said. "Johann—a crowbar or a pickaxe! Müller, you stay here and let the doctor in!"

Müller nodded. Johann came back in half a minute with a pickaxe and followed the detective inspector through the dining room. In the door between this room and the bedroom adjoining the study the key that had locked it was likewise on the inside. Just as Horn, after uselessly calling out and pounding, had wedged the blade of the pickaxe between door and frame, the bell rang downstairs. The door to the bedroom burst open with a loud crack. Johann hurried to open the shutters on the windows, and as the second shutter swung open Müller and the doctor arrived on the threshold of the room.

"The bed has not been slept in," thought each of them, and they went on. The door between the bedroom and the study stood open. The shutters at the windows of the study were likewise closed, and the lamp had gone out long before, yet one could see by the weak light that came from the open door to the bedroom a dimly outlined figure that was the professor, sitting at his desk. When Johann opened the shutters in the study, it was clear at a glance that Fellner was dead.

"Most likely succumbed to a stroke," said the doctor, after he felt the icy forehead of the dead man. Then he reached for the now stiffened hand that had already let go the pen in use at the moment of death, tipped back Fellner's head, which had slumped forward, and raised the half-opened eyelid. The eye had dimmed.

The three others stood around the doctor, silent. Horn had become rather pale, and his usually rather impassive face showed genuine distress. Johann was speechless and intensely upset—the tears in his eyes bore witness to this. Müller was unmoved. He looked like someone eavesdropping, someone who sees something the others don't; at least, only that would account for his usually slack features being as strangely tense as if his sallow face were made of metal. When the doctor spoke of a stroke Müller smiled gently, and his eyes were caught by the revolver lying to hand on the desk, but then, as if he were denying something, he shook his head, and finally he started—Horn saw him—at the moment when the doctor pulled the slumped-over body of the dead man upright.

At that moment, Müller said, "He died from a bullet."

"That's right," confirmed the doctor. Everyone could now see a miniscule round hole in the dead man's shirt. When the corpse was righted, the vest had fallen back into its natural position. The doctor pulled the fabric aside, and in the left side of Fellner's chest there was a small bullet wound. Only a few drops of blood had appeared; the wound had bled on the inside.

"He didn't suffer," said the doctor.

"Suicide. Suicide!" murmured Johann, now completely confused.

"Strange. He still had time to lay down the gun," remarked Horn, and without thinking Johann reached for the weapon. Before Horn could stop him he had grasped it. "You should have left the thing lying there. One never knows what might be important here," Horn reproved him, but then the doctor swung around: "You're not thinking of murder?" he cried out. "I see the key in that door too. It must have been locked, or you wouldn't have broken open the other door. Where's your murderer?"

"That's true. I don't see him either. Meanwhile, according to regulations we should leave everything undisturbed. Müller, you locked the front door, didn't you?"

"Here's the key."

"Johann, are there other keys to the apartment?"

"Yes, sir. Just one more, the third has been lost for many months. The one we still have must be in the top drawer of the nightstand in the bedroom."

"Müller, would you please look for it?"

Müller went. He reappeared soon and handed the inspector a key, visibly a duplicate of the one he had just given Horn. But he had found something else in the top drawer of the nightstand—a tortoise-shell hairpin—, and this lay well-protected in his pocket-book. Müller made no mention of it.

Horn turned to the servant.

"Have you left the apartment since yesterday?"

"No. I only left to come get you."

"And you locked up at that time?"

"You saw yourself, inspector—I had to turn the key twice to unlock the door."

Horn and Müller eyed the fellow closely, but he looked so harmless that both dismissed the idea that Johann had only pretended to unlock the door. What for, after all? If he were in league with the murderer, then the latter could get away much more safely during the night. Horn allowed his eyes to roam involuntarily around the room and said, "Well, then, the murderer is either still here, or..."

"Or?" the doctor repeated.

"Or we have a mystery on our hands."

Johann had laid the weapon down again. Now Müller reached for it. A few knowing inspections, and then he held the weapon out to the inspector.

"There's definitely been a murderer here. This revolver hasn't been discharged. All the bullets are still there. And there's no other weapon to be seen," he said quietly.

"Yes, murdered! It's as you say, the revolver is still fully loaded. So, to the hunt!" Horn was more excited than he wanted to let anyone see; that was clear by the way he spoke.

Johann looked around himself fearfully, but when he realized that the inspector and Müller, even the doctor, had begun to examine every corner, every cupboard, in short every place where someone could hide, then he also joined in. A quarter of an hour later the four men again stood in front of the dead man, having discovered nothing and no one in the interim.

"Doctor, I trust you will have the goodness to inform the detective superintendent and to arrange for the transport of the body. Meanwhile, we will look around for an explanation of this murder," said Horn, offering his hand to the doctor.

The doctor left. Müller showed him out.

"Don't you think that that fellow did it?" the doctor asked Müller in an undertone.

"He? No!" responded Müller dismissively.

"He looks too stupid to you. But that stupidity could be an act."

"It's real, doctor."

"What do *you* think? You, who have such a finely developed sense for these things that it recently got you into trouble!"

"So you don't believe me either?"

"About Mrs. Kniepp, the wife of the forest superintendent? No."

"And yet I'm right. She was a perfectly ordinary suicide."

"Restrain both your imagination and your tongue, Müller! You know that rumors about people whom the grand duke has favored are unwelcome. Besides, ... tell me instead what you think about *this* case," the doctor added, and gestured backward toward the rooms they had just left.

"There's a woman mixed up in this."

"So, you're imagining grand stories already? Well, no one will be so sensitive about this case. But just don't disgrace yourself again, my dear Müller—your position hangs in the balance, don't forget that."

And with that the doctor left. Müller smiled bitterly and murmured to himself as he locked up behind the doctor, "By God I won't forget that, and that's why this time I have to repair what the subtle gentlemen of the court call 'the damage' even though it's not. And the Kniepp case isn't closed yet."

When he got back to Fellner's study, he found Johann sitting in a corner, staring dully into space. Horn was bending over a piece of stationery that lay in front of the corpse. The latter must have been busy with it shortly before the shot struck him, since the pen had fallen from his hand as he died. It had left a black mark on the paper, of which only one page had been covered with a delicate, almost feminine handwriting. Horn motioned the detective over, and both of them silently read the following words:

Dear Friend,

I have been challenged with pistols. It is a matter of life and death. My enemy is as bitter as he can be. I, on the other hand, have no wish to die. But doubtless I will be the one to fall, so I have refused the duel. Admittedly I have gained damned little, because the man in question will have a need for revenge that will pursue me nonetheless. I don't dare to spend a minute unarmed anymore; his threats after my refusal lead me to fear the worst. I have a horrible foreboding. I'm leaving early tomorrow. I have freed myself from my duties unter the pretense of settling a pressing family matter. Naturally I will never return. You will, I hope, in my place, dissolve my household here; I'll tell you everything else later, perhaps in person. At the moment I must hurry, I still need to pack. If anything should happen to me, you will know who brought about my death—the terrible man is call....

Here the letter broke off. Müller and Horn looked at each other without speaking, then their eyes dropped to the dead man.

"He was a coward," the detective said coldly, and turned away. Horn repeated mechanically, "a coward." With an expression in his eyes as changed as Müller's, he looked down at the handsome, soft, face of the dead man, framed by golden curls, whom so many girls and women had adored, and whom men as well had been inclined to like because they believed he was a decent fellow.

Quietly, and with a detachment born of their disenchantment, the detective inspector and Müller continued their investigation. In the stove in the bedroom they found a clump of loose ashes. Letters and other trifles had been burned here. Müller carefully retrieved the pieces that were still stuck together, but the writing had become indistinguishable with the exception of a few unconnected syllables. In the wastepaper basket Horn discovered an assortment of envelopes. He collected them and looked especially for any which might bear a postmark from the last few days, but they were all letters that had been mailed more than a month ago. They found nothing else that could give them even the smallest clue with respect to the criminal.

Only the letter of the murdered man made it clear enough that "revenge" had driven him from this world.

Horn took possession of that portentous letter, and then, followed by Müller and Johann, he left the room to examine the rest of the house, as far as that was possible—the third floor was barricaded by a strong iron gate fitted out with an artful lock.

"Is the house locked up during the day?" Horn asked the servant.

"On the street side, yes, but not on the garden side."

"Has anyone ever intruded on that side?"

"Never. The enclosure around the garden is quite high. It's especially secure on the promenade side."

"But there's a gate there."

"Yes."

"Is it usually locked?"

"Almost never with the key. But it has a combination lock that you can only open if you've been shown how."

"You were at the theater last night."

"Yes."

"With the permission of your master, naturally."

"Yes. For a year now he's given me money every Saturday to go to the theater. He was so good to me."

"And when you came home did you enter the house from the front or the garden side?"

"From the garden side. The theater's on the promenade."

"And you didn't see anything unusual? No footprints?"

"No. I didn't see anything. But it occurs to me—the house is always locked at night on the garden side. It was locked last night too, and I found the key— that is, we only have one key to the door on the garden side—in the same hiding place where I always had to leave it when I went out in the evening."

"Where is that?"

"In the first water bucket in the wellhouse."

"You were told to leave it there?"

"Yes, my master wanted it that way. He often went out himself and some-times came home again through the garden."

"And besides him nobody else knew of the hiding place for the key?"

"No one. We've been alone in the house for nearly a year. Who else would find out?"

"When you looked through the keyhole into the study, could you definitely tell that your master was still alive?"

Johann looked up in surprise.

"Well, I couldn't definitely tell, that is, I thought that he was writing or read-ing, but—my God, he was sitting just like that today, after nearly twelve hours," stammered Johann, to whom it seemed horrible, looking back, that he had seen his master last night around midnight sitting at the desk as a corpse.

"He must already have been dead when you came home. Or could a shot be fired without your hearing it?"

"No, inspector, it's as you say," murmured Johann. "But even if the mur-derer had been able to get into the house, how did he get into the apartment?"

"With a third key, a key you didn't know about," Horn replied, and turned to Müller. "It's much more puzzling how Fellner could be shot, since the shut-ters were closed and intact and both doors were locked—with the keys on the inside."

Horn inspected Müller's expression surreptitiously while he spoke, but in that quiet face he couldn't find the least clue to Müller's thoughts. That annoyed and pleased the experienced detective inspector. It annoyed him, because it wasn't inconceivable that Müller already had a clear opinion of this case and was just cleverly keeping it to himself. But it pleased him too, because he secretly hoped that Müller's otherwise unfailing scent for the truth had been daunted by his (admittedly only) mistake—the case of Mrs. Kniepp, which everyone had taken very badly—and that this time he wouldn't be so quick to step forward with an opinion. That was just fine with the inspector, who was a little vain, because how-ever little he wanted to admit it, he was jealous of the growing respect that Müller enjoyed with his superiors.

So he was pleased when Müller responded to his observation by shrugging his shoulders, and the latter was still looking into space, lost in his thoughts, when the doctor reappeared in the company of the detective superintendent, a clerk, and two orderlies. The superintendent ordered the circumstances of the case officially recorded, and soon the dead man had been put on a stretcher to be taken to the hospital under the supervision of the doctor.

Müller helped Horn into his coat and handed him his hat and cane. Only then did Horn notice that the detective himself had given no indication of leaving.

"Well, what about you?" he asked, astonished.

"I was hoping that I might be allowed to remain here for a while?" Müller responded shyly.

"But you know we have to seal off the apartment officially," countered Horn, unpleasantly surprised and thus irritated.

"I don't need anything in these two rooms."

"Don't let us disturb you, my dear Müller," the superintendent interrupted placidly. "We'll give your keen sense free rein *here*."

Müller winced nonetheless. The emphasis told him that even this most powerful superior at his workplace had taken it badly that he had uttered the suspicion that Frau Kniepp went freely to her death, an utterance which had also come to the attention of her husband, who was on good terms with all the highest officials, and had deeply embittered him.

"You'll see, he'll turn up something else," said Horn to the superintendent once they were sitting in the carriage.

"Then let him. It's his job to see even more than we do," the old, stout man smiled contentedly, "and that's why he'll always have to sit in the outer rooms, forced to make faultless obeisance to us."

"Always? I would have thought he'll advance."

"Never," the superintendent said with determination. "He'll move, yes, but always in a circle. He'll never advance the way his intellectual talents deserve. His genius—and the man *has* genius—will always make concessions to his heart in that moment in which it could achieve great things, and success slips away."

Horn stared with surprise at the pleasant old man, so feared among the police.

"I forgot that you've known him so long," he remarked. "What's the problem with Müller's heart?"

"It always makes its presence known at the wrong time, so that he's often been the source of a nasty shock to those who paid for his talents. As long as he doesn't yet have the criminal, he's after him like a bloodhound—and one who never goes astray, and so he's been invaluable for the cause of justice, which is generally blind. Some he's proved innocent, others he exposed as hypocrites. He's nearly an idol to everyone who has someone or something to find out, but unfortunately that goes for the criminals as well, because he nearly always warns them when he's sure of their guilt and has proved it. Maybe he's trying in this strange way to take away the bad taste, the feeling of baseness, that comes with the irresistible urge to investigate evil. But in fact he has badly harmed himself. In the capital they got tired of him and wanted to get rid of him. He has my weakness for him to thank that it never came to that."

"That's right, you brought him with you when you were transferred here."

"But I didn't do him any great favor: in this one year here, where nothing ever happens, he's nearly faded away."

And thus occupied the men rode back to the police station. Meanwhile, the man they talked about sat in Johann's little room and had a short conversation with the servant.

"How long has your master been accustomed to giving you money to go to the theater?"

"The first time was on my last name day."

"Which one? There are so many Johanns."

"Johann of Nepomuk."

Müller took a small calendar notebook out of his pocket and turned the pages.

"It falls on the 16th of May," said the servant helpfully.

"That's right, the 16th of May, it was a Saturday this year."

"Yes, a Saturday."

"And since that time you have been allowed to go every Saturday?"

"Yes."

"How long has the owner of the house been away?"

"Since April—his wife, who has a lung disease, had to go away. They went to Italy."

"So only the two of you have occupied this house since April."

"Only the two of us."

"There's no caretaker?"

"No, a gardener comes in to take care of the garden."

"You don't have any dogs. At least, I saw no sign of them."

"No, the professor didn't like animals. But once he must have intended to buy a dog, because I saw a new dog whip among his things."

"Someone could also just have left that behind. At least, it seems to me that one buys the dog first and then the whip."

"That's true, but no one could have forgotten it here, because at that time my master had no visitors."

"And how do you know that so exactly?"

"That was during the hottest part of summer, when all his colleagues and other acquaintances were out in the country."

"Really? Well, never mind the whip. Tell me instead about any ladies your master knew."

"Ladies? I don't know of any. I only know that my master frequently visited his colleagues, some of whom were married or probably also had other female relatives."

"And the professor never received letters from ladies?" Müller interrupted the garrulous servant.

Johann thought a while, then admitted that, owing to his own poor writing skills, he didn't understand other people's writing very well, but that delicate letters with small and finely-written addresses had come now and then.

"Do you still have the envelope from such a letter?" Müller inquired, but Johann was definite in his denial and added that Fellner, entirely contrary to his habit, had never left these letters lying around.

"And your master definitely never received visits from ladies?" asked Müller, urging Johann with the directness of the question.

Johann appeared decidedly stupid in that moment. In both his simplicity and his unconscious refinement he thought the question a very useless one to ask. He answered it only with a shake of his head. Müller smiled slightly at the fellow's visible discomfort, but didn't allow it to lead him astray.

"Your master has only been here a year. Where did he live before that?"

"In the capital."

"You were his servant then?"

"I've had the post for three years."

"Did the professor have any lady friends when you lived in the capital?"

"He had what was, I suppose, a fiancée."

"Why didn't he marry her?"

"I don't know."

"What was her name?"

"Marie—I don't know the rest."

"Was she beautiful?"

"I never saw her. I only knew about her because my master's friends spoke of her."

"Did your master have many friends?"

"Well, at least he called a lot of people his friends."

"Come with me into the garden."

"Certainly."

Müller took his overcoat and hat and led the way into the garden. It occupied a fairly large area and was broken up by shrubs and groups of trees, their tasteful arrangement evident even though the bare and denuded branches bent heavily under a blanket of snow.

The two men went down the path that led straight to the gate in the fence. It had a secret lock, but it was difficult neither to locate nor to decipher. Müller, at least, got the gate open without any instruction. Beyond it, completely empty at night and during the winter, stretched the promenade, leading on the one side to the city and on the other to the main road into the countryside. It was a well-preserved boulevard, lined on both sides with trees and footpaths and it took one, after a half-hour's walk, to a little village in which the grand duke possessed a charming and well-used hunting lodge. For this reason, the village had additionally been provided with a train station, at which, admittedly, only slow trains or specials stopped.

Müller disliked exerting himself in useless speculation, and therefore left the gate and the promenade and began to search the garden, first in one direction, then in the other. Nowhere did he find even the smallest trace of a night intruder.

"Which water bucket is it where you used to keep the key to this door?" he asked, gesturing toward the door from the house to the garden.

"The first one on the right. Watch out, there's a nail sticking out of that post there where the wind tore away a piece of wood yesterday—"

The warning came too late. Müller's sleeve sported a gaping tear even as Johann spoke; the detective had already plunged his hand to the bottom of the bucket, a movement which took very little effort since this bucket hung much lower than the others. Annoyed, the detective asked for a needle and thread in order to repair the damage at least enough to get home.

"Oh, you don't want to sew it up. I'll lend you my extra winter coat," Johann offered in a friendly fashion. "I'll carry the torn one home for you; I'm not staying here alone, it's much too horrible for me. I'm going to stay with a friend; you can find me there any time, as often as you need me. You can take the apartment key with you at the same time and leave it with the police."

Johann had become garrulous again as he and Müller went up the steps. The detective, whose sewing skills were pitifully bad, was in complete agreement with the suggestion. He merely wondered how Johann had come to possess such an elegant coat, and put his thought into words, whereupon Johann began to sing the praises of his master again and showed Müller in detail a goodly number of articles of clothing, the possession of which he owed to Fellner's generosity. At the same time he gathered up all sorts of necessary items and packed them, finally declaring himself ready to go. He could not be dissuaded from carrying Müller's torn coat. Müller finally gave in. With much to-do they locked up the apartment and the house, and left for the center of town. Müller lived there in the police station.

As they walked across the main plaza, it occurred to Johann that he had no tobacco with him. He was a passionate smoker and moreover had many days of forced idleness ahead of him, so he stepped into a tobacco shop to resupply himself with that dispeller of cares. Another customer had to be there, too, judging from the large mouse-gray mastiff wandering around in front of the shop. The dog was unafraid, almost overfriendly toward Müller, and he seemed to have the soul of a body-servant, because he not only let Müller pet him and rubbed his great head against him, but almost refused to be separated from Müller when Johann came out of the shop and the two men turned to leave. They had gone a fair distance when a whistle sounded behind them and the dog, whose ears pricked up quickly, became restless. Still, he wouldn't leave Müller until a strong voice called out "Tristan" repeatedly. Müller looked around him briefly and saw that Tristan's master was a well-built man in an elegant fur coat. It was impossible to make out a face at this distance and through the drifting snowflakes, and Müller wasn't interested anyhow; his mind was full of thoughts, all clamoring for attention. After Johann had told him his new address and added that he would pick up his coat when time allowed, the two men went their separate ways.

* * *

The next day the following announcement appeared in the legal columns of the city's daily newspaper.

The Golden Bullet. *Scarcely did we announce with great sorrow the death of a bloomingly lovely lady, when we must inform our fellow citizens once again of a strange and inexplicable circumstance. Professor Paul Fellner, a member of the faculty at our preparatory school, was found dead at his desk yesterday. His death was first thought to be suicide, since the doors and windows were locked fast from the inside and one of the former had to be broken down in order to reach the dead man. A revolver also lay to hand.*

But this revolver still contained all its bullets, as the gentlemen from the police commission soon confirmed, and another gun could not be discovered. Yet the corpse had a bullet wound in the left side of the chest.

The strangest part occurred at the autopsy. It is nearly unbelievable, but the bullet which brought about the death of Professor Fellner was made of gold.

We are faced with a complete mystery. Only one thing appears sure: this murder was an act of revenge.

That was the report in the newspaper.

The whole city busied itself with the strange case. A gentle excitement even permeated the police headquarters. The official rooms were full of talk of the golden bullet and the rooms locked from the inside. In the waiting rooms servants, guards, and citizens who had come to report things all put their heads together.

Müller, who performed even more quietly than usual the clerical duties for which he was occasionally used, was passing through Horn's office the next afternoon with a bundle of files for his patron, Detective Superintendent Bauer. Horn, whom Müller had visibly avoided since yesterday, scrutinized the latter as he went. He saw only the protruding yellowish ears, the spare hair on the detective's uncommonly broad skull—but just then, he made an observation that startled this practiced observer: Müller's usually bowed head shot up into the air, the yellowish ears went suddenly blood-red, and the hand carrying the papers began to tremble so much that the papers rattled. For one moment Müller stood still, rubbed his forehead with his right hand and murmured, "The dog—the dog." His quickly moving thoughts obviously blinded him to everything around him, but then he recovered himself and went quickly into Bauer's office. When he came out again after a while, he was as pale and quiet as ever, and as he shut the door he left behind him a jealously upset Horn.

"The dog, the dog," Horn murmured to himself again and again that afternoon, but despite all his ruminations he did not know what to make of it. Toward evening he went home in a bad mood.

We find Müller in his office. As he does every evening, he is busy putting away the books and files that were used that day. When he has tidied everything and is reaching to turn off the gas lamp, his glance falls accidentally upon the blotting pad that Horn uses, and then he looks at it more carefully and finally breaks into loud laughter. What has he seen?—on the white paper, in many different styles of writing, the same phrase, again and again. It's not a woman's name, such as the smitten everywhere have tenderly sought to immortalize—but rather, written about a dozen times: "the dog."

* * *

Days had gone by. Fellner had been buried. The court had secured the possessions of the murdered man, and summoned his heirs. Fellner was not rich, his affairs were in perfect order, and thus the estate could be dealt with quickly. Until its disposition Fellner's apartment remained under judicial lock and key.

There was nothing else to be done: the court officials, who had been in the apartment repeatedly, had not been able to discover anything new. The murderer must have felt perfectly safe.

A day after the appearance of the newspaper article already mentioned, Müller went to Bauer and asked for a leave of absence.

"For the Paul Fellner case?" the detective superintendent asked, with his incomparable calm, and Müller responded affirmatively. In two days he was back again. He had brought nothing besides a solitary page of notes.

"Marie Dorn, married name Kniepp," was written in his notebook, and next to it were some numbers which referred to the dates of the young woman's marriage. They made it clear that Marie Dorn had been the wife of the grand duke's forester for about two years. And, as Müller discovered during the days that followed, about a year ago Professor Paul Fellner had had himself transferred to the city which lay scarcely a half-hour from the residence of the young and beautiful forester's wife, who had once been his beloved. And in this city, Fellner had found himself housing in the quiet neighborhood closest to the grand duke's hunting lodge, had not cultivated the acquaintance of any ladies, but had become a passionate tourist, and had finally, since the time that he alone occupied the house, sent his servant to the theater every Saturday. And every Saturday Forester Kniepp's bowling club met at the other end of the city, from which event he was accustomed to return home only after midnight with the slow night train.

Meanwhile, hours of fond memories could be reenacted in Fellner's apartment, and there was nothing to prevent the professor from accompanying his beloved lady home through the walled garden and the deserted promenade, which, as we have heard, led one to the grand duke's hunting lodge. And once—once, Johann had found a dog whip in his master's waiting room, and the forester, Leo Kniepp, possessed a magnificent mouse-gray mastiff, who could scarcely be persuaded to disattach himself from people who wore Fellner's cast-off clothing! And in the nightstand of the murdered man was a tortoise-shell hairpin, and in the vestibule of his house a bluish mother-of-pearl glove button, one of the sort which had become fashionable this winter as a result of the scarcity of mother-of-pearl manufacturers and which every elegant lady thus aspired to wear. Mrs. Marie Kniepp was an elegant lady, and precisely this lady, some days before the professor was murdered, had fallen from the third-story window of her apartment and since that day, her husband, just as sensitive as he was passionate and eccentric, had not been the same.

Exactly a week after the murder it was—and therefore a Saturday again—when a merry dance of snowflakes took place on the capricious steep roofs, gables, and oriels of the ducal hunting lodge. The weathervanes creaked, and the old trees in the park shook their mossy heads over the mad wind.

An old peddler had fled the ever more angrily howling storm for the shelter of the lodge wall. He walked alongside it so closely that one could not perceive him despite the light from the snow. Finally he disappeared completely behind one of the huge pillars which protruded every twenty paces from the magnificent age-darkened wall. But from time to time his head could be seen; it had the attitude of someone keeping a lookout for something.

The dark thoughtful eyes looked indifferently down toward the village which spread itself along the side of the lodge opposite the city and whose most remarkable building was the small train station. The peddler's glance lingered often upon that station and the lights wandering to and from it. But it was most frequently drawn to the gate which broke the semi-circular facade of the wall here. It was a high, cast iron gate, upon whose baroque decorations the snow lay, and behind whose openings the sizeable body of a dog, wandering back and forth, occasionally appeared. The dog was a large, mouse-gray mastiff.

For a long time the peddler stood almost motionless behind the pillar, then he drew out his watch. "It's time," he murmured to himself, and looked down toward the train station again, where the traffic had begun to increase.

At that moment the noise of a door opening became audible, and then steps came crunching through the snow. A man, clearly a servant, opened a small gate next to the big gate for another man.

"Will you be returning with the night train, sir?" he asked respectfully.

"Yes," the gentleman replied, and in a friendly fashion he pushed away the dog, which was trying to accompany him.

"Come in, Tristan!" the servant called out, and pulled the dog back, bowed to his master, who waved briefly to him, closed the small gate and went back to the house.

The forester struck off in the direction of the train station. He walked slowly, with bowed head and uneven steps. He did not look like someone who is happy to be going out for amusement, and yet he was going to his club.

A half hour, perhaps, had passed since the departure of the train, when the listener stepped out of his hiding place and went noisily past the gate. What he expected, happened. The dog went for the gate, barking loudly. But from a large leather bag, which he carried on a stick over his shoulder, the peddler took out a silk gentleman's scarf and held it out to the dog and the animal quieted immediately. Tristan became completely gentle, allowed his huge head to be stroked and appeared to find it entirely in order that the stranger rang the bell.

The same fellow who had accompanied the forester appeared from a stately wing of the lodge. The peddler managed to look so frozen and at the same time so dignified that the young man did not dare to send him away. On the other hand, maybe he only let him in because he hoped for a little diversion.

"Who do you want to see?" he asked, nonetheless.

"The chambermaid of the deceased mistress."

"Oh, … you know?"

"Yes, I know of the misfortune that happened here."

"And you think Nanette might have all sorts of things to sell?"

"That's it, that's why I'm here. With my cigar holders and the other odds and ends I have I won't do much business here, so close to the city."

"Cigar holders? Well, maybe we'll be able to do a little business after all. Come on, then. My, look how trusting the dog is with you!"

"He must be like that with everyone. Not a watchdog!"

"Oh, now there you are wrong. Tristan is usually only so forthcoming with people he has seen a lot. I'm very surprised that he's letting you go up to the house without a fuss."

And with this conversation the two had reached the steps to the entrance. The peddler held the servant back.

"Tell me, where did she fall?"

"From the last window up there."

"And was she dead on the spot?"

"Right away. At least, she was unconscious when we came down."

"Was the master at home?"

"Oh yes. It happened in the middle of the night."

"In a fever, right?"

"Yes."

"Had she been sick long?"

"No. She took to her bed that day all right, but we thought she was only temporarily indisposed."

"Yes, that sort of thing often develops surprisingly fast," the old man remarked with an air of wisdom, and added, "this case has caused a sensation throughout this area, and I would be very grateful if you could tell me a little about it, naturally only what you can mention as a loyal servant. My customers would be very interested."

"You already know everything anyhow," remarked the servant, visibly annoyed that there was nothing left for him to tell that could affect the peddler's gratitude. "There are no secrets here. Everyone around here knows that our master and mistress lived in the most wonderful harmony with each other, and even if there was a small disagreement on that tragic day, it was complete coincidence and definitely had nothing to do with the mistress's being upset."

"So there was an argument after all?"

"Is there talk of one?"

"I've heard things to that effect. And the argument has even been called the cause of the suicide."

"Stupid gossip," the servant fumed.

His genuine distress just then made quite a favorable impression on the old peddler. During this conversation they walked down a corridor; now the servant was laying his hand on a doorhandle.

"Will I be able to talk to Miss Nanette alone?"

"Alone? Oho—I'm her fiancé."

"I know that," the stranger said, who appeared to be very well informed about relationships and happenings in this house, and added, "and I'm an old man. I only meant whether any of the other servants would be present?"

"I can keep the cook away, if you want."

"A third party isn't good for business," the old man remarked, and then they went in. It was a cozily decorated and pleasantly warm room. There were two people in it, a pretty young woman and an old woman. Both looked at the old man astonished.

"Who have you brought us there, Georg?" asked Nanette.

"This man is a peddler and might have some things we can use. You can both take a look at his wares."

"Now, Lene, you need a thimble," remarked Nanette, and the cook waved the peddler over to her.

"Well, show us, what do you have?" she said in a friendly but condescending way, and so the old man dug his wares out of his pocket. There were thimbles and scissors and colorful ribbons as well as all sorts of soaps and pomades, brushes and combs, smoking supplies and other things enticing one to buy. As the women, always eager to shop, were selecting various articles, they noticed how the old peddler leaned against the stove, shivering from the cold, and they felt sorry for him. "Sit down," Nanette invited him, and she pushed a chair over to him. Lene got up to bring him something warm.

The peddler looked meaningfully at Georg and the latter nodded.

"This fellow wants to see what the master gave you from the mistress's wardrobe," he said to his betrothed.

"Are you interested in buying such things?" Nanette turned to the peddler.

"For the moment I only want to look at them, if you don't mind."

"I would be glad to be rid of them. But I'm not going up there, I'm much too afraid."

"Well, if you want, I'll get them," Georg offered, and when Nanette nodded in agreement he went.

Scarcely had the door shut behind him when the peddler began to undergo a remarkable transformation. His head, bowed with age, shot up, and his bent frame straightened itself with youthful elasticity.

"Do you love your fiancé?" he asked Nanette, who was backing away in astonishment. Finally she stammered, "Yes. Why do you ask, and who are you?"

"Never you mind about that, dear child, but just answer me every question, the plain truth, otherwise it might occur to me to tell Georg that he's not the first man you've loved."

"What do you know?" she whispered, terrified.

The peddler laughed. "Oho, he's jealous. Well, all the better for me. The forester was jealous too, right?" Nanette stared fixedly at him, horrified.

"So, the truth—and make the other two go away, I have to talk to you *alone*. You'll *have* to arrange that, otherwise I'll tell Georg about the handsome cooper's apprentice in Moor Street, or Franz Schmid, or—"

"Be quiet, for God's sake, be quiet. I'll do anything you like."

Pale and trembling the girl sank down onto her chair, as the peddler, once again old and tired, went back to the stove. By the time Georg came into the room with a large traveling-basket, Nanette had recovered enough to busy herself unpacking the toiletries her mistress had given her.

"Please go and keep Lene in the kitchen," Nanette asked Georg with well-feigned evenness. "She could make us some tea."

Georg smiled understandingly and went.

"I'm primarily interested in your dead mistress's gloves," the peddler said, once they were alone again.

Nanette looked at him, surprised, but, still intimidated by his threats, she hunted among the various boxes and packages for the one that contained the gloves. Soon they lay in front of the old man, who began to examine them. Finally he shook his head. "There must be some more gloves there," he said with certainty, and so Nanette hunted anew, and found—she wasn't surprised that they were there, merely that he knew they were—yet another narrow box, this one containing fine leather gloves. They were gray Danish gloves, upon which there gleamed bluish mother-of-pearl buttons. Three pairs lay in the carton, one had been worn, and on one of these a button was missing.

"These," said the peddler, and lay them aside, and then he asked, "Your mistress often took walks alone, didn't she?"

The girl's pale face suddenly became intensely lively, and she stammered, reddening, "You know about that?"

"You do too, I see. Did you know *everything?*"

"Everything," Nanette murmured.

"So it was you and Tristan who always accompanied the lady on her walks?"

"Yes."

"I thought as much, she would have had confidantes. So, and what do you think about this murder?"

"The professor," the words burst from Nanette. "Yes—yes—what am I supposed to know about that?"

"The forester was probably desperate when he learned of the relationship?"

"He still is."

"And how did he behave after the—let us say, after the accident."

"It was as though he was out of his mind."

"I've heard that he looked after his business nonetheless, that he traveled."

"This time not for business. Otherwise he was often gone for weeks on business—"

"And on those occasions your mistress was especially inclined to go on these outings?"

"Yes," Nanette whispered.

"Well, and this time?" the peddler continued. "Why did the forester go away this time?"

"He had some personal business to do in the capital."

"Do you know this to be certain?"

"Yes. He even went twice. I think he just couldn't stand it here anymore and was trying to distract himself. He even went to the casino today."

"And *when* did he go away?"

"The first time just after the mistress's funeral."

"And the second time?"

"Two or three days after he returned."

"How long was he gone the first time?"

"Just one day."

"Good. Now, get hold of yourself. I'm going to fetch Georg by telling him that you've become unwell. Naturally, you are to say nothing about our private conversation. How do I find the kitchen?"

"Turn right, and it's the last door in the corridor."

The peddler went. Nanette sank down upon the closest chair. She was completely confused. Georg found her pale, but not in serious condition, and thought it was entirely natural that the memory of her unlucky mistress should have caused her to become indisposed. He invited the old man to come back during the next few days, before the now unnecessary Nanette was to leave the household. Thereupon the peddler sold a few things to the cook, drank a glass of tea that Lene pressed upon him, and took his leave.

When he was halfway from the lodge to the town and found himself completely alone, he took off the beard and the wig and used snow to wash the false wrinkles off his face. A quarter of an hour later Detective Müller, burdened with a large carrying-bag, walked into the village train station, into which the night train shortly thereafter thundered. He got into a compartment and rode to the capital.

By midnight he had reached his destination; he checked into a second-class hotel, and left it the next morning accompanied by suspicious glances on the part of the staff, for a traveler so constantly in motion necessarily had to have something unpleasant either ahead of him or behind him.

Müller went to police headquarters right away and requested the guest lists from the hotels for the twenty-first of November. Mrs. Kniepp had been buried on the twentieth. He quickly found what he was looking for. "Forester Leo

Kniepp" from * had stayed in the Hotel Imperial on the twenty-first of November. Müller went to the Hotel Imperial, where he was known from an earlier case. After a few questions he knew what had brought the forester to the capital.

Kniepp had had dealings with a goldsmith.

Müller was pensive too, by the time he, having been to see the goldsmith, once more boarded the train that took him home. He had a short conversation with Bauer, who subsequently gave him the golden bullet and the key to the murdered man's apartment and himself got ready to go out. An hour later the detective superintendent and the detective met in the garden of Fellner's house. Bauer had come from the promenade side. Müller had explained to him the mechanism of the lock on the gate. They went up to the apartment together, which naturally proved to be extremely uncomfortable and icy cold.

This circumstance did not bother the two men, who were all too occupied with their errand. Above all they inspected in the most exacting fashion the two doors that had been locked. The keys still stuck in both, on the inside. They were large, rough keys of the sort that are used with high, old German doors of a certain style with deep grooves and beautiful, wrought iron decorations. Indeed, the whole villa had been built in this pleasant, solid fashion. After the locks had been examined, Müller lit the lamp that hung over the desk and closed the shutters.

Initially Bauer had smiled and shaken his head over the actions of his young protégé, but he wasn't smiling any more; suddenly he understood what Müller was doing. The latter sat down at the desk and looked intently at the door directly across from him, which led to the dressing room.

"It's true," he said, and took a deep breath.

Bauer, who while watching Müller had sunk down upon a couch, jumped up. "Through the keyhole?" he cried out.

"Through the keyhole," Müller answered.

"That's hard to believe."

"Shall we try it out?"

"Do it."

By now the jovial old policeman was breathing more heavily, too. Müller took a small roll of paper and a small pistol from his pocket. He unrolled the paper and fastened it with thumbtacks to the high back of the chair on which he had been sitting earlier, and where Fellner had met his death. On the paper was the target-practice outline of a French soldier.

Suddenly Bauer raised an objection. "But the key was in the keyhole."

"Yes, but in such a way that the beard was turned either to the right or the left. Johann saw the ray of light through the hole, and could himself see through into the room. When the murderer put the mouth of the pistol into the keyhole, the person who sat here was directly in the line of fire of the shot. The murderer didn't need to aim."

Bauer's objection had been laid to rest. Müller continued evenly, looking into space like a clairvoyant: "The murderer, bent on revenge and disturbed to the point of madness, found Fellner here after the latter refused to meet his challenge to duel. He slipped into the house and the apartment. He must have known exactly what the household arrangements were here, and knew that the professor, whom he had come to know as a coward—"

"A coward! Is a fellow a coward when he doesn't want to duel with a madman?" Bauer interrupted the detective. But Müller merely looked up, startled, and said with certainty, "Fellner *was* a coward."

"Then you know more than you've told me."

Müller nodded. "That's true," he admitted, smiling, "but I can only tell you more when I have all the proof in my hands."

"And meanwhile the villain gets away."

"He has no idea I'm after him."

"Now, be smart about this, Müller."

"Forgive me my reticence, even if I insist upon it with you. I don't want to be cast as a dreamer again."

"As in the Kniepp case."

"As in the Kniepp case," the little man repeated with a strange smile. "Allow me to make sure of everything first. Tomorrow I'll tell you."

"Tomorrow, then."

"Can I go on speculating now?"

Bauer nodded, and Müller went on: "The villain, hungry for Fellner's blood, was determined to have it at *any* cost."

"And thereby resorted to assassination."

Müller nodded evenly. "Admittedly it would have been nobler of him to make Fellner aware that his enemy was there, but then the whole thing might have gone wrong. One could barricade oneself, call for help, and with the *one* crime prevented, *another more shameful one* would not have been avoided."

"Fellner, a criminal?"

"More about that tomorrow, my protector! Now, the test. Please lock the door behind me, just as it happened."

Müller left the room, taking the pistol with him. Bauer locked the door. "Like that?" he asked the detective standing outside.

"Yes. I can see a wide round section of the room, the whole desk. Please stand to one side."

For a moment there was complete silence, then a slight noise was audible, as of metal being put to metal, then a crack, and immediately afterward Müller returned via the bedroom. He found Bauer bent over the silhouette of the French soldier. It had a hole in the left side of the chest. The bullet that had caused it had buried itself in the seat back of the chair.

"It's true, the chief said, and shook Müller's hand. "But why a *golden* bullet?"

"Tomorrow," the detective said, and looked at his superior with a pleading expression.

Soon afterwards they left the house. An hour later Müller traveled back to the capital and went to the goldsmith's shop.

"Well?" The goldsmith received him with a single word, which expressed extreme excitement. Müller handed him the golden bullet.

"Here's the gold object," he said, paying no attention to the goldsmith's astonishment. The latter quickly composed himself, took a ring out of a secret compartment, and prepared to test the contents of the two objects. For this he needed a scale and a file, some physics and chemistry, and when he turned again to Müller the most complete certainty shone in his clear eyes. "It's exactly the same gold, of rare old French alloy that we can't produce anymore to this degree of perfection. Moreover, the bullet has exactly the same weight as the ring."

"Well! You could testify to that under oath if you were called as an expert?"

"I can defend my judgment."

"Good. And now here's my written version of what you told me yesterday. If I've made a mistake in *my* account, correct it, because you have to attest to it with your signature."

Müller handed the goldsmith his notes, neatly written, and the latter read, loud and slowly, "On the twenty-second of November a gentleman appeared here who gave me a wedding ring with the request to make him an identical one. He laid especial weight upon the speed with which the work was done (it was to be picked up two days later), and upon the exactitude of the color of the gold, the form, and the engraving inside it: the copy was supposed to be deceptively identical to the original. He explained his desire by saying that he wanted to ease his sick wife's distress over her lost wedding ring. The original would then turn up one day and relieve her sadness altogether. Just as he said, the gentleman reappeared punctually two days later and I gave him the two completely identical rings.

"He left after paying, extremely satisfied and visibly freed of this worry, but I was uneasy, because I was conscious of my own guilt. I had deceived the stranger. I could not succeed in reproducing the alloy of the original ring, but because I believed in good faith that I could restore the sick woman's peace of mind through my actions, and in no way profited from them, indeed took upon myself extra work for which I could demand no payment, I produced two new rings just like the original he had left me, engraved them, and gave them to my customer with the conviction that I had been of service to him. Today, December 7, 1890, I hereby give the original to Mr. Joseph Müller, who has revealed himself to me as a police detective, and I am prepared to be available to the court at any time."

"And are you?" Müller asked, as the goldsmith had read the document thoughtfully.

"Naturally."

"Do you want to add anything?"

"It says everything. I'll just sign it."

He did so, secure in the knowledge that he had harmed no one, and gave the detective the ring and the bullet.

* * *

When Müller got back to the police headquarters after several hours, he saw the windows of the superintendent's apartment brightly lit.

"What's going on?" he asked Bauer's maid, who was just hurrying up the steps.

"Oh, don't you know? Tomorrow is the mistress's name day—that's why we have guests tonight."

"Well!" said Müller and went up to his room. He was already thinking that it would be unpleasant for his protector if he asked the latter to excuse himself for a talk. But duty took precedence over pleasure. Müller took off his coat and washed up, made himself a little more presentable, then took up the goldsmith's statement, made sure he had the ring and the bullet, and went down to the second floor, a quiet side wing of which was occupied by the detective superintendent.

He announced that he was here to see the superintendent, was shown into his study, and sat down, deferentially, in a corner. The room adjoined a larger chamber, an elegantly appointed, masculine room, to which the smokers and card players had withdrawn. There were, perhaps, a dozen men in it at the moment. Various cries betrayed the eager card game, political discussions resounded in between, and the sound of music drifted from the salon.

At that moment the master of the house walked in. He was not alone; Forester Kniepp was with him.

"Please, my dear friend, make yourself at home here," Bauer said to his guest, who had begun to find the company too loud, as he pushed a small table with cigars and wine over to Kniepp. In so doing, he caught sight of Müller, nodded, and remarked pleasantly, "Good thing they put you in here. You're probably frozen through after the journey. Wait just a minute while I say goodbye to the doctor's wife, then we'll go to my office. Kniepp, my dear friend, I'm going to send Horn in to you. He's a friendly, chatty fellow, and will soon drive away your melancholy."

As Bauer left the room, the forester watched him. But then, coincidentally, he caught sight of the other man, unknown to him and shabby-looking, who had risen at his entrance and was still standing.

"Do sit down," he said in a friendly tone. Yet the object of his offer didn't move, but merely stared steadily at the man whose lot in life it was his task, still today, to make so miserable.

Kniepp was made uncomfortable by the rigid stare. "What do you find so peculiar about me?" he asked, trying to seem lighthearted.

"The ring, the ring on your watch chain," Müller stammered.

"That's a remembrance of my dead wife. I have worn it since the hour of her death," the unhappy man replied, with an icy calm. Nonetheless, the question embarrassed him and he tried to distract the strange man. Müller's face kept changing color and he was shivering with the cold. Kniepp urged him, "Drink a glass of wine. You've been traveling, and you need to warm yourself."

The drink was offered with such goodness and kindness, and yet its intended recipient turned away almost fearfully and shuddered. The forester stood up. "Who are you? What kind of report are you here to make?" he asked, his voice growing uncertain. At this, Müller jerked his head up, as if he had just come to a decision.

"I am a detective, and I spy upon people—not just because it's my job, but because it's my nature. And I've just come from Vienna bringing the last of the proofs necessary for your arrest. Nevertheless, you are a thousand times better than the coward who stole your wife's honor and then hid behind the law, and so—and so—" Müller's hoarse voice died away, and he could say no more.

Pale as death and motionless Kniepp stood and listened, and when Müller stopped he went on, "… and so you want to rescue me from prison or the gallows. I thank you. What is your name?" The unhappy man had spoken as peacefully as if he were scarcely affected by this topic.

The detective said his name.

"Müller, Müller," the forester repeated, as if was very important to him not to forget this name, and then he held out his hand to the detective.

"Thank you. Oh, I do thank you," he said with a passionate expression, and added softly, "Do not be afraid that you will have any unpleasantness on my account. You can find me at home."

At these words he turned away and sank down in his chair again. As Bauer, at that moment, returned, Kniepp drew on his cigar with a expression of the greatest ease.

"Well, then, Müller, I'm ready. And our Mr. Horn, my dear friend, will be here any moment to amuse you. He's right behind me."

The superintendent waved at the forester and left the room by the other door. He could not have seen Kniepp's deathly pale face, wreathed as it was in a cloud of smoke, but when Müller, following Bauer, threw one last glance at the man he had just warned, he saw Kniepp's eyes, sad as death, turned upon him with an expression of intense gratitude, and the forester nodded to him, and waved.

* * *

"My dear Müller, you're being awfully long-winded today. Can't you see that you're torturing me?" Bauer said, after an hour, to the detective. But the latter would not be moved and continued as he had begun, and after a further hour Bauer finally knew that the man whose name Müller had let him wait so long to hear was Leo Kniepp.

He was extremely surprised, as one could tell from his amazed face and his unsteadiness as he rose. "And I'm supposed to have him arrested in my own house?" he cried out in horror.

At that Müller said, quietly, "Hopefully you won't have any opportunity to do that anymore, superintendent."

"Müller! You wouldn't have—"

"I *have*. I have warned another unhappy soul. You know, don't you? that I can't do anything against my nature. You'll find the forester in his apartment, by the way. He promised me."

"And you believe him?"

"*He'll* keep his word," Müller said quietly.

And Forester Kniepp did keep his word. When the authorities got to the hunting lodge after midnight, they found the horrified servants clustered around the body of their master.

"Well, Müller, this time you were lucky," Bauer said, the next day, to his protégé. "This last trick has made your career as a police detective completely impossible, but you can put that behind you, since Kniepp has provided for you so handsomely in his notorious testament."

The detective had not expected such a reward. He was completely in a whirl over the luck that had suddenly befallen him. Today, twenty thousand guldens were his, who yesterday had been a poor and careworn devil, and not his *mind,* but his *heart* had brought him this fortune! Full of intense gratitude he thought of the poor fellow who had been ruined by the dishonor of two other people and his own passionate nature, and again and again he read the letter that was found, bearing his address, next to Kniepp's body, and which had been turned over to him this morning. It read:

My friend!

You have spared me the shame, the shame of being condemned and executed. I thank you once more for this from the bottom of my heart. You will also receive a legacy from my estate, because you should be a free man and a poor man is never free. Yes, I forced my wife to commit suicide, after I forced her to admit her shame. And yes, after I learned from her how she went to visit her lover, I sneaked into his apartment after I saw his servant leave the house. And yes, when I saw that false, scoundrelly face before me, that miserable man who refused me satisfaction, I shot him like an assassin through the keyhole, and continued to play the grieving spouse in order to avoid suspicion. Yes, I acted like a criminal, and in spite of it I still feel less vile than the two people I executed in a mad fury, just as I will execute myself today with a calm hand.

That I can still do this, I owe to you, and I bless you for this, you, who see into the souls of men and understand their most secret motives, and who are not merely clever, but also have a heart. You alone, I hope, will think kindly of him who is grateful beyond death, your

Leo Kniepp

With this letter, which Müller kept like a religious relic, the "Kniepp Case" was closed.

Joseph Müller really was dismissed this time. Not even Bauer's well-meant patronage could rescue him. So now Müller lives, quite well in his modest style, from his "pension." But now and then letters or telegrams arrive and he leaves in a hurry, to be gone for a little while, or maybe longer. Is it possible that the officials who cannot retain him officially, because of his strange habit, perhaps still use him unofficially for important missions?

Maximilian Böttcher
(1872–1950)

Maximilian Paul Richard Böttcher was born on June 20, 1872, in Brandenburg, the son of a wealthy businessman and a descendant of Johann Friedrich Böttger, the inventor of porcelain. He was educated at home and at two preparatory high schools, studied agriculture, and after completing his compulsory military service took up residence in Berlin about 1892 as a free-lance writer.

Böttcher spent many years editing various literary magazines as well as writing. He produced amusement literature, for the most part. Satire and humor seem to predominate among Böttcher's publications, although there are a few serious novels and plays, and a drama, *Vaterland*, received an enthusiastic mention in a 1914 review of new literary accomplishments. Among his writings were only a few pieces of crime fiction, including the novel *Wer war's? (Who Was It?)*, 1899, and one called *Schuld auf Schuld (Guilt Upon Guilt)* of 1909 and marked as "freely adapted from the French," perhaps a clue to Böttcher's attitude toward adopting material from other literary sources.

Böttcher's sense of humor and borrowing habits are both clearly in evidence in the following 1899 novella, *The Detective*. We have included it because it is an obvious adaptation of Sir Arthur Conan Doyle's Sherlock Holmes story, "The Red-Headed League," and it gives some indication how well known Sherlock Holmes had become in Germany by the last decade of the nineteenth century. Lest we think harshly of Böttcher as a plagiarist, let us not forget how much Conan Doyle himself owed to Edgar Allan Poe. Poe's "The Purloined Letter" supplied material for "A Scandal in Bohemia," as did Poe's "The Gold-Bug" for Conan Doyle's "The Adventure of the Dancing Men."

The Detective
by Maximilian Böttcher

About eleven o'clock on the morning of the 24th of December, I visited my friend Victor, the proprietor of a private detective business, in order to consult with him as to where and how we two lonely bachelors should spend Christmas Eve.

I had just taken a seat next to his desk and lighted one of his incomparable imported cigars when his servant entered and announced the visit of a lady, on whose somewhat grimy visiting card the rare name "Anna Müller" could be read.

Victor liked to initiate me into the secrets of his business because a few times, especially in difficult cases, which captured all my interest, I had given him good advice that had contributed more than a little to the clarification of the entire affair. For when Victor, with his eminently gifted detective's mind, came up against a seemingly insurmountable obstacle, I sometimes easily helped him over it with my writer's imagination and psychological insight. So this time too, he asked me right from the beginning to attend the interview with his new client.

We heard steps coming from the reception room, quickly assumed our impenetrable professional expressions and thus received the woman with the rare name of Anna Müller, who thereupon entered. It was a mild winter and warm rather than cold outside, so it really didn't surprise us that our lady wore only a light summer jacket and no gloves.

The detective becomes accustomed to observe his visitors sharply and searchingly as soon as they enter, so that from their appearance and clothing, their manners, facial features and other slight indications that cannot be more closely defined, he can draw conclusions as to their profession, character and habits and afterward, during the course of the interview, amaze the visitors by demonstrating his knowledge of things that really only those quite familiar with the clients' affairs could know.

Mrs. Müller entered and inclined her head somewhat clumsily first to me and then to my friend.

"Please, take off your jacket, madam, for this room is a little overheated, and as our conversation could possibly last for some time, you could easily catch cold afterward," said Victor, who had risen swiftly to his feet and was assisting the woman, obviously of modest circumstances, to remove her jacket with the same winning and chivalrous courtesy that he showed to ladies of the foremost social classes.

"There—and now take a seat and tell us your story."

The woman, about forty years old, whose otherwise nice-enough face was unfortunately distorted by a severe harelip, first drew out a handkerchief and with it fanned her cheeks, reddened by excitement and fast walking.

"First calm down completely—we have plenty of time," my friend continued with his deep and sympathetic voice. "You are the proprietor of a grocery store that you inherited from your deceased husband—or am I wrong?"

Mrs. Anna Müller stared at Victor in amazement.

"How do you know that?" The words proceeded from her distorted mouth in almost inaudible astonishment.

"So, I'm right.... And recently you have done a lot of work with a sewing machine. Am I right?"

"Yes, indeed, sir ... but ... you were a complete stranger to me until today. How in all the world do you know these things?"

"Perhaps I'll tell you later.... You're also left-handed, if I'm not mistaken?"

"Yes, but..."

"And in the past once lived in South Africa?"

"Sir ... I am ... I think ..."

"Where your husband was probably a master carpenter or mason?"

"Only a journeyman! He had the misfortune that a falling timber crushed his foot, so that he became unable to continue his acquired trade. With the compensation money that the builder had to pay out to him we returned here to our country and with it bought the little grocery store on the corner of Lynar and Schiller streets, in which we led a happy and satisfactory life until my Oscar died three years ago."

"I thank you for this information, which completely verifies my preconceived conclusions, and now I beg you to present the matter that has led you to me."

"Won't you first tell me, Mr. Detective, how...?" The client hesitated and lowered her gaze in embarrassment.

"Well, my dear Mrs. Müller, so that you won't think I'm a sorcerer or have made a pact with the devil, I will betray my secrets to you. I could tell three things by looking at your hands. First, that you keep a grocery store, for only someone who must frequently dip his hands into the brine for herring and dill pickles can have such peculiarly red fingers and such strange fingernails, almost bluish in color. Second, that you are a widow, for you are wearing two wedding rings on the ring finger of your right hand. Third, that you are left-handed, for your left hand has the muscular sections more strongly developed than the right one, while usually exactly the reverse tends to be true, the truth of which you can convince yourself immediately by observing my friend's hands and mine.

"That your husband was a carpenter I can tell by looking at your nickel watch-chain, obviously inherited from the departed, for on this chain hang silver replicas of a carpenter's tools: plane, saw, square and measuring stick.

"How do I know that you were in South Africa? Only there could you have acquired the characteristic tattoo of a snake on your right wrist.

"And that you have recently done a lot of work with a sewing machine I could see from the fact that the right lower sleeve of your bodice is frayed up to the elbow, while the left one on the contrary is frayed only up to a certain line above the wrist. So you see ..."

"That you must certainly be a very smart man if you can discover so much in a moment by looking at a simple woman like me, and I am confident that you will advise and help me. So this is my story:

"One day—it must have been about a month ago—a man with a briefcase came to see me in my store and had the following tale to tell: in America, some years ago, a German lady had lived whose face, like mine, but much worse, was disfigured by a harelip. Because of this the lady had remained single, had devoted herself to business affairs, accumulated a large fortune, and at her death had left the income of her gigantic estate as a legacy for those German women and girls who suffer from the same facial disfigurement as she did. By this she had desired to give them a small recompense for the many disadvantages that disfigured and ugly ladies have compared to their pretty and charming counterparts. But this legacy was not to fall into the laps of the recipients without their working for it. Those chosen by the committee, who had to be distinguished by a blameless life, had the obligation of sewing clothing for small children for four weeks long without interruption from nine o'clock in the morning to eight o'clock in the evening at a location in Schröder Street, in order to receive the inheritance. The clothing was destined for a charitable purpose, namely as gifts for poor mothers. Did I have the desire, under these circumstances, to be an applicant for the legacy, which consisted, from case to case, of three annual payments of 3,000 marks each? As compensation for the four weeks of sewing I would in any case receive 400 marks, payable every Saturday in a sum of 100 marks!"

Mrs. Müller, overtaxed by her unwonted long speech, stopped for a moment to catch her breath.

"A remarkable story," my friend said, turning to me.

"Yes, I thought so too," our client continued, "and told the man with the briefcase straight out that it was probably a swindle. But he was not at all upset by this rudeness, opened up a notebook, on the title page of which was written: 'Dispositions in the inheritance affair of Miss Angelica Kaufmann of New York,' and allowed me to examine the relevant paragraphs after he had first made me give my word of honor that I would not breathe a word of their contents to any other person. But even after reading the document I made all possible objections, so that the man finally slammed his briefcase shut and cried furiously, 'Well, if you absolutely refuse, then we'll just have to convoke another general meeting of the committee members and decide what should happen. So far as I know, there are no regulations as to how we should behave toward those candidates for the inheritance who *don't* want to take the money. The candidates are chosen by lot from the carefully prepared lists of all the women disfigured by harelips, and ...' Here my clerk, Mr. Emil Lange, joined the conversation.

"'I don't want to influence you, Mrs. Müller,' he said, approaching us, 'but in your place *I* would at least give it a try. A *try* at least cannot do any harm.

Four hundred marks a month can't be earned so easily in these bad times. And then the prospect of the nine thousand! Devil take it, I wish I was a woman with a harelip!'

"Well, I must confess that my clerk, Mr. Emil Lange, holds a certain influence over me"—and here Mrs. Müller blushed a little—"and his remarks began to wipe away my scruples.

"'Yes, but in the four weeks I'm away from morning to night, who will guarantee that my business will be cared for properly?' I asked suddenly, wavering again.

"'Well, I think in this regard you could have a little confidence in *me*!' Mr. Lange returned in an offended tone.

"'Moreover,' the man with the briefcase began again, 'we are also prepared to furnish you with a substitute, who ...'

"'Oh, no, that's not necessary. I have complete confidence in Mr. Lange ...' I interrupted quickly, endeavoring to conciliate my truly capable and faithful employee.

"'So we can expect you tomorrow morning at nine A.M. in our office at 210 Schröder Street, second floor?'

"'All right, then, I'll come.'

"The stranger bowed courteously, asked again whether I wouldn't forget the address, and went out the door.

"The following morning I arrived punctually and found everything the way it had been described. I immediately began to sew away on the machine that had been placed at my disposal and I completed a good amount of work, too. From time to time the man who had been in my store came into my room and inspected the state of my work without saying a word. At eight o'clock that evening he dismissed me, with directions to be on the spot quite punctually on the following morning. When I got home I found my business in good shape—Mr. Lange had substituted for me to my complete satisfaction, and the day's intake in the cash register was even a few marks higher than usual.

"So things went on for a week, and on Saturday I really got the first hundred marks in cash counted out correctly on the table. My inspector reminded me again expressly to continue in the work as conscientiously as before and above all not to even consider leaving the room before the agreed time had elapsed. Then I could be certain of the three-year legacy, in all probability.

"Three weeks went by in the same way. Three times I was paid my money down to the last pfennig, which was very pleasing to me, and thanks to the reliability and efficiency of my Mr. Lange, my store remained in the best of shape. The day before yesterday the fourth and last week began in the usual manner, and I was already certain of the 9,000 marks, as I really had worked very hard the whole time, when this morning upon my appearance at 210 Schröder Street, the familiar door, which I might say I had become really fond of, was not immediately opened by the stranger when I rang, as I was accustomed to. Only after my repeated, almost desperate ringing was the door finally opened by a cleaning woman with a mop in her hand, who asked me if I could be Mrs. Anna Müller. When I answered this question affirmatively, she pulled a letter out of the pocket of her dirty dress, gave it to me, and then slammed the door in my face. In breathless excitement I tore open the envelope and found this message in it. Please, read it yourself!"

Our client handed my friend a large square sheet of paper on which the following was written in somewhat illegible but powerful and energetic handwriting:

Dear Mrs. Müller: The bank which manages the estate of that noble and generous lady, Miss Angelica Kaufmann, has failed, and we have lost everything, everything. Console yourself over the loss of your honestly earned legacy with us and the innumerable others who were to share in it over the course of the centuries.

Respectfully,

Albert Seidel, Chair of the Kaufmann Foundation

Victor had read this letter aloud and now placed it on the desk next to him and burst out in a self-assured laugh, his eyes sparkling eerily, as they always did when he thought he was on the trail of a criminal.

"That's what I thought from the start, that's the way I thought it would end. Ha ha ha!"

I looked at my friend with no less astonishment than did his new client, for what he, with his detective's mind, had found so convincing when he had read that letter was extremely mysterious to me.

"Where did you go after reading this letter, which certainly must have acted upon you like a dash of cold water?" he then asked the amazed Mrs. Müller.

"To the landlord of the house at 210 Schröder Street, of course. I told myself, you see, that it was easily possible that the stranger had simply absconded with the legacy that perhaps had already been allocated to me. Upon my inquiry about him, the landlady reported that the man was an underclothing manufacturer, had rented the flat in question for only a month as an emergency measure, and last evening had had his office furnishings and sewing machine removed again. He had dutifully paid the rent in advance and at the time had said that his shop— at 194 Linden Street—was being renovated and for that reason he had to locate his private office here. So now she had sent her cleaning woman to the flat to have it cleaned so that at the beginning of the quarter she could rent it again, this time better and for a longer period of time …

"I hardly heard the landlady's last words, I was off in such a rush, without even saying goodbye, to go to 194 Linden Street…"

"Where, of course, no one had ever heard of an underwear manufacturer by the name of Albert Seidel!" Victor interrupted in decisive tones.

"Naturally, not at all! Now I was all the more certain that somehow I had fallen victim to a swindle, and, as I felt hungry and weak, went to a pastry shop where I ordered a cup of coffee and a roll and nervously turned the pages of the newspapers lying around. At that time my eye fell upon your advertisement, that advertisement in which you offer your services for clarifying and uncovering all mysterious affairs, and so I came here to tell you my story!"

"I thank you, my dear Mrs. Müller, and I hope that you will not regret taking this step. Even if in doing so you perhaps only helped to prevent a crime!"

"A crime? For heaven's sake! What kind of crime? Holy Father in heaven, all my life long I've never done anything to anybody..."

"Nor will anyone do anything to *you*, I'm firmly convinced. Before I let you go, however, I'd like to request that you answer a few questions about your Mr. Emil Lange ..."

"Oh ... you certainly can't be thinking that Mr. Lange is connected with the crime?!" cried Mrs. Müller with decisive indignation.

"For the time being I don't think anything at all, my dear lady, except that Mr. Lange probably expressed to you the opinion that it is not good for a person to be alone, and that in the future he therefore would not be averse to managing your grocery store not as your clerk, but rather as your husband ..."

"Ah ... you know that, too?"

"That's obvious, my dear. But please, let's get to the facts. How long has Mr. Lange been employed by you?"

"For about two months!"

"So we can say: since one month *before* the stranger with the briefcase appeared in your store!"

"Quite right!"

"How did you come to hire Mr. Lange?"

"On the basis of an advertisement that I placed in the *Intelligencer!*"

"You probably had a great number of applicants from this advertisement. Why did you engage Mr. Lange in particular?"

"Because he had brilliant references and only demanded half the salary that the other young people asked for."

"Excellent! Capable people who work for half the usual salary are rare these days! Does Mr. Lange have any peculiarities?"

"Not that I know of!"

"None at all?"

"At most, only that he is a great lover of mushrooms!"

"Excellent! He obviously started a mushroom bed in your cellar?"

"My dear sir! You must certainly be familiar with the conditions of my house."

"Only what you have told me."

"But ..."

"Mr. Lange sleeps in your house?"

"Certainly."

"And he often works a long time at his mushroom culture in the cellar?"

"The only fault he has!"

"Have you seen his mushroom bed?"

"No ... he always keeps the back part of the cellar, which he uses for it, carefully closed off."

"Bravo!"

"But several times already I've had to cook mushrooms that he harvested from his beds."

"If I am not mistaken, my dear Mrs. Müller—you see, I know your section of the city very well—the Cologne Commerical Bank building is next to the house you live in?"

"Quite right!"

"Well, Mrs. Müller, now I've got the complete picture. A band of burglars that your Mr. Emil Lange also belongs to, has deceived you. The noble bandits plan a burglary of the bank, which—as I know because of my profession—is to pay a loan in gold on the first of January to a foreign power. The gold resides, packed in iron chests, in the underground vaults of the bank, completely inaccessible from above for outsiders. Now, so that your Mr. Lange could make a short subterranean connecting tunnel underneath the foundation between your cellar and the cellar of the banking house, he naturally had to spend a lot of time in the cellar, and therefore asked you to allow him to use the back part of it, which was probably little used, for mushroom beds, of which, of course, there is not a trace in reality. The mushrooms he brought you to cook he simply bought. But so as not to be disturbed and surprised at his burrowing, he had to keep you away from your store and cellar. Therefore the somewhat complicated scheme with the inheritance story about Miss Kaufmann from America, which, however, the more I think about it, was really ingeniously constructed. For it would hardly have been possible to keep you away from your business for weeks in any other way. Right? You may now be convinced that during your regular absences two or three men would regularly descend into your cellar and work on finishing the tunnel that Mr. Lange had begun or at least made preparations for!"

"Oh, this is terrible ... terrible! But no, sir, I don't believe all of this, at least as it relates to Mr. Lange. Mr. Lange is a good person, a noble person, who is not capable of anything wrong. If you saw him ..."

"I certainly will do ..."

"Oh, I have a photograph of him with me ... Please, convince yourself."

Mrs. Müller pulled out of her handbag a leather case, which she flipped open and handed to Victor. He examined the picture contained in it for a long time. Then he turned to me and said:

"Just look, my boy ... this characteristic criminal physiognomy, this low forehead, these prominent cheekbones, these unreasonably large ears. Alas, my dear Mrs. Müller, you are not the first who was made blind by love!"

Our client broke out in sobs, and then suddenly sprang up as if to start for home.

"I can't allow you to do that, my dear, for you would be in a position to spoil my planned capture of the scoundrels by warning Mr. Lange. So you will remain here, if not willingly, then by force, and leave everything else to me!"

At these words, spoken in very energetic tones, Mrs. Müller sank back in her chair in despair, like a broken woman.

Victor handed me the photograph of Mr. Lange and said, "Would you be so good as to open up Series 6 of our criminal album, 'Foreign Criminals'? This face seems so oddly familiar to me." And sure enough! Mr. Lange was revealed to be a notorious burglar by the name of Anton van den Bergh, who had been sought by the Dutch police for years.

Thereupon my friend gave me the letter of the "Chairman of the Mercantile Institute" with the remark that his graphological knowledge could not leave him in doubt for a moment that the writer of these lines must also be an individual dangerous to society. I agreed with him.

After Victor had paced back and forth silently for a while, he suddenly stopped before me, grasped me by my upper coat button and said triumphantly: "See how these criminals, no matter how smart they are, always make a mistake that does them in. If these people had been smart enough to let our good Mrs. Müller work at her sewing machine through today, then they probably would have been able to carry out their plan undeterred."

"So you think ..."

"That they plan to break into the bank tonight. First, because these people have given up their "office" in Schröder Street, but second—and this is the more compelling reason—because tonight is Christmas Eve. At such a time, everybody likes to stay home in the bosom of his family, and the bandits can—or rather could—be pretty certain that they wouldn't be disturbed at their work. And in addition, tomorrow and the day after tomorrow are holidays when the bank stays closed. So the theft couldn't have been discovered until the third day at the earliest; and then the scoundrels would have been far away, over the border."

After we had left Mrs. Müller securely guarded, we drove to the director of the Cologne Commercial Bank to inform him of the planned break-in, and from there to police headquarters to request some policemen to assist us in our nocturnal adventure.

That evening at 10:00 we took our positions, ten men strong and armed to the teeth, to wait in the subterranean vaults. We had to wait three hours in vain in the impenetrable darkness. Finally a noise was perceptible beneath the floor, and a stone slab was raised, clearly visible to us from the shine of a lantern rising from the subterranean tunnel. Four men, among them Mr. Lange, crept out of the hole and were just about to start their work when, at a signal from Victor, suddenly all four of them felt themselves seized from behind by two men and in a trice were thrown to the floor and fettered.

The bank director that very night handed my friend the sum of 10,000 marks as a reward, of which Victor, upon returning home, placed 3,000 marks at the disposal of the anxiously waiting Mrs. Müller, "as compensation for the legacy she had lost." The woman was deliriously happy and in her joy seemed to have forgotten completely the sweetheart she had also lost.

When Victor and I then, toward three o'clock in the morning, sat together chatting over a bottle of Moet and Chandon, my friend suddenly cried out:

"Apropos Christmas! When Mrs. Müller came this morning—or rather, yesterday morning—we were just debating how we should spend the evening! Didn't we spend it in a very interesting way?"

"Well, that depends on how you look at it. That waiting time down in the dark cellar ... three hours that seemed like three days to me! Brrrrr ... I still shiver when I think about it!" I answered, emptied my glass and filled it up again.

Balduin Groller
(1848–1916)

Balduin Groller is the pseudonym of the Hungarian-born Adalbert Goldscheider. Goldscheider went to high school in Dresden, where he was taught by, and came under the influence of, the poet Albert Möser. In Vienna, Goldscheider studied law and later philosophy and aesthetics. He began his career writing about art. Later he turned to fiction, producing novellas and novels while continuing his journalistic activities. He served for years as the Vienna representative of the *Gartenlaube* (a very popular German weekly literary newspaper during the years 1853–1943), and was known in Vienna for being one of the city's most beloved feature writers.

In 1890 Groller turned to crime fiction. Noting the popularity of Sherlock Holmes, Groller set out to create a Viennese version of that master sleuth, a detective with Holmes's keen eye and brilliant methods, but with a personality more suited to the liveliness and gaiety of Vienna's fin-de-siècle high society and its romance with its Austro-Hungarian nobility. Dagobert Trostler is an independently wealthy bachelor in his fifties, with two passions in life: music and criminology. His crime-solving genius makes him a sought-after confidant of those noble and wealthy Viennese whose romantic indiscretions or financial peccadilloes threaten scandal or ruin.

Dagobert's interactions with the Viennese police provide a foil to his genius. Although he enjoys the friendship and confidence of Chief Superintendent Dr. Weinlich, other police officials are portrayed as clumsy and dimwitted (much like the overzealous police detectives who irritate Sherlock Holmes), especially that notorious bungler Superintendent Dr. Thaddäus von Strinsky, who makes his first appearance here, in *The Vault Break-In*.

The original eighteen Dagobert tales, of which this is one, were published together ca. 1909 in six volumes under the title *Detektiv Dagoberts Taten und Abenteuer* (*Detective Dagobert's Deeds and Adventures*). A further four novellas were published as *Neue Detektivgeschichten* (*New Detective Stories*) in 1914. There is also an unpublished war novella, *Detektiv Dagobert auf dem Kriegspfad* (*Detective Dagobert on the Warpath*) set in the early days of World War I.

The Vault Break-In
by Balduin Groller

It was the Tuesday after Pentecost. The Grumbachs had their old friend Dagobert to dinner again. That was nothing new; indeed, it happened twice a week. The clock struck a quarter past six, and the three were already eating dessert, talking about the events of the holidays, when a servant announced Mr. Kienast, the head cashier at the G. C. B., who wished to speak to the master immediately about an extremely urgent matter. Everyone in Vienna, among them, naturally, the servants in this household, knew what those three letters meant, so it was easy to understand that people preferred their brevity while speaking and writing to the wearying awkwardness of "General Construction Bank." Mr. Andreas Grumbach, the well-known president of the Industrialists' Club, was also the president of this bank. His friend Dagobert Trostler, the man-about-town, music lover and passionate amateur detective, had done Andreas the favor of taking a position on the Board of Directors at that bank.

Violet, Grumbach's charming wife, who presided over this small gathering—there was no one else present, apart from herself and the two gentlemen—was more than a little startled at the unusual announcement, and before the master, of the house could say anything she directed that the gentleman who had just been announced come in at once.

The head cashier, an older man with a reddish beard, heavily streaked with gray, and watery blue eyes fitted with gold-rimmed glasses, betrayed his great distress at first glance, and to this was then added his visible embarrassment. He was clearly in a great hurry, his errand very urgent, and yet he wasn't sure whether he should or was allowed to speak. In his confusion, he tried to make it clear by means of looks and gestures that he actually wished to speak to the president privately.

"What's happened, then, Mr. Kienast?" Mr. Grumbach asked, now roused himself by the sight of his excited head cashier.

"Mr. President, if I might be allowed—"

"Has something bad happened?"

"Something bad has happened, Mr. President, and if I might be allowed—"

"Something—in the bank, and—of a business nature?"

"Yes, Mr. President, in the bank, and of a business nature. If I might be allowed—"

"You want to speak to me alone?"

"If I might be allowed!"

"There would be no purpose, Mr. Kienast. Just sit down and tell us. I would simply have to tell it all over again to my wife, and as far as friend Dagobert is concerned, he is on the Board of Directors and will have to learn everything anyway. In fact, I think it will be of value for him to know everything from the beginning. What has happened, then? I hope it won't cost us all our heads!"

"Mr. President, we have had a burglary!"

"You're not trying to tell me someone forced his way into our vault?"

"Just that—into our vault!"

Grumbach struck the table with the flat of his hand. "Well now, *that* was really worth spending all that money!" he burst out. "Not even a year since we spent eighty thousand kronen to build a steel-plated, underground, fireproof, and burglarproof vault, so that we can sleep soundly in our beds at night, and at the first good opportunity the burglars just stroll in, as casually as if it were a coffeehouse, and carry away our money. How much is gone, then?"

"I don't know yet, Mr. President!"

"You don't know? Sir, pull yourself together and explain!"

"When I came into the bank this morning, there was a lot of work to do because of the two holidays, and the end of the month is also near. I took care of everything over the course of the day, and shortly before six, after the tellers' windows were closed, I went down to the vault, as is my custom, to lock up the valuables and cash that had come in during business hours."

"Surely you didn't go alone?" Dagobert asked, interrupting.

"Naturally not, Mr. Trostler. I was accompanied by the head bookkeeper, Mr. Höllerl, who has the second of the two required keys."

"Go on!"

"As soon as I unlocked the door I could see the whole tragedy at a glance."

"What do you mean?" Dagobert probed further. "It's as dark as pitch in that vault."

"That's just it! All the electric lamps were turned on. The burglars did their work by those lights and didn't even take the trouble to turn them off when they left. So I saw right away that the strong-box for cash—that's the smallest one—was broken open."

"How much was stolen?" Mr. Grumbach asked again.

"I don't know, Mr. President," the poor head cashier moaned.

"What does that mean, you don't know? You're our head cashier! You see a strong-box broken open and it doesn't interest you in the least how much has been taken from it?"

"I beg your pardon, Mr. President! When Mr. Höllerl and I saw what had happened, we talked about what we ought to do next, and came to the conclusion that we shouldn't go inside the vault before we notified you and the necessary official scene-of-crime examination had taken place."

"It would have been your duty to determine at once the amount of the loss," the president was heard to say, unkindly.

At this, Dagobert interceded: "Don't excite yourself unnecessarily, Grumbach. I think the gentlemen have dealt with this situation entirely correctly. It is always better for an investigation if the first impression hasn't been muddied by any incidental tampering. It should be able to begin on virgin soil. We have no need to rack our brains over the amount of the damages. Mr. Kienast, do you know approximately how much you had in your strong-box?"

"Exactly, Mr. Director. I had calculated the salaries and wages and all the other sums due at the end of the month, 164,000 kronen in all."

"Thus we calculate the amount of the damages—164,000 kronen. Nothing could be simpler. If I break into a strong-box containing only cash, then I clean it out, I don't leave anything behind."

"We can assume that the burglars were at least that intelligent," Grumbach admitted. "But we ought to go over there now, quickly, and have a look at the mess ourselves. I'm just glad that we already have Dagobert here."

"We're not going to do it like that, my dear Grumbach," said Dagobert, after thinking about it a moment. "The G. C. B. is an institution accountable to the public. We cannot permit ourselves to make an error in form just because I'm possessed by a private passion. We would doubtless have the right to look at the thing first ourselves; the matter does involve us directly and we are the masters of that house, but it's nonetheless more correct, as matters now stand, if we allow our praiseworthy police the first move. So, Mr. Kienast, you are going to betake yourself immediately to the criminal department at police headquarters— take my carriage, it's in front of the house—and with my respects to my friend, Detective Superintendent Dr. Weinlich, ask him to appear at the scene of the crime. From there you can go directly to the bank with him. Grumbach and I will be at the bank waiting for you, and will meet you at the main gate. Do you agree, Grumbach?"

"Completely."

The head cashier did as he was directed, and Grumbach went to ask that his carriage be readied immediately. Violet used the opportunity to ask Dagobert to persuade her husband to let her come along on this expedition. It was of enormous interest to her to be able to follow the matter just as exactly as they did. Dagobert had nothing against this, and when the master of the house came back, he immediately undertook this diplomatic mission: "Say, Grumbach, you know this evening rightfully belongs to our hostess. If we abandon her and leave her alone, she'll be bored. We can't let that happen. I suggest that we invite her along—provided she doesn't have any objection, of course. But one doesn't see freshly burglarized strong-boxes every day. Wouldn't you enjoy having a look at such a thing, dear lady?"

Violet was definitely in favor of the idea, and after some resistance Mr. Grumbach gave in. He directed that the landau be harnessed instead of the two-seater, and not too many minutes later they drew up in front of the main gate of the handsome edifice where the G. C. B. was located. Mr. Höllerl, the head bookkeeper, was already waiting there, pale and trembling with distress, yet standing guard until the relief the head cashier had promised should arrive. He had not gotten far with his hastily reported version when the rumble of Dagobert's sleek rubber-wheeled carriage announced its arrival, followed with difficulty and considerable rattling by a fiacre at a gallop, from which two uniformed security guards and two detectives descended. The first carriage had brought the head cashier, with Detective Superintendent Dr. Thaddeus v. Strinsky. The head cashier explained that Dr. Weinlich was not yet back from his Pentecost vacation, and that the latter's colleague, Dr. v. Strinsky, had been assigned instead.

The detective superintendent took charge of the whole matter as soon as the greetings and introductions were completed. He sent a detective to the doorman, directing that the latter come with the keys and open the offices. The man came, no longer in his ceremonious, gold-festooned doorman's livery, but rather in his slovenly janitor's attire. After all, his workday was over. A train of people followed the doorman up the stairs, with President Grumbach and the detective inspector close at his heels and Dagobert bringing up the rear, Violet on his gallantly offered arm. The two of them were conversing in whispers.

"We're out of luck, dear lady," Dagobert said softly. "Weinlich would have been infinitely preferable to me. Strinsky is a catastrophe."

"In what way, Dagobert?"

"He's a cretin. He won't discover anything in his whole lifetime."

"But—if you'll permit me—he's a detective superintendent and has a Ph.D.!"

"He might be ideally qualified for the lost and found, or the registration office, but he hasn't got the slightest clue about crime work—sheer lack of talent! I know him very well."

When the vault was opened—which one reached, from the offices, by going down again two flights on a special staircase—it was truly a sensation, despite the fact that the onlookers ought to have been prepared for the sight. The room was flooded with bright light. The electric lamps, twenty-four of them, were still functioning without fail and every detail in the steel-plated room could be plainly seen.

Eight large strong-boxes stood along the walls in weighty majesty. It was obvious that no attempt had been made to violate them. Only the smallest box on the narrow side wall across from the door had been attacked. It had been turned over and lay with its front on a pile of sand. A hole large enough for the purpose had been chiselled out or sawn through the back of it. Everyone immediately began to hurry toward it, when Dagobert categorically intervened: "Stop, gentlemen! Not a step! Let us not make the detective superintendent's task more difficult!"

The detective superintendent was visibly flattered by Dagobert's so impressively offered recognition of his criminalistic authority, and moved solitarily toward the strong-box. He stuck his arm through the hole and ascertained that the box had been completely emptied. With great satisfaction he collected various *corpora delicti* from the floor: a set of fine English tools for breaking and entering; a trouser button with the stamp of an English maker; a scarcely-smoked havana cigar; two elegant collars; and a cuff, in which a cufflink still stuck.

"Mr. Trostler, if I may be so bold," he called out to Dagobert. "You are familiar with such things, I believe—the cufflink isn't real gold, is it?"

"It's valuable," Dagobert decided, after a short examination. "That is real gold and the gemstone in the center is just as real."

"Even better! That just reinforces the opinion I formed at first glance. The gentlemen might as well have left their visiting cards!"

"You think you can lay hands on the burglars, detective inspector?" asked President Grumbach.

"I believe I can already guarantee you that. Come a little closer, Mr. President, so that I can explain precisely and virtually reconstruct the course of events, that is to say, the method used by the burglars. The others can all come closer now, too—"

He had not yet finished his sentence when the entire company received a sudden fright. A fiery, blinding light lit the room suddenly, making the faces look pale as death and the electric lamps look like weak night-lights. One could easily believe an explosion had taken place, but Dagobert had merely ignited a magnesium cartridge and taken a flash-lit photograph. The detective superintendent was not the least of those thus frightened, and he was less than charitable as he turned to Dagobert: "Pardon me, Mr. Trostler! I, too, appreciate gentlemen amateur photographers, but I think the occasion is a bit too serious for that sort of hobby. We have more important things to do right now. If you would be so kind, Mr. President?"

Grumbach stepped forward, and all the others followed him and stood on the pile of sand, in order to see more clearly. The detective superintendent then lectured one and all about how, in his opinion and according to his observations, the break-in had taken place. Frequently during this oration he cleared his throat; it was an accusatory action, discreetly but perceptibly aimed at Dagobert, for the flash-cartridge had generated not only a substantial amount of smoke, but also a pronounced stench.

"In general, we are in luck, Mr. President," he concluded his revelations. "The criminals have left traces which will ease our investigation considerably. However, they could already have quite a jump on us. We have had two days holiday, and we cannot know whether the crime took place yesterday or the day before. But with the clues they had the kindness to leave behind, I'll find them, even if they are at the ends of the earth!"

During his lecture he had led the president, now joined by his wife, in a circle around the violated strong-box. The sand crunched under their feet and made the detective superintendent particularly irritable.

"But really," he mused, annoyed and furrowing his brow vigorously, "how did this pile of sand get in here?"

The head cashier could speak to this. A short time ago, two niches in the room had been walled in, and the sand, which was left over from this operation, hadn't been removed yet. Moreover, as far as he could remember the pile had been beside the wall opposite the strong-box, in the vicinity of the door.

"The thing is clear," the detective superintendent explained. "The burglars shoveled the sand over to this location to dampen the sound from the strong-box falling over. For us it's unpleasant, of course; it's simply disgusting to have to march around on this crunching sand. I've never been able to stand that. As for the rest, my dear fellow," he turned to the doorman, "could you at least sweep the sand away a little, around the strong-box?"

The doorman had no broom handy, but he made the best of it by taking off his blue work-apron, getting down on his knees, and wiping the sand away with the apron as best he could. At that moment the magnesium flash-light flared again. Dagobert had taken another photograph.

The detective superintendent was furious and became decidedly frank.

"This is outrageous," he said sharply, "disturbing the course of the investigation with such silly games. I have had enough of being the victim of the passions of an amateur photographer. We won't be able to stand it in here much longer. I must ask Mr. Trostler emphatically not to make things any more unpleasant for us!"

Dagobert shrugged his shoulders and withdrew wordlessly. He went up to the doorman's apartment, which he found unlocked, and waited for the others to return. The detective superintendent merely felt all the more emboldened by Dagobert's withdrawal to parade his authority and give voice to his disapproval with many an expressive "Outrageous!" and "Unbelievable!" Turning to Mr. and Mrs. Grumbach, he said, "Those are the manners of the dilettante criminologist, and I believe I may say that they are bad manners." Thus was Dagobert rebuked, and it afforded the detective superintendent particular pleasure to have had the opportunity to do this.

Indeed, the air in the smoke-filled vault was becoming unbearable, and so, after a few minutes more, the detective superintendent gave the sign to depart. By the time the procession reached the main gate, Dagobert had left the doorman's apartment and was waiting there, to help Violet climb into the carriage. A considerable crowd had already gathered in front of the building, for the arrival of the police had indeed caused a certain sensation.

Dagobert helped Violet into the carriage and said: "I'm inviting myself for a cup of tea later this evening, dear lady."

"Aren't you coming with us now, then, Dagobert?"

"I have a few things to take care of, madame. I'll come later. You'll be at home, too, Grumbach? We'll have some things to discuss."

"Certainly I'll be at home, especially since you say you're coming!"

* * *

It was nine-thirty that evening, scarcely an hour since they had separated in front of the G. C. B. building, when Dagobert arrived again at the Grumbachs'. Violet, knowing that Dagobert never wanted to discuss "business" as long as the servants were coming and going, ordered the supper table to be laid, not in the dining room, but right in the smoking room. The tea needed no further assistance—as the lady of the house she preferred to pour it herself—and they could likewise easily manage alone with the few cold platters of food.

Thus they were completely undisturbed. Violet sat in her usual favorite spot by the marble fireplace, the samovar and cups before her, Dagobert in his usual place across from her, and Grumbach more in the center of the room in his comfortable easy chair at the smoking table, where a place had been laid for him alone.

"Now, madame," Dagobert began, "did you find that nice criminal investigation amusing?"

"It was extraordinarily interesting, and I thank you for taking me with you."

"It was an expensive amusement, at any rate!" Grumbach grumbled into his beard somewhat peevishly.

"We're not to that point yet," Dagobert comforted him. "But what do you think of our wonderful detective superintendent?"

"My God, what was he supposed to do? What could anybody do?"

"That's what I say," remarked Violet. "I think he did what he could. You shouldn't be unjust, Dagobert. Naturally he was furious at you; you really did irritate him."

"I had to do what I thought was necessary."

"Fine, but the second time was too much!"

"That was even more necessary!"

"What do you have against him?"

"Everything!"

"That's a little too much. In that case you must have the goodness to explain yourself more clearly."

"That's why I'm here. How did I put it so pointedly to you, madame, when we saw him? I think I called him a rhinoceros!"

"I really don't remember, Dagobert."

"Then it was an error of omission which cannot be rectified too often. Even the way he pulled up with that parade of security police was idiotic. Of course people will stop and stare and talk about it. We could have had an interest in keeping the thing quiet temporarily, or it could have been important to the investigation."

"That's true, Dagobert, he shouldn't have flourished the police like that."

"Onward! He strides into the vault with his horde and doesn't interest himself in the least in the question of how the burglars—and he was certain from the beginning that it was burglars, plural—could have gotten in there."

"You know, you're right, Dagobert, he didn't even think of that!"

"And I told you, madame, that I was prepared for a great deal, considering his stupidity. But he exceeded even my keenest expectations. By the way, even if he had thought of it, he wouldn't have found anything. I examined the keyholes. Fine, it's true that they bore no traces at all, but it's important to know even that. One can draw certain conclusions from the fact."

"What sort of conclusions, Dagobert?"

"That's perfectly clear," Grumbach entered the conversation now. "It follows that either the doors weren't locked, or that they were unlocked, that is to say, they weren't broken open, and that they were unlocked either with the original keys or with copies. If they were the original keys…."

"Let's not hold things up with these keen investigations. We don't need them anymore!"

"Don't need them anymore?" Violet cried out. "Dagobert, you're behaving as if you knew everything already!"

"I know some things, dear lady, but let me proceed systematically. So, he overlooked that. Fine, sometimes that happens. But what cannot be allowed to happen was everything he did after that, once he was finally inside. A bull in a china shop can behave that way, but not a detective superintendent at the scene of a crime! He came within a hair's breadth of spoiling everything for me!"

"Yes, but Dagobert dear, he wasn't doing it for you! Most of all, he took possession of those objects left behind. I would have done that too. They're really very important. Just imagine, two shirt-collars, so there must have been two burglars; two elegant collars, so they weren't common blackguards. The havana cigar, the button with the English stamp, the cuff with the real, valuable cufflink, the fine English tools—all this is already a big success for the investigation, if not a complete one! Now we can assume that they weren't ordinary local robbers, but rather traveling burglars, elegantly dressed and international, probably English. Really, those are very important points of reference!"

"You might conclude that, madame. You are a lady and have never been in the position of conducting a criminal investigation. You therefore have the legal benefit of numerous mitigating circumstances. But when a detective superintendent is similarly fooled right away in such a well-intentioned and harmless fashion, then I would retire him from the force immediately, if I had anything to say about the matter. That is to say, at first glance I came to totally different conclusions."

"Now, I'm all curiosity, Dagobert!"

"Two shirt-collars—therefore, only *one* culprit; two elegant collars—therefore, one ordinary fellow, or at least a man who never wears fashionably high collars, never wears cuffs with expensive cufflinks or smokes havana cigars. The

English stamp and the fine English tools—which, I might remark in passing, had never been used—therefore, a local scoundrel, whom we must locate nearby."

"That's your opinion, Dagobert, which might indeed have some points in its favor, but isn't proof by any means."

"Well then, we'll stay with your assumptions, madame, for which I won't blame you. So, it was two traveling international bank robbers, probably English. We can assume that they are a clever, completely unscrupulous pair. Stupid fellows are of no use in such a business. You'll admit that?"

"Naturally they have to be cunning scoundrels!"

"Fine. That's already evident in their choice of occasion. They had already chosen the Pentecost holidays, and they probably got to work on the first day. They had two days and two nights when they could be sure of being undisturbed. So they had plenty of time. Absolutely nothing indicates that they were driven, head over heels, to a hasty flight, and so could have lost their heads so badly that they left behind an entire arsenal of extremely important identifying objects. But if they weren't in a hurry, why leave behind revealing clues that could be at least extremely dangerous if not utterly damning?"

"Oh, they didn't care about that anymore!"

"Fine, they didn't care about that anymore, but they did have to worry about something else—how they would get out of there unsuspected. Not in the dark of night—they would have had to pass the doorman in his apartment. That was too dangerous. So they had to leave during the day, unnoticed. We have established that they were clever fellows. I ask you, then: would it have been clever to leave behind a whole collection of revealing objects unnecessarily? Furthermore, we know that they were elegant persons. They wouldn't have any large bags or trunks to carry away. What they took they could hide comfortably in their breast pockets. So now I ask: if they were really elegantly dressed, wouldn't it draw attention if they allowed themselves to be seen without their shirt-collars? And wouldn't they have had reason to want to be inconspicuous?"

"Yes, actually you're right about that, Dagobert!"

"Clever burglars don't proceed like that. That comedy was arranged simply for the detective superintendent, as if the burglar—and there really was only one—had suspected that it would be Strinsky, who then really did fall for it right away. And, if Strinsky has his way, he will pursue those clues for weeks and months and finally, actually—"

"Catch the culprit?"

"Not that, but find out where the collar was purchased and where the cuffs were laundered last. He's full of confidence; he remembers a glorious case of precedence and gives himself up to the sweet madness of thinking that he'll be just as successful this time."

"What case was that, Dagobert?"

"The Gröschl case. That was a burglar whose specialty was plundering the city apartments of persons who were away enjoying a summer respite. A nice, comfortable specialty, it's true! After he had operated with complete success more than a hundred times, he made a small mistake in his last undertaking—it was at an apartment in the Schottenhof. He left a cuff at the scene of the crime. The detective superintendent—it wasn't Dr. Thaddäus von Strinsky—sent a detective out with this cuff to go down the list talking to washwomen—to every single one in Vienna, if it was necessary. You see, on the inside of the cuff a mark had been made with ink, a letter and a number, and they had to find out which laundress or cleaning woman used that mark. After two weeks, the woman was identified. She recognized her mark—laundresses have a memory for such things—and knew the name of the customer to whom the cuff belonged. There was nothing more to do but collect Mr. Gröschl from his apartment."

Dagobert Trostler went on. "It was a pretty case, I admit. Strinsky will now follow this method. But while he dreams of his future victories, I have chosen to come to an understanding directly with the burglar."

"Dagobert!"

Mr. and Mrs. Grumbach had cried out simultaneously. The former even jumped up, bursting out in his excitement, "You know the culprit? I hope it's not one of our officers?!"

"Who is it, Dagobert?" Violet pressed him.

"Really, these salmon sandwiches are excellent!"

"Dagobert, you're just horrible!" Violet exclaimed.

"Tell us!" the president implored, excited.

"I have in mind to do just that, but one can't get a word in edgewise with you two. It has to be told in the proper order, and one really ought to let a fellow finish talking!"

"Have you arrested him, Dagobert?"

"Arrested? Am I the detective superintendent, that I can arrest people just like that?"

"So then you haven't arranged anything?"

"I've done a thing or two. I've brought the stolen money with me."

"Dagobert!"

"Here it is." Out of his inside breast pocket he pulled a rather voluminous package wrapped in waxed linen, and handed it to the president.

"There, count it up, Grumbach!"

The president counted it and then said, with a sigh of relief, "Yes, it really is all there. One hundred sixty thousand kronen!"

"Not everything, Grumbach. Four thousand kronen are missing. You have a prophetic spirit, and your prescient heart did not deceive you when you said this was an expensive amusement. It was for me, at any rate. Namely, I'll pay the four thousand kronen; the pleasure was worth that much to me."

"Dagobert, now you really do have to tell us how everything happened!"

"You can imagine, madame, that I paid complete attention when the investigation began, all the more because I had not the slightest trust in our detective superintendent. The many objects he found were suspicious to me from the first. It seemed too planned: specifically, like a plan to lead us astray. Two collars! After all, even if there were two culprits, why should both of them have forgotten their shirt-collars? But onward. The strong-box lay there crookedly. If two people had been at work, then according to the rule of the parallelogram of strength it would have fallen straight forward. And for one man, turning over such a strong-box is quite an achievement anyhow, practically an unbelievable one."

"I'm also inclined to disbelieve that a man could manage that alone, Dagobert," Mr. Grumbach remarked.

"There are technical aids, my dear man. I also noticed marks on the wall where the strong box stood which indicated clearly that someone had used an iron bar and exploited its potential for leverage. Naturally our detective superintendent missed all this. The bar wasn't there anymore. Strange! The burglar forgets not only his shirt-collars, but also the fine set of tools; but the coarse, bulky iron bar, which is not only heavy to transport but difficult to hide, this he takes with him!"

"That *is* strange, Dagobert; what do you make of it?"

"That the man with the iron bar didn't have far to go. But the most important thing, for which our solid criminologist had no eyes, was the footprints in the sand. I looked very closely, but there were footprints of only *one* man, one of the right foot, one of the left, very easy to distinguish, but always of the same man. Now that was evidence! We could do something with that! So what does the competent criminologist do? He lets his whole parade of people trample all over the footprints! That did it. The real clues were lost and the lofty officials led astray by the false ones."

"But you shouldn't have let that happen, Dagobert!"

"I felt absolutely no compulsion to protect the detective superintendent from a well-deserved disgrace. Furthermore, I did my part when I at least photographed the most stunning footprint at the last minute."

"How will that help if you haven't got the exact dimensions?"

"I didn't need them in this case. What I needed had already been secured. I had thought about it for a long time. The burglar had revealed considerable carefulness and cleverness. I looked for the one act of stupidity or carelessness that, according to experience, even the most cunning criminal occasionally commits. And I found it."

"What was it?"

"I found it, and then, when I was thrown out with a flourish, as you recall, I didn't care anymore. The investigation was closed, as far as I was concerned. I had my man, and I took care of the matter pretty quickly, which you've already seen for yourselves. After I saw you to your carriage, I went to see the doorman, who was sitting at his table in the middle of the room when I walked in. I closed the door behind me and began in an extremely determined tone: 'So, Hartwanger! Where's the money?'

"'What money?' he asked brusquely. I don't know anything!'

"'Don't play the innocent with me, you scoundrel! The money you stole from us!'

"'I haven't stolen anything,' he uttered with a dull voice. 'Who says I've stolen something?'

"He got very red while he was speaking, but it wasn't the gentle red of shame, dear lady. It was a mad rage rising in the man. The blood vessels in his forehead began to swell, and his blood-shot eyes acquired an eery glow. All of a sudden— I don't know where he got it—he had a long knife in his hand."

"For God's sake, Dagobert, what kind of tales are you telling us?" cried Violet, pale with fear.

"Well, then. I'm not exactly an admirer of such tricks. I can become very unpleasant about them. And I did. First I tore my revolver, which I had at the ready, out of my pocket and pointed it at him, and then I told him a few things, in such a way that—madame, if you had heard me, I don't know whether you would still have poured me a cup of tea tonight! But it worked. It brought the fellow down to size."

"'What? You miserable gallows-fodder?' I screamed at him,—I'm only repeating the gentler expressions, my dear lady—'Is it not enough that you're a thief and a robber?'—really, only the finer expressions, madame!—'you want to be a murderer, too? Then just look here, you scoundrel!' And then I shot just past his ear at the wall-clock, so that a shower of glass poured down upon us.

"'Look at that, you jackass, how I've shot out the middle. Do you really think I couldn't hit such a clod as you? You will throw the knife under the bed this instant!'

"He still hesitated, but I didn't slacken.

"'At the slightest move,' I continued, 'I'll fire. Don't believe for a moment that I'd shoot you dead. That would be too bad, before we have the money back. And maybe that would be just fine with you. I wouldn't do you that favor. No, I'd just shatter the kneecap a little, that would suffice. Are you going to throw that knife under the bed?'

"Now he obeyed. His resistance had worn down. My stay in the room had not been exactly pleasant—here the smoke and the stench were also nearly intolerable. I admit, sometimes I'm a decidedly uncomfortable guest, dear lady. I sat down at the table and let him stand in front of me, three strides away, and I gave him a little lecture: 'Don't think, Hartwanger, that I'm going to burglarize you the way you burglarized us, or that I'm going to take the money by force, or even—how disgusting!—that I just want to extort some from you. I don't do things like that. I'll only become nasty if you force me to. That's right, if you come at me with the knife. Otherwise we can talk quite calmly. You are entirely secure with me. I'm not going to arrest you, I'm no police detective. I just want to get our money back. If you don't want to give it to me, that's fine too. I can't make you. Then I'll just leave, with everything unresolved.'"

"'I didn't take it.'"

"'We'll come back to that later. I think I can convince you that you did. For the moment, I just want to say that it would be much better for you to deal with me than to let things come to the point where the police busy themselves with you. But as I said, no force. If you don't want to, you don't have to.'"

"'I can't confess to anything if I didn't do anything.'

"'Naturally not, in that case. I'll tell you something, Hartwanger. Maybe you can twist a detective superintendent around your little finger, but not me. The detective superintendent really does believe that it was two English burglars; but I know that it was you alone.'"

"'I'd like to see someone prove that!'

"'Of course! That's what I'm going to do.'

"'I'd like to see the man who could move a strong-box like that alone!'

"'Why not, if he's as strong and skilled as you, and if he has as good an iron bar as the one you used. It's of excellent quality and completely unsuspicious. It's used to lock the cellar door, and it's lying in your kitchen behind the stove right now.'

"That had an effect. I noticed this at once and used the fact to my advantage.

"'But perhaps that's still not proof,' I continued. 'Not sufficient proof, I admit. You can quibble about it, Hartwanger. There are a lot of iron bars in the world. You can explain satisfactorily how that one happens to be there, and it would be difficult to prove that precisely that one was used for the burglary. Very difficult, although it was naturally very nice for me to find it there. I have something better, though, something that will assure that you cannot get away from me, however much you want to.'"

"I knew you had something up your sleeve, Dagobert," Violet interjected.

"Something very important, dear lady. I cannot take much credit for it; it was pure luck. Some investigations go quickly, some are plodding; I admit, it's often a matter of luck."

"Not entirely, Dagobert. It's a matter of luck, but in the way a general must have luck, in order to be a good general. Why didn't the detective superintendent have any luck?"

"So I played my trump card. 'Pay close attention to what I'm about to say, Hartwanger,' I continued, 'and then tell me whether I've caught you in an iron vise or not. You managed the sand heap as cleverly as you arranged everything else. That beautiful soft yellow sand! But you let one bit of carelessness trip you up. You didn't think about how wonderfully sand retains footprints! So now you're smiling, and pleased, and thinking, in that thick skull of yours, that I could run after the culprit and the money for a long time if I didn't have anything better to do. But that smile will fade from your face, my dear fellow; I'd put that in writing and you can bet your life on it, if doing that brings you particular pleasure.'

"'Where are these footprints?' he said, quite calmly.

"'To be sure, I know the detective superintendent and his faithful team trampled all over them and destroyed them, but you'll remember that I photographed the best one at the last minute, before it was destroyed. I also know what you'll say now. One can't do anything with a photographed footprint! That's no proof! My God!—according to a photograph it could just as easily be a small foot as a big one! Right? You see, I'm admitting everything to you. But you will also remember, my esteemed burglar, that I took another photograph when you knelt down and wiped away the sand. So that doesn't disquiet you? Well, it's nonetheless something. If the two pictures should happen to resemble each other—but I'll still admit, lots of shoe soles can look very similar. Every reasonable person would have to admit that.

"'Certainly! And I believe I'm not an unreasonable person. But now the main thing. Pay attention, Hartwanger. There was a line across the middle of the footprint in the sand. It was an old, resoled piece of footgear, a boot or a shoe, that the burglar was wearing. Furthermore, there was a fine, diagonal line beginning behind the ball of the foot and running over toward the point of the little toe. So: the burglar has the peculiar habit of abusing his soles in the vicinity of his right big toe—the soles of his boots, that is, because you wear boots—and because you are a thrifty man, you didn't have the entire sole resoled, but merely had a patch put on the damaged area. When you knelt down, I had the distinct pleasure of seeing this patch in all its glory and photographing it. And now, tell me whether you can get away from me. Have a nice look at your right sole, if you don't believe me.'

"He really did look at it, and then he capitulated after all. He threw one last glance under the bed, and then another quick one at the small firearm that glittered on the table in front of me, and then he gave up and began to whimper and beg.

"I let him talk it over with me. As far as I was concerned the main thing was to recover the money, and I proceeded with that in mind. My mind ran quickly through all the possibilities. It would have been unwise to drive the man to desperate measures. He couldn't really do anything to me, but he could force me, by means of a crazed attempt to escape, to shoot at him. One doesn't like to think of such things. There would have been wearying explanations in that case, just as there would be if I now turned him over to the police. Who knows whether he wouldn't have reconsidered his position and merely served his few years in silence without first revealing where he had hidden the money?

So I showed myself to be flexible and let him negotiate. I told him I was no official and had no power over him. But it would be decidedly better for him to make do with me than to force me to turn him over to the authorities. I just wanted the money back, and everything else was all the same to me, but that wasn't the case for the police or the court. For them punishment was just as important as the money. He only needed to hand over the goods, and then I would show him that I wasn't inhuman and that I could still do something for him.

"The man was difficult to deal with. But finally I got him to the point where he was 'done.' He led me into the cellar and retrieved the package with the banknotes from its hiding place. I was able to follow him with no uneasiness. He carried the lantern, and it was he who was illuminated, not I. Then we went back up to his apartment. I counted the notes and they were all there, 164,000 kronen. I gave him four thousand."

"But Dagobert!" Violet cried in an accusatory tone.

"Dear lady, I already said it was an expensive amusement, but I'll repay the bank, naturally."

"It's not that, Dagobert. But wasn't it morally wrong?"

"Perhaps, but I had promised to do something for him, otherwise I really might not have reached my goal, and a promise must be kept, even to a scoundrel. So I gave him the money and told him to find himself a gallows somewhere else. I would, of course, be obligated to inform the authorities at once, but I strongly suspected that I would be out of luck and wouldn't be able to locate the detective superintendent again this evening.

"I hadn't even finished talking when the man was out the door and had vanished into the darkness. I found one servant still in the bank. I installed him in the doorman's lodgings and came over here. I've done my part, as well as I could. The nasty business of catching the criminal I gladly leave to Detective Superintendent Dr. v. Strinsky."

Works Cited

Primary Literature

Böttcher, Maxilmilian. *Der Detektiv. Kriminalnovelle.* In *Willkommen!* Vol. 10 (1899), pp. 180–195.

Groner, Auguste. *Zwei Kriminalnovellen: Der Neunundsiebzigste. Die goldene Kugel.* Leipzig: Philipp Reclam, 1893.

Groller, Balduin. *Detektiv Dagoberts Taten und Abenteuer.* Ein Novellen-Zyklus. 2 parts. Leipzig: Philipp Reclam, 1909.

Ludwig, Otto [Emil Freiherr von Puttkammer]. *Der Tote von St.-Annas Kapelle. Ein Criminalfall.* Reprinted from *Urania. Taschenbuch auf das Jahr 1840.* Leipzig: Brockhaus Verlag, 1840 [1839]: 289–422.

Müllner, Adolph [Amandus Gottfried]. *Der Kaliber. Aus den Papieren eines Kriminalbeamten.* Leipzig: Philipp Reclam, n.d. [Universal-Bibliothek 34].

Streckfuss, Carl Adolf. *Der Sternkrug. Criminal-Novelle.* Berlin: B. Brigl, 1870.

Secondary Literature

Boileau-Narcejac. *Der Detektivroman.* Trans. Wolfgang Promies. Neuwied und Berlin: Hermann Luchterhand, [1968?]. Paris: Payot, 1964.

Chesterton, G. K. "A Defence of Detective Stories." In *The Defendant.* London: R.B. Johnson, 1902.

Colbron, Grace Isabel. "The Detective Story in Germany and Scandinavia." *The Bookman* 30 (Sept. 1909–Feb. 1910), pp. 407–412.

Depken, Friedrich. *Sherlock Holmes, Raffles und ihre Vorbilder.* Anglistische Forschungen 41. 1914. Amsterdam: Swets & Zeitlinger N.V., 1967.

Freund, Winfried. *Die deutsche Kriminalnovelle von Schiller bis Hauptmann.* Paderborn: Ferdinand Schöningh, 1975.

Gerteis, Walter. *Detektive: Ihre Geschichte im Leben und in der Literatur.* Munich: Ernst Heimeran, 1953.

Gross, Hans. *Handbuch für Untersuchungsrichter als System der Kriminalistik.* Munich, Berlin and Leipzig: J. Schweitzer, 1893.

Haycraft, Howard. *Murder for Pleasure. The Life and Times of the Detective Story* (1941). New York: Carroll & Graf, 1984.

_____, ed. *The Art of the Mystery Story* (1946). New York: Carroll & Graf, 1992.

Hügel, Hans-Otto. *Untersuchungsrichter, Diebsfänger, Detektive: Theorie und Geschichte der deutschen Detektiverzählung im 19. Jahrhundert.* Stuttgart: J. B. Metzler-Poeschel, 1978.

243

Liang, Hsi-Huey. *The Rise of Modern Police and the European State System from Metternich to the Second World War*. Cambridge: Cambridge University Press, 1992.

Nusser, Peter. *Der Kriminalroman*. (Sammlung Metzler M191) Stuttgart: J. B. Metzler-Poeschel, 1980.

Reinert, Claus. *Das Unheimliche und die Detektivliteratur*. Abhandlungen zur Kunst-, Musik-, und Literaturwissenschaft 139. Bonn: 1973.

Sayers, Dorothy L. "Introduction." *The Omnibus of Crime*, ed. Dorothy L. Sayers. New York: Harcourt, Brace, 1929. Pp. 9–38.

Schönhaar, Rainer. *Novelle und Kriminalschema: Ein Strukturmodell deutscher Erzählkunst um 1800*. Bad Homburg: Verlag Gehlen, 1969.

Skreb, Zdenko. "Die neue Gattung: Zur Geschichte und Poetik des Detektivromans." Zmegac, *Der wohltemperierte Mord*, pp. 35–96.

Spencer, Elaine Glovka. *Police and the Social Order in German Cities. The Düsseldorf District 1848–1914*. DeKalb: Northern Illinois University Press, 1992.

Vogt, Jochen, ed. *Der Kriminalroman. Zur Theorie und Geschichte einer Gattung*. 2 vols. München: Wilhelm Fink, 1971.

Wright, Willard Huntington. "Introduction." *The Great Detective Stories*, ed. Willard Huntington Wright. New York: Charles Scribner's Sons, 1927. Pp. 3–37.

Zmegac, Viktor. "Aspekte des Detektivromans." *Sinn und Form* 24 (1972), pp. 376–394.

_____, ed. *Der wohltemperierte Mord. Zur Theorie und Geschichte des Detektivromans*. Frankfurt a. M.: Athenäum, 1971.